Dear Merryn and Jo

I'm rather proud of
my photograph of you
(opposite page 80.). Your
kindness to me during our
time together will always
be a precious memory.

All the best,

Deidre

The Suffragette's Daughter
Betty Archdale
Her life of feminism, cricket, war and education

Captain Betty Archdale (*right of centre*) leads the English women's team onto the Melbourne Cricket Ground, 7 December 1934. (Courtesy of the Herald and Weekly Times Ltd)

The Suffragette's Daughter

Betty Archdale

Her life of feminism, cricket, war and education

Deirdre Macpherson

ROSENBERG

First Published in 2002 by Rosenberg Publishing Pty Ltd
P.O. Box 6125 Dural Delivery Centre NSW 2156 Australia
Phone 02 9654 1502   Fax 02 9654 1338
Email rosenbergpub@smartchat.net.au
Web www.rosenbergpub.com.au

National Library of Australia
Cataloguing-in-Publication data

Macpherson, Deirdre, 1947- .
The suffragette's daughter : Betty Archdale : her life of
feminism, cricket, war and education.

Bibliography.
Includes index.
ISBN 1 877058 09 2.

1. Archdale, Betty, 1907-2000. 2. Abbotsleigh (School). 3.
High school principals – New South Wales – Sydney –
Biography. 4. Educators – New South Wales – Sydney –
Biography. 5. Women educators – New South Wales – Sydney –
Biography. I. Title.

373.9441092

Set in 11 on 14.5 pt Bembo
Printed in China by Everbest Printing Co Limited

To the enduring kindness of my family,
Andi, Sholto, Rory, Minto and Arabella,
with great love

Our deepest fear is not that we are inadequate.
Our deepest fear is that we are powerful beyond measure.
It is our light, not our darkness, that most frightens us.
We ask ourselves 'Who am I to be brilliant ... ?'
Actually, who are you *not* to be? ...

Margaret Williamson, *A Return to Love*
(Thorsons, 1992, pp. 190–1)

CONTENTS

PREFACE

The value of this book is in showing how the changes in how we earn our living will bring about changes in everything connected with us such as education and status.

I was lucky to have a marvellous mother. She had no doubt at all that a woman could do virtually everything a man could so I was brought up to choose what I wanted to do in life regardless of sex. I was never told 'Girls can't do this' but did what I wanted to do.

And how right she was. One of my earliest memories is visiting her in prison for breaking windows in support of votes for women (I'd gathered the stones).

I liked both boys and girls and had crushes on men and women. I never married but had plenty of friends, both men and women. It was not until I moved into a retirement village that I felt any regrets of not having a family of my own. I was the youngest and last.

Deirdre has been a first-rate friend and her book shows a great understanding of changes during my life.

All the best to it and may thousands read it.

Betty Archdale
24 February 1997

PROLOGUE

On that first day I didn't realise that the descent into Galston Gorge to see Betty Archdale would always mark a suspension between my ordinary suburban existence and that of her earthy individuality.

On the outskirts of Hornsby the ridge tops are covered by a dry forest dominated by scribbly gums, white stringy-barks and angophoras with their smooth orange-pink trunks. Their understoreys are sparse. A broad view across the gorge looks to ridges on the far side, all smothered in trees. Above them the vast sky, on this dull day, was subdued.

Four days earlier I had rung Betty and said I had been approached to write a biography of her and that, if she felt happy about it, we'd talk. 'Fair doos,' she laughed nervously.

We were both tentative. Betty had been my headmistress at Abbotsleigh, Wahroonga, 30 years previously. Then, with a largesse of spirit, she seemed eccentric, wearing instead of twin-set and pearls a sheepskin coat with its ghostly protrusion of the clothes hook on which it was habitually hung. This big persona drove not a Rover, but a tiny van, a mud brown, corrugated deux chevaux Citroën.

In the suffocating constraint of the 1950s she was able to generate profound changes in her students, stirring us up to enjoy being ourselves, to throw away fear of the unknown, encouraging us to believe that we could do anything we chose, to embrace the world. We wore a jaunty pride in her as a controversial public figure, notorious for saying exactly what she thought to the press and in private conversation. We were proud that she held prestigious positions in the community; that she was regarded as a great educationalist. For many, her breadth of knowledge and enthusiasm, the throwing back of her head to heartily laugh away the pettinesses of life, established her as our heroine. Of course she had her detractors …

My grey van, quickening down the steep slope, had to be reined in with care to negotiate the six hairpin bends to the floor of the valley. On the high side of the road were outcrops of Hawkesbury sandstone, honeycombed by erosion. Here and there were the gaping mouths of caves. Cicadas drummed amongst the primeval banksia, hakea, the fine-leaved geebungs with their pendulous bright yellow flowers, the bushfire stumps and trunks of old trees.

Betty's past was vague in my mind. Her mother had been a suffragette, and I wasn't sure of her father; she often referred to a wonderful school in Scotland. Abbotsleigh had boasted that she had been captain of the first English women's cricket team which toured Australia a long time ago. In World War II she had been with the WRNS in Singapore and Mombasa, and after the war the principal of the Women's College at the University of Sydney before becoming a headmistress. But the core person behind these acts of bravado was curiously shy and elusive.

The temperature dropped slightly and the air felt more moist as the van descended into the sheltered gully. Christmas bush and blueberry ash and turpentines indicated a gradual change in flora. Stands of wattle and young, feathery casuarinas formed a dense thicket beside the road— lush and green—watered by the creeks and sheltered by the ridges. Colour flashed in the dense growth beside the creek and a chattering—crimson rosellas. In the ferny gully, the van rattled the thick wooden planks of a narrow bridge over Berowra Creek. And then the ascent began beside the rocky escarpment with a canopy of trees embracing above the carved-out road.

Betty and my mother had been friends, and in some ways were alike—their readiness to be amused, their lack of desire to fully comply with social expectations, their warmth and alive interest in the world around them, their tilting at authoritarian stances. For these reasons Betty was a familiar type, and in my apprehension it was this that I trusted as I approached her home.

Curiosity was another driving force. What intrigued me most was the question: Was it genetic inheritance or the environment which produced a woman regarded as being a person ahead of her time? How had Betty developed the capacity to leap the boundaries of her society, and to keep on leaping them as those boundaries moved with social change? And most mysteriously of all, how did she manAge to influence and generate personal change in so many people without seeming to be actively doing so?

Emerging from the gorge I turned right into Crosslands Road, drove past rustic acreages, and then turned into the rough driveway of Northis.

It was obvious that, at Northis, Betty lived in modest harmony with nature. The lanky front iron gate was held permanently open by a covering of purple twining pea. The five-acre block topped with ironbarks and white stringy-barks sloped down to untouched bush at the bottom. The rectangular house was built by Betty and her actor brother, Alexander, by ramming earth between saplings selected from the property. It was painted a musky pink and against its rough walls were propped garden tools. Boxes of unused parquet tiles were left weathering outside.

At the sound of the van pulling up, Betty emerged through the front door, laughing off uncertainty. With much of her hair still dark around a thinning face, she looked younger than her 82 years. She was dressed in a sloppy joe, torn blue nylon slacks, tan checked socks and sneakers.

Together we entered the house. It consisted of a large main room with a long front wall of sliding glass doors overlooking her land. Immediately in front was a flagged terrace where magpies darted at crumbs she had recently thrown. The back wall was covered in books. When I later climbed up on an old electric organ in stockinged feet to peer in the gloom at volumes near the ceiling I discovered that rainwater had matted them together. At one end of the room was a small kitchen which opened into a bathroom. At the other, two monkish cells, bedrooms for Betty and Alec.

The chief impression on entering the main room was the strong smell of smoke from hundreds of fires. Its source was an open grate with a fire laid ready to be lit, under a copper flue. To one side was stacked a mass of eminently flammable dry twigs. It all looked dangerous … The ceiling seemed to be propped up by a central sapling. On it was an electric outlet from which four different cords ran. There were no overhead lights, and on this overcast day an attached upright light with a straw lampshade refused to cooperate.

As we sat down to coffee I noticed the walls were hung with large, oval, unglassed sepia photographs of ancestors. Betty wasn't sure who they were. She sat in a huge, grey brown wool-covered chair.

The whole setting was given a dash of class by an enormous walnut desk which belonged to her grandfather, Alexander Russel, an editor of *The Scotsman*. Broad and high and multi-drawered, it was strewn with papers. On one corner was a rotating bookstand, beautifully carved and holding religious books, capped by *The Guardian*. A fine layer of dust covered all her possessions in this comfortable but primitive room. The house appeared to be in a state of entropy, with nature reclaiming its own. As we talked, mice ran comfortably along the bookshelves. Betty, unperturbed, was at one with her world.

Although we conversed well, a feeling of settling-in was apparent. But after several hours we had already developed an air of conspiracy.

'Would you like a sherry?' she asked.

As we raised the full Vegemite glasses to our lips, little did we know that that drink was a toast to a nine-year conversation.

This is the story that emerged.

1

FALLING IN LOVE

Betty Archdale's story would have been simpler, less passionate, if it weren't for the boxes. It is understandable, in repeatedly summarising her life in interviews, that the stones of her path had become polished. The boxes gave a different picture. They came out from under the beds of the rammed-earth house on the brink of her moving to a retirement village in 1991. They were nothing much to look at—stained cardboard with dried mud rubble sprinkling the exposed papers—but the contents seemed to radiate energy, as if their voices could be repressed no longer.

Amongst them was the unpublished autobiography of her mother, Helen Archdale, 'An Interfering Female', describing with ardour her life as a suffragette. Two letters (one 40 pages long) from Adela Pankhurst saying how impossible it was being the daughter of Emmeline. Photographs of Betty alongside prominent feminists from America, England and Australia on the steps of the League of Nations in the 1930s when agitating members for reform for women. Affectionate letters from Viscountess Margaret Rhondda, owner of the English political and literary journal *Time and Tide*. A memoir by Betty's actor brother Alec on the beginnings of the Marion Street Theatre in Sydney. Then there were Betty's own writings—of her involvement in the evolution of women's cricket, in education, in the conscience of her society.

The boxes also cast new light on the courtship of Betty's parents.

In her conversations Betty said, 'Mother married in the days when girls from England used to go on trips … to India and collect a husband en route. It was … the correct thing to do in such circles. Mother collected father, on one of these trips.'[1] Whether her mother's later suffrage activities tinted her understanding of the events of 1900 or not, the true story is much more romantic.

Betty's father, Theodore Montgomery Archdale, was of the Archdales of County Fermanagh in Ireland. Here they had lived for two and a half centuries—ever since the forfeited lands of the Irish earls were distributed amongst King James's subjects. Their lands bordered the east shore of Lower Lough Erne, an extraordinarily beautiful area where the land, clothed in forests of oak and ash, seems to rise slowly out of the lake. The mood is one of brooding stillness where, in Yeats's phrase, 'peace comes dropping slow'.[2]

The Archdales' main occupation was farming, usually after a spell in the army. They became one of Fermanagh's leading families, improving facilities, building roads, bridges and churches. They represented Fermanagh in parliament for an unbroken period of 154 years.[3] Even so, the Archdales generally were and are fairly eccentric. According to Betty's nephew, Audley: 'they will say what they believe—very forthright—almost to the point of rudeness. They will basically help pretty well anybody that's got problems, usually to the detriment of their own condition. They do have a tendency to trust people, and talk with any level of society and be equally at home.'[4]

Theodore was born into the institution of the Archdale family on 24 September 1873.[5] With his family's firmly established social status, his lifestyle was predictable. The culture of the Anglo-Irish in the seventeenth and eighteenth centuries followed closely the traditions of Britain. He was educated at Repton, entered the Royal Artillery in 1894 and progressed steadily through the ranks. The fact that Theodore's good-humoured eldest brother Edward Mervyn (his senior by twenty years) sat in parliament for North Fermanagh as a Unionist, was made a Privy Councillor, the first Minister for Agriculture in the Ulster parliament and Grand Master of the Orange Institution indicates that the family very much followed the conservative and responsible ways of their forebears.

At the age of 22 Theodore's diaries reveal him to be an aesthetic person who enjoyed the arts, young women, animals and physical fitness. A year after joining the army he holidayed in Rome, where he visited museums, called on an array of women, had regular singing and fencing lessons, attended a hunt, danced till early morn, and picked snowdrops and berries in the fields with a young woman. Back in Ireland he attended meets, dances and teas. He played hockey and billiards and went to Crystal Palace for the Association Cup football final. In view of his daughter's later success it is ironic to note that he wrote: 'afternoon—ladies cricket match at the Bainbridges. Rather amusing—gentlemen only using left hand.'[6]

After his father's death Theodore lived with his mother, brother Frank and sister Ellie on a farm, Clover Hill, at Clondalkin just outside Dublin.[7] But in the autumn of 1899 he sailed for the Cape and the Boer War, where he fought at the Battle of Tugela and the relief of Ladysmith.[8] He was mentioned in despatches and awarded the Distinguished Service Order, earning a medal with three clasps.[9] He was also wounded and by May 1900 he was back in London with a damaged eye and a bandaged ankle. In October he was ordered to attend a medical board at the Royal Infirmary in Dublin and was given six months leave. Surgeon Bennet, who examined him, recommended a voyage to New Zealand.[10]

Instead, Theodore decided on an exotic cure at the sulphurous baths of Cairo.[11]

One of Betty's Archdale cousins said she inherited her name from the Archdales and her intelligence from the Russels.[12] Whether this is true or not, there seems no doubt that the conservative influence on her life came from the Archdales, and the urge to reform from the Russels. For while the Archdales had the social status of the landed gentry, the Russels had notoriety for different reasons.

Betty's mother, Helen Alexander Russel, was born a few weeks after the death of her father, Alexander Russel. The editor of *The Scotsman* newspaper, Alex was a born fighter who gloried in getting into the thick of any public controversy. He had a marked intellectual capacity and energy, reading and conversing widely. His appeal was not only due to compact, graphic, even racy writing, but also to his exuberance of humour. 'The charm of his wit lay in its spontaneity, in its bubbling up, naturally, out of the soil of the subject that was in question,' wrote *The Scotsman* after his death. 'What he really wanted to do was to prove his point. For the same reason his humour was essentially genial and sympathetic, not biting and acrimonious. It was ideas not persons, "measures not men", that he was earnest for or against.'[13]

Alexander Russel had been brought up on the Whig school of politics and supported his party with ardour, but after 1868, when the Household Suffrage Bill was passed by a Tory government, he swung his support to the Liberal Party and it was his articles in *The Scotsman* more than anything else that produced an overwhelming majority for the party in Scotland. This added tremendously to the prestige of the paper and Russel was admitted to the highest social, literary and political circles. Near the end of his life he was elected a member of the Reform Club, a prized reward for distinguished services to the Liberal Party.[14]

He seemed to be known by everyone. Once, when he had been to the Nest on an angling trip and was driving to Galashiels, he heard a voice crying, 'Russel! Russel!' The shout came from a ploughman, who pulled up his horses, left his plough stilts, ran down to the roadside hedge and asked over it: 'How is the Irish Church Bill getting on?'[15]

Alexander Russel died on 18 July 1876. Just over a month later, on 25 August, his daughter Helen was born. His widow, herself an early feminist, having been one of the first women to attend medical school, was left with a lack of funds.[16] Because of its good educational facilities and economic living conditions, she settled with her two sons and daughter in St Andrews.

Helen was sent to St Leonard's School in St Andrews, itself a pioneering institution and the first girls school in the United Kingdom to echo the character of the greater public schools for boys, with strong academic ambitions and compulsory sport. Helen admits she was lazy— her natural intelligence carried her lightly over academic problems both at school and at St Andrews University, which had just opened its doors to women.[17]

Due to her late father's position, Helen led a full life in the Scottish manner. She met a great many distinguished people, she danced at balls, she was accomplished at fly-fishing, like her father, and had a man's handicap of nine on the Old Course at St Andrews.[18] But for all that, Helen was dissatisfied and wrote in her autobiography: 'The fact that I was the only daughter and that my mother was a widow was dressed up as all sufficient explanation of why I made no effort "to do anything", why I stayed at home. Almost I became a martyr to this mythical sacrifice. Occasionally I was seized with gloom, accompanied by floods of tears. Then really bored by this time, I became an invalid. I now believe this invalidism to have been as mythical as its predecessor, the sacrifice, but it worked. Spas in Britain, winter in Italy and on to Egypt, proved for a time cures at least for boredom.'[19]

In November 1900, Theodore arrived in Egypt. He made his way to Hulwan, a centre of prehistoric and Pharaonic settlement and known from early times for its mineral springs. At one stage the desert submerged them, then in the 1800s the sulphurous springs were uncovered and baths built. After 1900 the centre flourished as a spa.[20]

Although today Hulwan is a suburb of Cairo, in 1900 it was a more remote village of low-lying, white, square buildings, with mountains forming a distant backdrop. It was devoid of vegetation apart from a small, localised cluster of trees. The Bath Establishment, as Theodore called it, stood apart from the village, a series of rectangular, horizontally striped buildings further ornamented by a multi-arched portico at the front and a large spear-headed dome above its core.[21]

On his first morning at the Grand Hotel, Theodore saw Dr Page-May, who estimated six weeks was needed for healing. In the afternoon he took a sulphurous bath which he said smelt horrid, and had a massage. Although it was not quite the season, on 27 November Theodore noted the presence of W. S. Gilbert (of Gilbert and Sullivan fame) in the hotel, badly crippled with rheumatism, with his wife and his adopted daughter, Miss Nancy McIntosh.

Despite being disturbed by occasional bad news from the war, it was an indulgent life. In the hot, close days, Theodore bathed, had Arabic lessons from a 'negro', walked, saw donkeys race ('rather amusing to see the populace'), attended dances in the hotel and played golf. It was a pleasant but unexciting time. Then on Monday 17 December, three weeks after his arrival, he wrote:'Dined at Des Baines, only 12 people—Mrs Russel, Miss Maun, Mrs Langlands, Mrs Rickard and self at one end of table—dinner good and short'.[22]

Mrs Russel and her daughter had arrived for their second winter in Egypt. No doubt they were fragile emotionally, because just before coming Michael, the oldest son, had died. Having been such a close family unit after Alexander Russel's death 24 years earlier, Michael's death would have been felt all the more keenly by them both.[23]

Whatever state Miss Russel was in, Theodore was quick to notice her. Four days later he wrote, 'up to dance in evening at other hotel with Miss Russel'. The next day he walked with 'Miss R' in the afternoon to a deserted graveyard outside the town. From the courtyard of the police station they saw a procession of Arabs on the eve of Ramadan. The day after that Theodore again met with 'Miss R' in the afternoon, walked up the hills with her and gathered fossils. They shared Christmas day, going to an early service at eleven and a pleasant dinner and dance till twelve, by which time the band was drunk. He went for a walk with her on New Year's Eve and danced with her that night until the singing of 'Auld Lang Syne'.[24]

On 1 January 1901 the doctor told Theodore that he was better but advised him to stay on in Hulwan instead of moving to Aswan. So in the rarefied atmosphere of hot sulphur baths, of the imposing pyramids, of heat and exotic culture, of the idiosyncratic pastimes of the English, and of timelessness, the courting of Miss Russel continued. They became more daring and Theodore noted on 8 January:'After lunch Miss R and I went as hares on an ass paper-chase, no donkey boys—the field could not find our trail—never even looked for paper, so we had no pursuit … After dinner to other hotel to play Progressive Hearts—I won a 2nd prize … and Miss Russel tied for 1st.'[25]

The many photos Theodore took of their expeditions show Helen Russel as far from sickly. Her dark brown hair was pinned in a bun at the back of her head, a straw boater jauntily tipped forward, a significant bust, thin waist and a flair about her dress. On the visit to Wady Aboush

with Miss Hall and Mr King, her long skirt of black and white check
and a stylish mutton-sleeved white shirt with a high collar are held into
a neat waist by a wide black belt with an elaborate buckle. A dramatic,
multicoloured tie round her throat sets her apart as being less conservative
than her female companions. In all the photographs she looks squarely
at the camera, free of guile, with not a hint of coyness but with the air
one who challenges—a sense of derring-do. Even a century later the
photographs reveal her to be a spirited young woman.

This was also evident in Theodore's diary entries, but time was
running out. After examining Theodore on 24 February, Dr Page-May
stopped further baths and massage. Yet it was obvious that the couple's
involvement was deepening. Theodore manfully attempted to objectify
emotional swings in his diary, summarising, 'row with Miss R but squared
up'. Eventually on 24 March, fourteen weeks after first meeting Miss
Russel, Theodore wrote: 'lovely day. Walk with Miss R to palm tree after
tea—proposed, accepted—saw Mrs R after dinner and wrote home.'[26]

It was an unremarkable way of describing the climax of weeks of
mutual pursuit. Helen Russel related it differently in her autobiography:
'in the second winter in Egypt there appeared the man with whom I fell
head over ears in love, and in a few months married. Blandly, now, I
decided that the one excuse an only daughter could have for leaving her
widowed mother was marriage, so conscience and convention were
quiescent and I was acquiescent.'[27]

In late March Theodore went to Cairo and bought Helen a gold
signet ring with what appears to be a stylised serpent on the front—an
ancient Egyptian symbol of commitment? Not at all. Inside the ring is
the inscription '1901' with 'Nell' (Helen) written above and 'Toots'
(Theodore) below. If one turns the front of the ring on its side, the
design can be seen to be an elaborate N (for Nell) with the stem of a T
(for Toots) inside it. Helen wore it on her little finger for the rest of her
life. A week later Theodore sailed for England. For the first time in his
diary he referred to Helen Russel, not as Miss R, but as HR.

Twelve days before proposing to Miss Russel, Theodore had been
promoted to the rank of captain in the Lancashire Field Artillery. He was
stationed at Sandhurst. The Russels returned to St Andrews a few weeks

later and whenever he had time off Theodore used to meet his fiancee and they would cycle the Scottish countryside. Plans for their marriage in October evolved in the woods where they drew up guest lists.

On Wednesday, 9 October 1901, Theodore wrote in his diary: 'Married 3pm—left at 5 for Perth'.[28]

2

FALLING IN REALITY

Helen later told Betty that she didn't know on the wedding night what the sexual act was. 'She couldn't understand what he was getting at—I ask you,' said Betty. 'She thought father was being funny!'[1] Despite this initial confusion, all evidence shows that Helen and Theodore enjoyed being together in an active, domesticated and social life. However, Helen started to have episodes of ill health, mainly neuralgia, according to Theodore's diary. Being ignorant of contraception, she may not have realised that she was already pregnant.

It was in Preston, Lancashire, where Captain Theodore Archdale was posted with the army, that the couple made their first and most satisfying home. Manor House, Fulwood, was a two-storeyed Georgian house in extensive level grounds. In them the erect newly wed couple posed with their dogs. Helen's arm is linked through Theodore's and his hand covers hers. Theodore looks very pleased with himself indeed. Quickly they became domesticated, Theodore buying Buttorpington cocks and hens, transplanting gooseberry trees, making gardens. Cigarettes arrived from Egypt.

While Theodore was engaged in army activities Helen visited neighbours, with Theodore noting their names in his diary at night. They both played a great deal of sport, including badminton, but mainly golf and hockey. In summer Theodore played cricket, and every Sunday

they went to 'kirk'.[2] Their first son, Nicholas, was born in July 1902
while Theodore was away with the 11th Battery on the Salisbury Plain,
down south. Nicholas was blond and blue eyed, like his father.

But soon this apparent family idyll suffered a mood change that
had permanent repercussions. In October 1903 Helen received a telegram
saying her mother had died suddenly. A church service was held the
following week and the family went to Edinburgh to Dean Cemetery.
Mrs Russel's grave was dug alongside her famous husband Alexander
Russel's monument, erected 27 years earlier. Only three weeks later Helen
was informed that her brother Ander had died in Jamaica.[3]

The death of her mother and brother only three weeks apart was
a serious blow to Helen and she later wrote: 'The deaths of both brothers
and of my mother were unexpectedly announced by cable and telegram,
without any previous intimation of illness, from India, Jamaica and
Scotland and I saw none of them before their deaths. We had always
been a close knit little family, only four years separating the eldest brother
from myself and the other brother coming in between. My marriage
and following motherhood were achieved in the dark ignorance of those
times. From this ignorance arose many problems which, being now bereft
of my family, I had to face in terrifying solitude. I passed into an unknown
life, surrounded only by strangers and with an innate reluctance to confide
in or to ask the advice of those strangers, however kindly or loving they
might be. This change in surroundings forced me to think for myself in
order to find how to endure the new experiences and the loss of all one
had known as home.'[4]

The decision to work things out for herself was the key to change
in Helen's life. Not that she was unfamiliar with such an approach. She
had been born and bred in liberal-thinking, progressive circles. Her mother
had been one of the first women to enter a medical faculty, and her
father's reputation for reform cast a mantle on her early life. What is
more, she witnessed her mother's brave independence during nearly three
decades of widowhood, determining a path for herself and her children
that was not answerable to anyone, particularly not a man. Yet Helen had
entered into the life of an officer's wife and she believed only those who
had experienced it could know what a restricted existence that can be.

Emotionally stirred by personal circumstances, seeking some outlet, some distraction, alleviation, occupation, she always found herself up against a wall of 'not dones'.

A man came to the barracks where the Archdales lived, to attend a course. He had travelled extensively in the Arctic and elsewhere and Helen found his talk a joy. This entirely innocent friendship was stopped by the remark, 'I will not have that man hanging up his hat in my house'. It was Helen's first harsh encounter with the attitude that assumes male dominance and female submission. The idea that she was not capable either of choosing her friendships or of dealing with any mistakes of choice she might make was new and startling to her. Not having had any male dominance in her childhood home, it hit harder.

In November 1903 Helen and Nicholas went to Ireland and stayed with Theodore's family. Theodore arrived in December and tried to take it easy, but Helen later observed that 'A series of visits among my in-law relatives showed it to me [the assumption of male dominance] in its stone age purity'.[5]

With no extended family of her own to extract her at intervals, Helen was very much at the behest of her husband's employer, the army, to do with her what it will. At least life at the Manor House was settled and busy, with the garden flowering and bearing fruit and vegetables for all seasons, the hens laying, pups playing with baby Nicholas, and the social life amongst the army fraternity widening. But even that security was stripped away when, in 1904, Helen left for India and a succession of army houses, none of which had the same ambience and sense of place as Manor House.

They sailed from Southampton to Bombay on the SS *Plassy* and then travelled to Jhansi where Theodore was stationed with the 4th Brigade of the Royal Field Artillery. From there he would go on manoeuvres throughout India. It was in Jhansi on 25 November 1905 that their second son, Alexander, was born.

Despite pleasure in her expanding family, Helen was growing increasingly restless. In India she found the life of the wife of an officer was even more restricted. She could understand how so many wives regressed instead of developing. Limited in almost all forms of intellectual work except private study, all forms of social work except visiting the wives of their own regiment, rank and file, they were left with dinners, dances, races, gymkhanas and the club—a round repeating itself perpetually. 'Small wonder that intelligence tends to atrophy, scandal to grow and boredom to lead to degeneracy,' wrote Helen.[6]

Concern for the bearing, rearing and educating of children in India preoccupied Helen as well, happy satisfaction turning into a fretting anxiety. The problem of whether the wife should stay with the husband or the mother with the children if the children were sent back to Britain was still unsolved, and arose afresh with every married officer on eastern service.

Eventually Theodore must have bowed to his wife's pressure. When Helen became pregnant a third time she returned to London specifically to have the baby. Theodore followed her later, reaching London just in time for the birth of his only daughter, Helen Elizabeth (Betty), on 21 August 1907.[7]

On their return to England the Archdales resumed normal garrison life, moving to one inadequate house after another. They had to hastily leave one house because the drains ran into, instead of out of, it. Another house had seven old wallpapers on its walls, affording the children occupation and delight to pull off.[8]

With a gap in Theodore's diaries from 1903 to 1914, the only indication of the family's whereabouts during this time is to be found on the yellowing cardboard pages of photograph albums. The first photographs of Betty show her in a simple patterned dress and bonnet running in the garden of Southfield House, Road, in 1909. Nearly two, she is determinedly trying to mount a toy camel three-quarters her size, or with her mother and Alec in a cart being drawn by a donkey. Her face is round with a snub nose, her cheeks plump, light brown hair coming from under her bonnet frames a direct gaze. The grounds of Southfield House were shared with an enormous pink pig, a family of five piglets, and Vic the dog.

Betty holidayed in France the next year, paddling naked with her two brothers, while clutching sandbuckets, in the streams near the Hotel Source de la Truite. In 1910 Theodore was with the army on the Salisbury

Plain. Another home seems to have been at Trowbridge. Betty often said 'we were a very happy family, although father was obviously away a lot'.[9]

And so it seems he was. Apart from soldiering, Theodore went on several stunning cruises, apparently without Helen. In 1910 he went to Stockholm and Amsterdam, and later that year to the Black Sea, Constantinople and the Bosporus. In 1911, when serving with K Battery, Royal Horse Artillery, at Canterbury, he went on a trip to Hamburg and Antwerp. It is amongst photographs of this trip that a poem 'The Happiness of the World' by Christopher Plantin appears, pasted in his album. The poem epitomises an ideal life:

To have a cheerful, bright and airy dwelling place,
With garden lawn, and climbing flowers sweet;
Fresh fruits, good wine, few children; there to meet
A quiet faithful wife, whose love shines through her face.

But Helen no longer appears in the albums—only photographs of distant lands, or army camps, or meets, or dogs and horses and Theodore's children.

The children are shown as scallywags, relaxed and happy at play with boxing gloves, or rugged up and running round the shores of Skelmorlie. They wore identical clothes of dark shorts and polo-neck jumpers. In earlier pictures the boys had crewcuts while Betty's hair was loosely held in two plaits. But in later photographs her hair is similarly shorn and the trio could be confused for being three little boys who are used to rubbing along together, having fun. Despite being the only girl, and the youngest, Betty seems to have kept up with the boys, although when she was upset she cried 'boo hoo' so loudly that she was soon nicknamed 'Boo'.[10]

At times Alec seems to have been in awe of Betty, two years his junior. In his autobiography he recalled: 'I was about four years old and was incarcerated with my sister in the kitchen for safety. My mother, with either Nanny or governess, heard from outside my loud wail of anguish. They came in to discover my howling and my sister, tied for further safety to the leg of the table, beaming with joy. Upon enquiry I tearfully informed them—"Betty hit me!" I believe now that my wail was one of protest at the unfair situation in which I had been placed. My dominant sister had hit me but inexplicably I was unable to hit her back, so, howls of frustration and lack of understanding.'[11]

Despite his complaint it was Betty who very early on became Alec's ally, and she frequently went to his rescue when the older Nick teased him. This partnership was reinforced when Nick went off to prep school as a boarder, leaving Alec and Betty to amuse each other.

In 1911 the family was at Sheffield. Theodore travelled in October that year to Rotterdam, Delft, Utrecht and Harzburg. And then in February 1912 he returned to India. His family remained in England.

The reason for Theodore's singular travels over the past three years, and his return to India alone, was that the pictorial record of normalcy belied the truth and a domestic earthquake was shaking the family to its core. According to Alec: 'By about 1910 we were all much in the hands of Nannies and Governesses, father was being kept very busy by the Army and mother found herself with little to do. This changed in one instant and she became a militant Suffragette.'[12]

3

DEEDS NOT WORDS

Helen Archdale's awareness of the women's movement must have been impeded by her time in India, because by the time she became involved it had been noticeably gathering strength for years.

In fact efforts had been made to win women's suffrage since 1870, all to no avail. After years of inactivity, Emmeline Pankhurst, a widow, believed that political power was a means of salvation and so with other women formed the Women's Social and Political Union (WSPU). 'Deeds, Not Words' was to be their permanent motto. In 1904, the first suffrage bill in eight years was submitted by the Independent Labour Party, at the behest of the WSPU. The members of parliament, by extending their debate on the Roadway Lighting Bill with silly stories and foolish jokes, ensured that the suffrage bill was automatically disqualified through insufficient debating time.

When years of Conservative rule ended in 1905 the WSPU hoped for greater sympathy from the Liberal Party when it came into power. To their chagrin they found the Liberals were hostile to them and the nature of confrontation changed alarmingly. The votes for women campaign of 1907 began with a Women's Parliament, called together in Caxton Hall. When the women met on the afternoon of 13 February they knew that the government meant to do nothing for women during the session ahead.'They went to the Houses of Parliament with the slogan "Rise up, women" with answering shout "now," wrote Emmeline Pankhurst. 'Suddenly a body of mounted police came riding up at a smart trot, and for the next five hours or more a struggle, quite indescribable for brutality and ruthlessness, went on. The horsemen rode directly into the procession, scattering the women right and left. But still the women would not run back.'

The newspapers were almost unanimous in condemning the government for sending mounted troops out against unarmed women. Angry questions were asked in parliament and the ranks of the WSPU increased in size and ardour. They launched their paper, *Votes for Women*, and selected the colours purple (justice), white (purity) and green (hope) to represent them. The WSPU became a national organisation. Its work at by-elections was such a new thing in English politics that the women attracted an enormous amount of attention wherever they went.[1]

Despite a vigorous militancy, and the press teeming with articles on the question of votes for women and with notices of the doings of the suffragettes, Helen Archdale was largely unconscious of their activities. She had just returned from three years in India, was absorbed with a new baby, as well as two other little children, and was cocooned in military barracks away from London.

But one day, when walking along a street in Edinburgh, one of her relatives pointed to a window and said, 'Of course one cannot have anything to do with these people, they go too far.' Helen glanced at the offending window and saw in it some copies of *Votes for Women*. The matter dropped, but some spark had been struck in Helen and on returning to the barracks where Theodore was stationed she sent to London for the latest issue.

When Theodore saw the publication he was horrified and thrust it quickly into a drawer, but Helen found it and read it. That issue included a photograph of Mrs Pankhurst being led along, arrested, by two burly policemen. 'Her face instantly blew the almost unnoticed spark within me into a blaze which still, after fifty years burns redly with frequent flares,' Helen later wrote. 'It seemed to me that a person enduring that physical contact and enduring it with the emotion that the face expressed had got hold of reality.'[2]

Inwardly, Helen queried whether she had been living in unreality. Certainly, she thought, there had been no conscious aim, no seen purpose in her life. Life was just lived, the pleasant things enjoyed, courage sought to surmount the unpleasant. Now, it seemed to her, she was seeing something much better, something living, real, worth doing and which needed to be done.

Helen Archdale's first ideas were very mild, running to the possibility of holding meetings, probably tea-party plus drawing-room, rising boldly to the heights of the local schoolroom. But alarmed by the suggestions, Theodore consulted his colonel. The colonel told him that he did not object to the wives of his officers working for votes for women provided that they did not do it in his district. That district covered about a quarter of England, but instead of damping Helen's little flame the qualification provided her with the impetus that sent her into the thick of the fight. To her it was unjustifiable interference that the two men should discuss and control her actions. While most military wives followed narrow conventional ways in dread of jeopardising their husbands' careers, Helen announced she would leave the district.

In the autumn of 1909, Theodore and Helen had decided to send Nicholas to Dunhurst, the junior school of Bedales school in Hampshire.[3] The time for his departure coincided with the fateful interview with the colonel and no doubt this coincidence had its influence on Helen's decision to go also. The two younger children had nurses to look after them, so Helen felt no uneasiness about them. Betty was only two years old but Helen 'was a magnificent mother,' Betty said more than 80 years later. 'I never had any feeling of neglect.'[4]

Helen doesn't record what Theodore felt about her departure, but to be left with the final responsibility of two little children in military barracks must have alarmed and confused him considerably. Meanwhile, Helen went straight to Clement's Inn, London, where the WSPU offices were located, and told them she had come to join. It was suggested she go to Edinburgh, where a procession was being arranged by the WSPU.

If Helen had any doubts about her decision, they were revoked by a single meeting. She wrote later:

When I returned two days later and was with Mrs Tuke again, I saw a woman standing in the window with her back to us. After some talk this woman turned round. She came forward. It was the figure that in the photograph had stirred my spark to a blaze. Hardly could I do the ordinary courtesies of handshakings and a few words. It was too soon to be talking to an inspiration. She said 'God bless you.'

Up till then my actions had been inspired by ... boredom, anger ... by a variety of rather incoherent emotions ... suddenly they were ordered and understood with a full consciousness. That first meeting with Mrs Pankhurst, who personified a great truth, showed the way. All the ... indignation and resentment ... were discovered to have had one cause, the subjection of women, and one cure, the emancipation of women.[5]

So inspired, Helen left the military world of her husband and joined another, but vastly different, army.

In Edinburgh Helen was soon absorbed in street meetings, paper-selling and sandwich-board parading. She heard relatives say that no-one with her fuller figure should be used for sandwhich boards. She saw friends and acquaintances suddenly turn and become absorbed in what must have been perfectly familiar shop windows so as not to notice the most unusual parade. But the cheeriness and encouraging remarks of the more general public combined to strengthen her often weak knees. The street meetings utterly shattered her, however, and she just managed to stand beside the speaker in a dumb misery that was not lessened by the chill of the northern evening.

Following the Edinburgh demonstration—a gigantic affair in the Waverley Market after a procession through the town—Helen was asked to go to Dundee with four others to try to upset a meeting for Winston Churchill.

It was in the days before the Dundee meeting that Helen saw, for the first time, the unpleasant sight of human beings losing control of themselves. The women had driven to a village where a Liberal meeting was to be held and when the open car reached the place, it was surrounded by men. They snatched the cardboard placards, stamped on the running boards, stabbed at the tyres with penknives and shouted silly things. Of such events, Helen wrote:

Once when I was doing my now accustomed job of standing beside the speaker, she, very neat and small, was on a chair and was afraid of stepping off it while speaking or of being pushed off it by a pressing crowd. A far deeper fear and one which I shared in dumb horror was that some of the spit (it was night time and dark) which we could hear my countrymen ejecting all round us might reach us and our garments. Another time, later, when I had become rather braver and ventured to speak, I was speaking at a dark corner one night and received a sod of earth full in my face which knocked my hat sideways. For some reason this seemed to me to be funny and I could only stand and laugh. Another time when no sense of humour came to me, my organiser and I were speaking from a carriage, again in darkness, when I smelt a dreadful smell, put my hand down on the seats to search and it went into something soft, wet and warm. I grabbed it (quite the bravest deed of my life) and flung it back to the crowd.[6]

On the day of Churchill's meeting Helen's instructions were to try and get through the barricade. At the appointed time she came forward, and as she made her way through the great crowd she saw one of her colleagues being marched off between mounted police. The woman looked supremely happy and continued to exhort the crowd all the way. Helen's own effort was very brief. With some of the crowd she approached the barrier but was quickly cut out and hauled through it. Firmly gripped by a policeman, she found herself in what she took to be the packing room of a publishing business. Near where they stood was a pile of Auntie somebody's Annual and her guardian expressed his opinion that she would be better employed reading that than bothering about votes for women.

'One of the five was also there, similarly held, some way down the room and now occurred the only time in my life when I ever hit any one in anger,' admitted Helen. 'A plain-clothes man came in and standing beside me began saying insulting things of the other prisoner. Being new to such behaviour, up came my one free arm and swung a backhander on to the man's neck. He fell sideways over a little table and then acted true to his type by twisting my free arm, rendering it near useless for several days.'

Finally the women were taken to a four-wheeler, where some of the crowd put their hands through the windows and made encouraging comments. The five women were taken to a courthouse, charged with disorderly conduct, granted bail and returned to the hotel to exchange experiences and sleep out the rest of the night. However, two of the five had been hidden in a room in a tenement which overlooked the roof of the meeting hall, and when Churchill began to speak they were able to shout 'Votes for Women' so as to be heard inside the hall. Men appeared on the roof of the hall and threw slates at the window where the women were. In time the police, accompanied by reporters, found the room and arrests followed. The women were shoeless so tenants below wouldn't hear them in a supposedly vacant room and one of the women had placed her shoes in the grate to be out of the way. When she bent down to retrieve them one particularly idiotic reporter described her as attempting to escape up the chimney. 'This "attempt" was later fastened on myself,' remembered Helen. 'I being so large that humour was found in the picture of myself getting into or up a chimney.'[7]

In court the next morning the women were given the option of ten days imprisonment or a fine. They refused to pay the fine. On the second day in prison, Helen was taken from her cell and put into a tiny cubicle. Within a few minutes the door opened and the governor was there. He explained that an aunt and a stepsister had come to pay Helen's fine. The new recruit recalled: 'I had heard just enough to know that paying fines was "not done" by suffragettes, so was horrified and burst into tears. The Governor hastened to say "it's all right, it's all right, I'm not to pit ye oot", explaining that without my consent he would not accept the fine. Much relieved and expressing real gratitude I went back to my cell. This particular aunt and step-sister had not been on speaking terms for years but the disgrace of their relative drew them together and they journeyed to Dundee and interviewed the Governor. Later I learned that they had chorused to him their opinion, the very lowest, of suffragettes, and he had stopped them with "not at all, madam, these ladies are actuated by the very highest motives". It might have been rather pathetic to see these two little ladies going home again from their adventure.'[8]

The women were kept in cells with no chair, no heating, a coir mattress on the floor, without their own clothes. Because they were striking, they were also very hungry.

Once out of gaol, Helen found that one of the most heart-warming experiences in those militant days was the unstinting kindness, the ever-ready hospitality of one member to another. It might be a single meal, a chance bed for a night, a ten-minute visit to change clothes or hat in order to evade pursuing police, or it might be sustenance for weeks, skilled care for months, but it was always gladly given. And so it was with that time in Scotland.

After a few days in the country near Dundee, four of the suffragettes went to Arran for further recuperation. 'We landed in Arran from a steamer and had about seven miles to drive in a horsed wagonette,' remembered Helen. 'It was pouring with rain and at every hill we got out and walked to ease the horse. As we trudged along we heartily sang the old song with the refrain, "She's off with the raggle-taggle gypsies, oh!" which to me at least seemed peculiarly appropriate. Then it became a question of "Where next?"'[9]

By this time Helen had been away from home for at least three months and her freedom of behaviour and movement was in such stark contrast to the prescribed behaviour of a wife in military barracks that she must have felt increasingly remote from her previous life. Even visually, there was a stark disparity. The year before Helen's Romany adventure Theodore had been photographed at Trowbridge with the staff of the 6th Battery, RHA. All thirteen men sport moustaches, even waxed handlebars. The soldiers are wearing an elaborate uniform of taut riding pants and tight braided jackets and holding busbies decked with feathers. Theodore's expression seems softer than his fellows'. He stands at home in the group, his wedding-ringed hand placed atop a sabre, his commitment unquestioned. There is not a shadow of a raggle or a taggle or a gypsy oh! in sight.

Helen soon began to realise that the militant movement into which she had flung herself did not merely consist of processions alternating with prison sentences, but that it included a great amount of slogging, continuous work. All over the country were stationed organisers, each responsible for a district. These organisers were to do all in their power to rouse the dormant to militancy. There was always plenty of dissatisfaction, but it was much less often translated into any effective action. It was in this groundwork that Helen eventually settled down with Adela Pankhurst, Emmeline Pankhurst's third daughter, as organiser.

Not only did Helen's confidence grow, so too did her physical presence. Helen's large size—a considerable change from the wasp-waisted woman photographed in Egypt—and accompanying strength had their uses, but also brought its embarrassing moments. In the middle of a Sheffield street a young Yorkshireman accosted her with, 'If tha cooms dompin' on me Ah'll gie thee t'voat'.[10]

Before she arrived in Scarborough Helen went home for the Christmas holidays after Nicholas's first term at school. As Theodore did not really like having the responsibility of the children and was also almost due for another move, she took the children and nurses to Scarborough and then to Sheffield, where they remained for a few years.

4

HARROWING HOLLOWAY

After a few years of working towards the growth of militancy in the north, Helen moved to London. Adela Pankhurst decided to distance herself from conflicting trends in the organisation of the suffrage movement by studying at Studley Horticultural College in Warwickshire. As Theodore had gone to live in India Helen had only the children and their education to consider in her private life. She took a house in Battersea where Jennie Kenney, teacher sister of the famous suffragettes Annie and Jessie, came as governess to Alec and Betty. Here they lived under a clumsy scrutiny.

Once when both Annie and Jessie Kenney had been staying with Helen they had all, including the children, gone away for a few days leaving the two maids in the house. On their return home they found that 'burglars' had entered but had touched nothing except the room occupied by the Kenneys. That was thoroughly ransacked. Clothes had been emptied out of the wardrobes and drawers, everything that could be opened or unfolded was open, thrown about. The only possession of Helen's touched was a silver coffee pot which looked as if it had been crushed. The two maids did not seem disturbed and when a police inspector came he merely said that it was not to be wondered at that they were burgled; had they not the treasurer of the WSPU in the house? The household had become accustomed to seeing a detective imagining himself concealed in the bushes in the park over the road and they now decided that the two maids were accomplices and that the whole thing was a clumsy police operation. So they tidied up the mess and sighed.[1]

The children settled to a new domestic scene. Apart from their mother and household staff, there was a constant flow of women, some familiar, some strangers—all filled with excited talk and a mission. The children, caught up by their derring-do, became accomplices. 'I remember early one morning gathering the stones she [Helen] was later to throw at the windows in Whitehall,' said Alec. Betty laboured at his side.[2]

Helen's opportunity to throw stones came when she was told to break windows at the National Liberal Club. Confident that a certain skill in athletics would make hitting a window a few feet distant quite easy, she was annoyed when several stones failed to break any glass. The windows were heavily mullioned besides which, Helen being nervous, she only managed to hit the building. Another unexpected happening was her evading arrest. The police were as nervous as Helen was, so she walked away to try elsewhere.

The whole affair started at 8 p.m. and at about 1 a.m., after greater success with anonymous windows, Helen went to the WSPU offices and asked what she should do, keep on or go home. She was told that while over 100 women were already arrested they wanted to add to the numbers, so Helen and four or five others went out together, determined to get arrested. They broke shipping office windows in Cockspur Street but still were not arrested. Then they took one window apiece in the Grand Buildings, where policemen were thick. They walked across Trafalgar Square, approached their chosen windows and were swamped by police.

'By this time I had thrown all the stones which the children had gathered for me outside the stoneless London streets and I was using a hammer,' said Helen. 'This resting up a sleeve, nearly let me down by sticking in the lining. I had meant to go close to the window and to tap it but found myself on the kerb with policemen rushing at me. Just in time the lining gave way and I threw the hammer at the window. The owner's subsequent description of the resulting damage, given at the Assizes, was beyond belief but at the time gratifying to me. Two almost hysterical policemen seized each arm, one pulling towards Bow Street, the other towards Cannon Row. I begged them to be calm and assured them I would come quietly either way but could not possibly go both ways. The Bow Street man won and off we went, to be bailed out, and so to bed for what was left of the night.'

They were a motley crowd that gathered at Bow Street the next morning, queued up to get into the inadequate premises. All had a bag or a box of some kind, expecting to be dealt with summarily. A footman attended one prisoner, carrying her bag. He moved beside her up the queue and when she reached a place where she could sit down and have the bag with her he was dismissed with, 'Thank you, John, that will do'. The women were put into the men's billiard room and overflowed into passages and up and down staircases. By evening the great majority had still not been dealt with and a bail fee of 2s 6d was demanded but the women refused, adding that the authorities could keep them there all night if they were going to make them pay for going out.

While waiting her turn to give particulars, Helen was behind a young woman who, in a marvellous brogue far too Irish to be genuine, gave an Irish name and an Irish address. 'I looked on her in admiration and the policeman solemnly wrote it all down,' said Helen. 'Her real name I found later was Smith.' In her own case, the disapproval of her in-laws turned Helen's thoughts to resuming her maiden name, but she decided against it after receiving an indignant letter from one of her Russel cousins saying, 'You have no longer any right to either name, you have disgraced them both'.

The relationship between Helen and Theodore must have been severely strained by this stage. One can imagine the gossip of the other officers' wives at Helen's most unconventional behaviour. Yet despite little reference to her husband, Helen notes his concern for her in her most difficult hours and hers for him:

At the Bow Street Police Court the damage done by myself and over twenty others was put at over £5 a piece so we were committed to the

Assizes, not due for two months. The terms of committal prevented any suffrage work. My husband was on the point of returning to India and did sail on the day on which I was sentenced at the Newington Assizes. He had been at Bow Street and was disgusted with our treatment there and so was worried about a possible long sentence. We went over to Ireland to his mother's home but there the subject of Votes for Women could not be mentioned and the strain on myself was too great.

One day I took refuge in a field which could not be seen from the house and inside its high hedges I went round and round, trying to work off steam. It was no use and I decided to return to London. The day I left, a local outside car was ordered and came about 7.30 a.m. to drive me to Dublin. No one got up to see me off but I found the old ruffian who drove the car to be a perfect 'gain the government' type and we talked rebellion and revolution all the way to my own great relief. I should like to know what he later reported in the village where my ultra conservative in-laws lived.

Finally the Assizes and two months dealt out all round. A telegram with the news just caught my husband before sailing from South-ampton.[3]

Despite the humiliation of being gaoled, Helen was developing a hostility towards men in authority. When utterly weary, and seeing the proceedings being delayed when a little man approached the desk beside the matron, she heard her voice ring out, 'Who is the little man?' As it was the governor, she was hushed and reproved.

She was also becoming more haughty, displaying an intellectual arrogance. The decision as to what books she might read rested with the chaplain who, Helen decided, was paternally minded and rather foolish. When she protested against his refusal to allow her to read certain books on child psychology for which she had asked, he said 'Oh! Mrs Archdale, I am a very broad-minded man'. Really, she noted, his mind was narrowed to vanishing point.[4]

Helen's request for books on child psychology is one of the few indications that she was concerned about the children. In her lengthy account of her militancy, very little reference is made to them. Maybe she felt the expression of maternal feelings was inappropriate to her history. Or, more likely, the physical and emotional demands of the militant life and her concern for the plight of her suffrage sisters were all-consuming. She did not record, for instance, the fact that the children came to visit her in Holloway, an occasion which remained vivid in Betty's memory.

'Not knowing what it was all about I don't think I had any idea what gaol was. It was just very nice to see mother,' recalled Betty, who was four at the time. Asked if Helen was distressed, Betty replied, 'Not in the least … she certainly hid it if she was. She had a lot of courage. They didn't get very long sentences … my recollection was that it was short. And of course in those days everyone had a housekeeper or a nurse—so your house kept on going.'[5] Betty's apparent equanimity is belied by the story that one of the warders told her and Alec that they could come back and fetch their mother in a fortnight. Betty burst into tears because she didn't know what a fortnight was.[6]

Among the women were many restless spirits and they all tried to smuggle things in or out. One day a fountain pen was found in a parcel of Helen's and the governor came to her and roundly accused her of 'not playing the game'; he allowed parcels and she was abusing the privilege. Helen told him not to talk nonsense. She was utterly alone, confined in a seven by nine foot cell; he had a staff to search and to watch everything and everywhere, and the whole power of government to back him. Playing the game, indeed!

One day the suffragettes staged a protest over the treatment of a fellow prisoner. To make their separation difficult, they gathered in close knots. In running to join her knot, Helen tripped and went headlong over. She was told afterwards that a flood of wardresses fell on top of her. It ended any resistance on her part and she was carried off and dumped in a punishment cell.

On Boxing Day the women were brought singly before the governor and the visiting magistrates. Helen was very cross. Her head hurt from hitting a stone shelf in the dark punishment cell and she was full of indignation. When the clerk reproved her with 'You must respect the chair', the chair being the governor, Helen hotly replied that she would respect him only when he deserved respect. In her memoirs Helen admitted that she probably said many other things, both wise and foolish, and she was given seven days solitary confinement which had one good result, that of curing her headache.[7]

By this time Helen was regarded as a troublemaker and when she sprained her ankle she was taken to the prison hospital on the pretext of receiving better treatment. On recognising that the authorities had simply put her there as a means of dividing those whom they wished to rule, she asked to be returned to her cell.

When Helen eventually came home she found a state of affairs which made relations with her relatives worse. Expecting and receiving a sentence which would involve a considerable absence from home and its duties, she had left Annie Kenney in the house with a capable domestic staff, a certain amount of money in cash and another amount in a deposit account with one of the large all-providing London stores. But when Annie used up the cash in hand before Helen's release she went off to a stepbrother of Helen's, who strongly disapproved of her behaviour, and asked him to come to her rescue with money. It is easy to understand the stepbrother's indignant refusal to hand over one single penny.

'This episode probably had its share in a later suggestion which came to me by chance,' said Helen. 'My mother-in-law had a habit of passing on letters from one member of her family to others, thus disseminating family news and gossip. Our two boys were staying with her in Ireland, and I, in England, received from her a letter from one of her sons, my brother-in-law, in which he suggested to her that now that she had got the two boys in her house she should hold onto them and thus get them away from "that pernicious mamma of theirs".'[8]

Helen stoutly clung to her new life, but instead of enacting militant deeds and going to prison herself she was to arrange the goings and doings of others. She was called the prisoner's secretary. It was her first executive post and her work included finding hospitality for those who came to London from distant homes, helping them in any personal troubles, attending the courts where they were tried, arranging bail and seeing that they had food during the long hours of waiting.

It was about this time, in March 1912, that the leaders of the movement—Emmeline Pankhurst, Christabel Pankhurst, Mr and Mrs Pethick-Lawrence and Mrs Tuke—were imprisoned on the charge of conspiring to incite certain persons to commit malicious damage to property. The government, resolving to crush the movement, intensified its repression, and in a new and subtle approach attempted to confuse and confound, divide and disintegrate its members.

Annie Kenney, who had been put in charge of the movement in the leaders' absence, said: 'When the leaders were released after having done a hunger strike my work seemed to grow and not diminish … They were ill and needed rest and change. Scores of the rank and file were still in prison and had to be got out. Had it not been for Mrs Drummond, my sister Jessie, Margaret Cameron, Mrs Sanders, Miss Kerr, Mrs Archdale, and that splendid Mr Arthur Marshall, the movement would have been weakened and discredited. We survived the storm.'[9]

Helen recalled: 'Certain occasions stand out in my memories of those days. One was of an older woman, obviously poor, who on receiving a longer sentence than she had expected showed much distress and, in great secrecy, in her cell under the Court, showed me a pawn ticket and begged that I should take it to the pawn shop and redeem the goods. Owing to her longer sentence the date for their redemption would fall due before her possible release. She had pawned the things to obtain money to carry her over the expected sentence. If any inclination had grown in oneself to pat oneself on the back for one's share in militancy, contact with such courageous sacrifice stayed the patting hand and fostered instead a deep humility, and a thankfulness that one had been privileged to meet such women.'[10]

Betty, who was nearly five years old at the time, would have observed these comings and goings through her hazel eyes, and quietly absorbed her mother's new perspective and the welling up of her respect for all classes of women.

By the summer of 1913 Helen felt compelled to leave England and escape to Europe. Theodore was still in India, the children were no longer babies and sustained militancy and the sustained domesticity which they now increasingly needed were, for the time being, incompatible. A break in school life was recommended for Nicholas.[11] They wandered first, during the summer months, in Italian Ticino, studying the many schools run on the Montessori system which were established in the Bellinzona district. On the borders of Switzerland and Italy they lived in inns and saw the way of life of a rather primitive people. At one place there was a Montessori school which was very well run and Alec and Betty attended it while their governess studied the method. The governess at this stage was Jennie Kenney. Betty later observed that all the governesses they had during the suffrage battle were suffragettes having a rest.[12]

With the coming of winter Helen and the children moved into a flat in Milan. Jennie Kenney went home and Adela Pankhurst came out from England to look after the two younger children. 'Mother was a very warm person,' Betty said, 'and people who needed help quite definitely gathered to her … they knew they could always gets a sympathetic hearing.'[13] Helen had taken care of Adela at Wemyss Bay, Scotland, in 1912 when she was at her lowest ebb—exhausted by the Votes for Women cause and disillusioned with her mother's violent tactics.[14] Now, it seemed, Adela needed special understanding again. She had left Studley Horticultural College and found a job gardening. It, too, was wearing and she was restless, so she joined the Archdales in Switzerland as governess to Alec and Betty. According to Adela's biographer, Verna Coleman, it was a role her mother disapproved of, believing it to be bad for the prestige of the family. Betty found Adela great fun, admitting that as a six year old she was excited by the suspicion that Adela was on the run.[15]

Although their friendship was a recent one, Helen had been struck at their first meeting in Dundee when Adela opened up a crack in Helen's conventional complacency by saying, 'Discontent is the finest thing in the world'. A born revolutionary, bred in an atmosphere of self-sacrificing agitation, Adela nevertheless had in her a strong streak of domesticity. This was partly expressed in the loving care she lavished upon Helen's two younger children when they were under her charge.[16]

Helen, on the other hand, had been reared in an unruffled atmosphere of domesticity and had in her a strong streak of revolution which found expression in the militant movement under Adela's guidance. Adela and Helen had started life from different points and moved on different lines with different aims, but they met when both were changing over. They mingled their similarities and had some great times together. It was this period of changing over that Adela was now going through. By fleeing England she was trying to escape from her mother and from the cause, which she perceived was becoming more fundamentalist in its antagonism to men. For instance, *The Suffragette*, Christabel's paper, began a series of articles on 'the great scourge, venereal disease, and the dangers of marriage, blaming men for all the ills of women'. 'Votes for Women and Chastity for Men' was now the slogan of her paper as she preached a sex war'.[17]

In two poignant letters (one 40 pages long) in 1945, when Helen was writing her autobiography, Adela spoke with a rare frankness about the reality of being the daughter of Emmeline Pankhurst:

> I have often lectured and written about the suffragette movement and my mother's life but have, as far as possible, eliminated personal matters and tried to present her work and her beliefs, apart from such details as her home and family life. What occurred to me and the rest of us concerned our lives and not hers. The truth is that we, her children, were never independent enough, we tried to pattern ourselves by her standards when, really we were creatures of another age …
>
> She, my mother, really made her attitude clear—that she would do as she thought right without considering us—we should have accepted that and done the same. Our slavish obedience and heart-searching loyalty was actually ridiculous.[18]

The Archdale company, enveloping Adela, moved from Milan to Berne. They knew trouble was brewing when Annie Kenney came from England to see them in Locarno, to chastise Adela for attracting the attention of a Milan journalist. He had mistaken her for Christabel, and wanted her to talk. Sibling rivalry was powerfully felt by Christabel, who was indignant and suspicious that Adela was trying to wrest the control of the movement from her.

In January 1914, both Helen and Adela were summoned to Paris to spend a day with Emmeline and Christabel Pankhurst. Here Emmeline indicated that she saw Adela as a failure, and instructed her that she should not live in England permanently. Instead, a fare had been secured for her youngest daughter to sail to Australia on the *Geelong* on 2 February 1914.[19] As Helen Archdale was returning home anyway, it was arranged that she should go directly to England with Adela and see her off. 'We went sadly to Tilbury and to see that lonely, little figure dwindle in the tender remains a clear but depressing memory,' Helen wrote.[19]

Another militant friend had joined the Archdales in Berne and she undertook to go with the children to St Malo. Exhausted by travel and emotion, Helen also returned to St Malo to rejoin her family. On the way she visited her mother-in-law at Bath but when she reached Southampton a gale prevented the overnight passage. The next day the sea subsided and Helen made the crossing. 'I can still clearly see the walls of the harbour [of St Malo] with a trickle of water between them,' Helen recalled, 'just enough to let our boat scrape through and there, in a little group on one wall were my kind friend with my three children. That was a good moment.'[20]

5

WAR

Helen Archdale moved into a furnished house in Hampshire near the school where the three children were to spend the summer term of 1914 as day pupils. It was intended that they should become boarders in the winter term, when a more permanent home had been found. Theodore was still in India and uncertain of the next move.[1]

The school was Bedales, the first coeducational school in England, which had been founded twenty years earlier. Its progressive curriculum included manual work, labour in the fields during harvest time, plenty of fresh air and cold baths; a combination of the idealistic and practical. It also stressed the arts. The headmaster, J. H. Badley, wanted to avoid the chauvinism of the older British public schools and about a fifth of Bedales students were from the Continent, recruited by Badley himself. It attracted people who were more forward-thinking.[2]

For Helen, who thrived on independence of thought in all areas of her life, it was not a surprising choice. Nick had already been attending the school, but the swelling of Archdale ranks didn't heighten the closeness between himself and the two younger children. Not only had Alec and Betty been tied to the furniture when infants to keep them out of mischief, but they had become bound to each other by being each other's sole companion, sometimes in the absence of either parent, throughout all the family moves. Alec explained: 'Whether it was for convenience or by reason of her feminist beliefs that my mother bracketed my sister and me together as a separate group from my brother, I cannot judge.'[3]

Betty confirmed the struggle between the brothers. It wasn't that they didn't love Nick, she said, but when he tried to bully Alec she'd always fight him.[4] The school records have many references to Nick and Alec, particularly in sport. By the time they reached the top of the school they were obviously gifted cricketing all-rounders.[5]

Initially Betty, aged six, and Alec, aged eight, entered Dunhurst, the Junior School. 'I always remember when I first went to Bedales,' Betty said. 'We all had nicknames ... Nick had rather bad legs, like I have, and he was called "Legs", so when Alec came, Nick was called "Legs Major", Alec (who had graceful and fine legs) was called "Legs Minor" and to my horror when I got there I was called "Legs Minimus". I had legs rather like I do now—nobody could accuse them of being minimus. The nickname "Legs Minimus" used to make me laugh and make my friends laugh too. Then I went on to St Leonard's and that nonsense stopped.'[6] However, Betty had learnt to laugh off her appearance.

Whereas Betty was ignorant of the significance of her mother's time in gaol at the time, she was aware of the suffrage movement when she started school. And at the age of 85 she still woke in the night in anguish and guilt over the matter, feeling that as a little girl she let her 'magnificent' mother down. 'Mother and I were very close, she did a wonderful job and yet she never sort of bullied us [into taking on her feminist ideas] but oh boy I've done an awful lot of things wrong ... the first was when I first went to Bedales preparatory school ... which was just when the suffragette movement was at its height ... the other boys and girls were very hostile about the suffragettes, they were terrible women who didn't know how to behave, etc. and I didn't stand up for them [the suffragettes] ... it's the sort of thing you regret after ... you do feel always a sort of responsibility for them [one's parents], don't you.'[7]

Betty settled into the prep school readily, winning a 'General Prize, Especially Garden' one year, and one for 'Repetition and Raffia Work' another. Her gifts were various, for in the lower middle she won a reading prize and the next year came second in the 'neat dive' at the girl's swimming and third in the running dive. She also discovered the fun of ball games and participated in soccer (as centre half) and also played cricket with boys as well as girls. At that age, she remarked, you suffer from no inferiority complex, either physical or mental, and can do anything a boy can.[8]

She was also constantly in trouble. Bad marks for being late, untidy and talking were added up. Ten bad marks a week meant no sausage on Sunday for breakfast. 'I must have saved the school pounds. It made me wonder about punishment in schools … I never thought I must remember if I stopped talking I might get a sausage—water off a duck's back.'[9]

With the children settled, Helen's thoughts turned again to votes for women. It seems that her year of abstention had given the flame of militancy time to burn down into her inmost self, to become a self-feeding furnace, never to go out.

She caused an uproar on the occasion of the old pupils gathering at St Leonard's school by sending in a resolution for the general meeting which asked whether it would wish to discuss the subject of votes for women. A noisy storm immediately arose and when Helen sought an interview with the headmistress she found her furious. The committee rejected Helen's resolution, but she was invited to the platform to 'explain' the circumstances.[10]

Helen had only a few weeks of picking up suffrage contacts and activities, interspersed with house-hunting, before the outbreak of war. There was considerable difference of opinion within the WSPU as to the rightness and wrongness of abandoning work for the vote and instead putting all energies into work for war. Their militant colleagues in the United States did not abandon their fight, but they were more geographically removed from the war.

The WSPU did stop work, indeed it dissolved, but the names of individual members were found in magnificent war work and in political and social, national and international activities. Helen was later to reflect that 'those years of enthusiasm, of discipline, of self-sacrifice, of giving all to a cause, have brought plentiful and magnificent fruit'. The recommendation that the vote should be given to all men of 21 and to women of 30 who fulfilled certain qualifications became law in 1918. Eventually in 1928 a Conservative government, responding to continuing agitation, gave women complete franchise equality with men.[11]

Occasionally Helen took Alec and Betty to Ireland to see her husband's family at Clover Hill. Theodore's mother, her spinster daughter Ellie and son Frank were kindly but constrained, eating meat that was smelly with age and going, without query, to their Protestant church every Sunday.

'I can always remember we were going to church and we saw a little boy who was a real Irish boy,' said Betty, 'a Free State boy dressed in green and gold—and I can remember Aunt Ellie absolutely ridiculing him—beyond the pale. The Roman Catholics were almost regarded as if they were coloured—a different race and inferior in every way—terrible really—and Alec and I were horrified. We weren't particularly good Christians at that age but we were just horrified at the attitude. All so unnecessary and a terribly difficult problem to solve because father's family was sent there by Britain to try and steady the Irish up—a lot of the Protestant side of Ireland were the same.'[12]

The rigidity of thought of Theodore's family contrasted starkly with the tolerance Helen and her family exercised in welcoming the shifting population of suffragette women, strangers of all classes and religious denominations, who periodically shared their London home. And yet the Archdales were kind people and if anyone was in strife they would help. They always entertained Helen and the children when Theodore was away with the army. Later they assisted Helen in paying for the children's education, despite privately being horrified by her militancy and incarceration.

Helen and the children were holidaying with the Archdales in August 1914 when the war started. On returning to England Helen went to Studley Horticultural College for Women, which began to train women to replace men on the land. Without sufficient capital, the effort died in 1916, but Helen thought those years were peaceful and happy as far as the children were concerned. Out of the path of enemy aeroplanes, out of the path of possible enemy invasion, she felt that the children didn't suffer.[13]

In September Theodore sailed from Madras to France, where he remained, mostly in the Ypres salient, until 1918. When, early in 1915,

Helen received a telegram informing her that Theodore was wounded and in hospital at Etretat, she managed to secure a passport and make her way to his bedside. Her militant training had taught her that it was possible to surmount any obstacles to her intentions. Despite indignation amongst the British and medical authorities, Helen was able to see her husband, who was most unpleasantly peppered from head to foot with minute particles of shell.[14]

During the war years it was not easy for skilled women to find employment commensurate with their skill. Helen recorded a classic reply by an official to an offer of medical help which epitomises the general attitude of the official world, military and civil, to the employment of women: 'My dear lady, the best thing that you can do is to go home and keep quiet.'[15] However, backed by friendship, Helen became an 'Assistant Lady Clerk' at the Women's Auxiliary Army Corps Headquarters at Devonshire House in Piccadilly, then under the Chief Controllership of Mrs Chalmers Watson, familiar to Helen at school as Mona Geddes. In this work Helen rose to be in charge of the registry.[16]

In the meantime Alec, about eight, had not gone to school as had been intended because he had broken a leg. It was a difficult fracture and after two attempts to set the break, Helen was advised the alternatives were to amputate or have a stiff knee for life. Instead, she cast round desperately for another answer. She had heard about the new science of osteopathy, which was widely practised in the USA, and she whipped Alec up to London to see an osteopath, Doctor Harvey Foote. After two years in Dr Foote's house, Alec was able to play football with great success.[17]

For Helen there was another trauma associated with the accident. Alec was recuperating with friends in south-east London when a bomb landed in the road in front of the house. A girl and a boy were killed. The other children, including Alec, were in a back room and were unhurt. Helen was telephoned in Westminster soon after the bomb dropped, but she was visiting friends just back from Serbia and they had been so deep in talk that they had scarcely noticed that a raid was taking place. The next morning she was called again and immediately went down to fetch Alec home.

It was fortunate that Alec was eventually able to join the others at school as it became increasingly difficult to house him in safety and for Helen to continue any kind of war work.[18] And even with all three at school Helen still had their holidays to plan for, and her husband's leaves. Theodore came over fairly regularly and when he was wounded a second time he came to Milbanke Hospital to be cared for. Theodore wrote to the children constantly, and they visited him when he was hospitalised, but he had become a remote figure in their lives. Helen had grown to be an indomitable presence and the children had been saddled to her in vivid travels through recent years.

In fact when Theodore came back to London he stayed at his club, but he visited the children at their London home. First in Gayfere Street, Westminster, near the House of Commons, a tiny two-storeyed but comfortable house with a small backyard. And then a house in Horseferry Road, Victoria.

By this time Helen was working in the Women's Department of the Ministry of National Service under Lady Mackworth (later Viscountess Rhondda) and the minister, Sir Auckland Geddes. Her role was to get in touch with and to classify the numerous women involved in various women's organisations (many of whom she had known as suffragettes or the milder suffragists) so that they could be easily available for call-up according to category. There were at that time some military and many civilian occupations in which men might be replaced by women, releasing men for the front, where the shortage was getting desperate.[19]

In the last summer of the war Theodore had been in England for a gunnery course. Before returning to France he had a fortnight's leave and, as was his practice, he planned to go to Ireland to spend the last two days with his mother. This was the first occasion on which Helen did not go with him. Early in the morning of 10 October 1918, a month and day before the signing of the Armistice, Theodore made his way from the Kingstown dock up the gangplank to board the steamer SS *Leinster*, one of the City of Dublin's mail boats, for its three-hour journey across the Irish Channel to Holyhead.

Theodore was 45 years of age, a lieutenant colonel with a

reputation for courage in the war. Before his visit his mother had had a premonition and had pleaded with him not to come over.[20] But the youngest of eight children, he was a dutiful son. He regularly wrote to 'The Mother' from wherever he was posted, both in and out of battle, in Africa, India, Egypt and France.

The weather was fine, although the sea was rough, and there was a full complement of 687 passengers and 70 crew. The atmosphere was thick and hazy, though not foggy, and the passengers gathered in groups on deck could not see any further than about three miles.

The *Leinster* was travelling at about eighteen knots when a passenger who was standing chatting with two others on the forward part of the ship saw a torpedo rushing towards the ship. It passed about ten yards away, but a second torpedo was fired and struck the ship on the port side, forward. It destroyed a large part of the woodwork but did not cause serious damage. Passengers ran to help in getting the boats away and were working at the tackle when a third torpedo was loosed at the ship.[21]

It struck her amidships—near the engine room—and seemed to cut the ship in two. The decks were covered with steam and water and there was a frightful explosion. The funnels were blown to pieces, some of which fell to the deck, killing many. There was a regular panic and confusion on board, according to an American, Frank Martin. One lifeboat was lowered, but too many got into it. People were jumping on top of each other. The bow of the boat hit the water first and she capsized and all on board were thrown into the water. Martin and some of the other Americans tried to lower the boats but without success.

Everyone was thrown into the water as the ship heeled over on her beam end and sank. According to one survivor, it took no more than two and a half minutes. Those who survived managed to save themselves by clinging to upturned boats and rafts, listening to the heart-rending screams of the men, women and children who were floating all around them. One of the most pathetic sights was that of a dead mother and child, the child with its little arms clasped tightly round the mother's head.

When all the survivors had been picked up, the work of searching for the dead was begun and carried on so long as daylight lasted. As the boats with the victims of 'Hun brutality' came into the harbour, one after the other, there were many moving scenes as the dead were laid out on the dock—young and old, of both sexes, who only a few hours previously had been full of happiness. They were all covered with tarpaulins, only their boots showing. Here was a row of women, there an elderly man or a boy and a child. Relatives sought to identify their loved ones by the footwear that was visible, and turned away with faint hope when they were unable to identify the missing.[22] Theodore was not amongst them.

The next day the *Irish Times* cried out: 'At the very moment of asking the Allies for peace and uttering copious promises of reform, Germany has committed one of her foulest crimes against humanity. The *Lusitania* was the first of her hideous landmarks in this war: the *Leinster*, we hope and pray, will be among the last. Both crimes were committed in Irish waters; from both of the stricken vessels the murdered bodies of men, women and children were landed on Irish soil. The hand that sank the *Leinster* has plunged hundreds of Irish homes into the blackest sorrow … Germany is a mad beast whose teeth and claws are turned against all the decencies of human society and all the sanctities of human life. She hates England as an enemy; she despises Ireland as a fool.'[23]

About 580 persons lost their lives and 197 were saved.

It was not until three days after the sinking of the *Leinster* that Lieutenant Colonel Theodore Montgomery Archdale's body came to shore—returning to Ireland once more. How he lived his last moments one will never know, but they would certainly be very different from his poetic desire 'to rest at home, and calmly wait for death'.[24]

As the waves lifted and dropped his fine fair hair, the conventional influence in 11-year-old Betty Archdale's life ebbed away. 'I was at Bedales and the house mistress told us,' she remembered. 'Alec was there and I suppose Nick was there too … of course it happened to someone almost every day. I think mother came down fairly soon. It was a shock but then it's no good pretending I loved father because I didn't know him. I loved him because he was Father, but I hardly knew him at all. I think I'd have just recognised him if I had met him, so it wasn't a sort of terrific shake-up in the family in the sense that it was for a lot of people.'[25]

When Helen went down to the children's school to discuss their future with them she was told by the matron of the different ways in which they had behaved on being told of the death of their father. Nicholas kept his grief to himself, worked and played as usual and had not even told his best friend; Alec cried quietly in the matron's room; and Betty talked of it and carried on outwardly as usual.[26] Restraint and suppression was a family pattern. Helen later confessed that, having bottled things up for so long, she could do no other. As for Betty's impression of Helen at the time: 'Mother never gave the faintest impression that it hadn't been a perfectly happy marriage … It wasn't until I grew up that I began to realise that things weren't. I don't know, she didn't talk about it very much and I never talked to her about it because I always sort of felt that it was a tricky subject.'[27]

However, looking back on things Betty could see that her parents had effectively parted before the war. In fact she wondered what would have happened if Theodore had survived it. 'He was a very fine man, there was nothing wrong with him, but of course mother was a suffragette and had strong views and he was an Irish Protestant and had strong views too.'[28] But there didn't seem to be any animosity between Helen and Theodore, and the children did feel secure. All of them had nice memories of their father visiting, bringing presents (Betty's favourite being a wooden doll from India which she called Jimmy). 'But looking back on it, when he came on leave in the war he didn't stay in our house,' Betty recalled. 'I don't know where he stayed, but I can remember him coming and seeing us and we were running down stairs and kissing him goodbye.'[29]

6

ST LEONARD'S AND VISCOUNTESS RHONDDA

When Helen Archdale was working in the Ministry of National Service the children would come home from Bedales to spend their holidays modestly. They were always very conscious that they were hard up and Betty can remember thinking they might be taken away from school.[1] Betty also recalls that, although she had many friends at school, she and her brothers were isolated when they went home to London. They read books from The Times Book Club, played war games with tin soldiers and dared each other to pinch things from the Army and Navy stores. Occasionally the family would escape the city. And it is from these interludes, travelling about the country in a horse-drawn caravan, that Betty drew the conclusion that she and her brothers had a very free and easy youth.[2]

On these jaunts Helen and her friends can be seen as rather imposing figures, often sitting heavily on a grassy mound with their hair in a long plait down their backs. Betty said they felt in no way different from other families in travelling the country with suffragettes in tow— so many of their friends were suffragette people that they faintly looked down on people who weren't—but she did experience feelings of dissimilarity for another reason. Although it was a happy time, her father's death meant her mother had to bear the brunt of responsibilities in a world which was unforgiving of women on their own.[3] At some point after the First World War Helen Archdale became an ardent Christian Scientist. Betty always had the feeling it was because it was started by a woman, Mary Baker Eddy. Helen thought that the Church of England was too dominated by men. While Helen didn't try to convert her daughter, Betty occasionally attended with her the rather dour Christian Science services at their church at Sloane Square.

Meanwhile at Bedales, Nick completed his secondary education and left to go to Oxford, where he went on to gain a modest MA and two and a half blues—in soccer and boxing. Alec was becoming involved in Shakespearian productions at the school, and in sport. Betty, in her final year of preparatory school, was on the wrong side of her house mistress. She had been behaving badly because she had a lot of energy. Things came to a head one night when Betty let the bathwater keep running and it flowed along the corridor.[4]

Helen next sent Betty to her old school, St Leonard's, on the shores of St Andrews in Scotland. With its imposing buildings, some of which date back to 1512, and its vast playing fields, the school had an air of quiet grandeur. It was regarded as pioneering because it was the first boarding school for girls to be run on the same lines as boys schools. Like Eton and Harrow it had a strong academic emphasis, including the priming for external exams (of the Oxford and Cambridge Joint Board) with the expectation of university beyond.

In upper social classes it was the norm for girls to be taught a bit of French and music and then sent to finishing school in France, but this was something that the St Leonard's girls scorned. They were proud of their school because it was treading new ground for women's education. Young and often brilliant women, generally from Oxford or Cambridge, came to St Leonard's to teach, attracted by its reputation for scholarship and advanced work.

The girls were given responsibility and leadership duties at a time when it wasn't considered quite right for a girl to be a leader. Apart from the facts that they learned, the school gave the girls the attitude that if they really wanted anything, there was nothing they couldn't do. Being a girl was no excuse for failure. One was expected to be independent, to behave like a free and equal and responsible person. 'If not, why not?'[5]

Betty remembers St Leonard's a Spartan. Despite the Scottish climate, ice and snow in winter, and the winds from the sea, it had no heating either in the classrooms or in the dormitories, where hot water bottles were not allowed. Only in the prep room was there a small coal fire at one end, around which the most senior girls of the house gathered. The girls grew used to being permanently cold, to wearing an enormous number of clothes, or to walking or cycling to keep warm.

Betty was thirteen when she arrived at St Leonard's in 1920 and was placed in Bishopshall East under the care of an august woman, Miss J. K. Stewart. While others found her large frame and fierce personality frightening, to Betty Miss Stewart was a familiar type. Not only had she been at the school at the same time as Helen Russel, but her strong personality was not dissimilar to that of the militants who peopled Betty's youth. What is more she had once been a games mistress, was enthusiastic about sport and coached her girls during matches.

For Betty, who had moved around considerably in her early childhood, St Leonard's was to prove a safe harbour in which to develop, away from her compelling mother and brothers, her own strong individuality. 'I remember her coming looking like a little boy, with her hair cropped like a boy and being very small,' recalled a friend, Diana Ashcroft. 'I admired her very much.'[6]

Despite rugging up, Betty became ill and suffered from pneumonia in her first term. She also suffered from homesickness for the first time, but she didn't express her longing to Helen because she believed her mother required her children to be stoic.[7]

Lessons took place in the morning, and every afternoon the girls played compulsory sport, then there was more school from 4.30 to 6.30, mostly prep and the odd lesson that didn't fit in earlier. There were music and plays and the school was run on the lines that if it kept the girls busy all day they'd be too exhausted to do anything wrong. They were kept at it and then sent to bed. The idea of having time to sit and think would never have registered.

For an energetic person like Betty, the program was ideal, the sports field being her main arena for enjoyment. St Leonard's was, par excellence, the school for games. The standard was extremely high and the team games—cricket, hockey and lacrosse—were enjoyed by the majority, many of whom continued to play after they had left school, some at international level. Several, including Betty, led sporting teams abroad.[8]

Team games were compulsory, but there were opportunities for other forms of sport too, including fives, which was just like squash, but with a gloved hand instead of a racquet—rather painful on a winter's day. There were good facilities for riding, and swimming in the (freezing) sea pool below Castlecliffe was a seasonal pursuit. During cold winters there was sometimes skating when the frost held. There was also fencing, and golf was popular with some, but time was limited and it was seldom possible to play nine holes. The girls used to chase the Prince of Wales round St Andrews golf course. He was most attractive, said Betty, and absolutely everyone fell for him.

The girls organised the games and there was intense rivalry between houses. However, there was virtually no competition from other schools. Very few away matches were played, but games were arranged against university and ladies' sides and occasionally against a Scottish national team.

It was on the sports field that Betty Archdale shone. The games mistresses reported that Betty was a brilliant goalkeeper in hockey. In cricket she was a powerful bat. Elizabeth Hake, a contemporary, believes that facing Betty's batting and fielding at point helped forge her (Elizabeth's) character … that her strong sense of determination was probably moulded by those experiences. Younger girls admitted to being scared when Betty started bowling and swiping at balls because they came at such speed. Nor was Betty the only talented player. It was at St Leonard's that Betty Snowball and Betty Green, who later toured with Betty in the English women's cricket team, became friends.

It was not only Betty's skill but her physical presence which made an impact. For as she moved up the school Betty grew into quite a big girl. She was 'a completely solid person,' said Elizabeth Hake. 'I remember her at goal in lacrosse. It was a very small goal and they were very heavily padded and there wasn't much goal left. Betty stood in it and one wondered where anyone found space for the ball.'[9]

By 1925 Betty was in the school hockey team, captain of the cricket team and head of school. A year later she was also in the lacrosse team and in show drill, the pick team of gymnastics, and in the team which won the foursome reel competition.[10] Because her program was so hectic, she remembered liking fielding in cricket because it was the only time she could stand and think about things. Diana Ashcroft said Betty's life at school was easy because anyone who was good at games had an easy life. But she was unique in that she wasn't a bit like the games hierarchy which Diana thought an intolerable group.[11]

In the classroom, the education was liberal, the curriculum wide, including Latin, English, history, geography, mathematics, Greek, French, German and science (including chemistry and some physics particularly for those wishing to qualify for the Bachelor of Medicine course). But because Betty's main focus was on games, she didn't shine academically. She spent most of her time in the middle of the three academic streams.

When Betty's teachers said that she could not pass any external examination, Helen Archdale, believing that they misjudged her daughter, urged them to try her. While most of the girls took the Joint Board Certificate, Betty took the London Matriculation and passed, which surprised the headmistress, Miss McCutcheon. Betty stayed on at the school, after her friends left, to sit for the McGill Junior Matriculation because she wanted to go to McGill University in Canada where her brother Alec was studying. The word was that she could not possibly pass in history. Nevertheless, she passed so well that she could forgo her fresher year.[12] Betty said, 'I wasn't recognised as being academically bright. I can remember overhearing a mistress who didn't know I was there— I was round the corner—saying 'Elizabeth passed' [the London Matric]— great surprise and laughter. I could tell, too, that when I went to McGill and got my BA and topped the year and got some scholarship—quite obviously Miss McCutcheon was surprised I'd done so well.'[13]

At school, Betty was seen to be a rather laughing kind of person, energetic and free thinking. To her delight, she found a kindred spirit who came to stay for a short time at Bishopshall East. She was an Australian girl, Mavis Mackenzie, from Goondiwindi in southern Queensland. Mavis was typically Australian, said Betty, in that she didn't think much of authority. 'We had a whale of a time. Rather inevitably, the social tradition of the school was conservative—she was a breath of fresh air. She was a fast bowler and I was terrified of her, and we were both very naughty together.'[14]

Betty's high spiritedness compelled her housemistress to tell Helen Archdale that she could not make Betty a monitor because she had no sense of responsibility. Helen countered that her daughter would shoulder any amount of responsibility, but if she was not given responsibility she would not seek it but enjoy life to the full. Helen was vindicated when Betty was made a monitor, then captain of Bishopshall East and gardening representative, head of sport of the house and finally head of the school.[15]

The headmistress was certainly taking a risk. Betty was independent in spirit and she wasn't going to toe the line just because she was head girl. However, Diana Ashcroft said: 'I can remember talking [about Betty] to Miss McCutcheon—a very wise old bird—she started smiling. She said, 'I made Betty Head of School because you will find in life the best thing to do with a rebel is to give them responsibility.'[16]

Betty 'was far the most impressive person in the school the four years I was there,' according to Elizabeth Hake, who believes Betty stood out because of her intellectual ability, her honesty, her absolute intolerance of anything dishonest and her down to earth practicality. 'To look at her she's extraordinarily unchanged, and her mannerism, this laugh, and throwing back her head and laughing the way she does, is what I remember about her at school. The headmistress always took prayers. We always had prayers in the hall and we had church services … And I can see her now [Betty when head girl] flopping in after the headmistress—just as she'd walk now, rather flat feet, always untidy.'[17]

It is obvious that Miss McCutcheon was not only well satisfied with her choice of head girl, but also impressed by her potential. Years later, in 1935, she wrote in a reference: 'Miss Archdale has not only excellent ability, as her achievements show, but she has to a marked degree the capacity for leadership and for organisation. Whatever is entrusted to her, she carries through without friction.'[18]

St Andrews in the inter-war years was remote and small. There were no girls schools comparable with St Leonard's within 200 miles and there was a danger that the community within the priory walls was too enclosed, too concerned with its own excellence, impervious to the currents and criticism of the wider world. The Seniors Weekend, when former students returned, served to keep the girls in touch with what was being done in the world outside. Helen Archdale was one senior who made her presence felt.

Betty said that when she went through school it was dominated still by the idea that one went to university to study something, not because you wanted to earn a living. It was still very much this leisure class atmosphere—which in itself was a good one—where they were interested in the right things, helping other people, art, music, literature, philosophy, the things that don't earn money. However, there was an assumption that after university the girls would all marry and have children. Because of the limited number of careers thought to be available for women, Betty said one of the reasons the girls wanted to get married was so they wouldn't become the maiden aunt or a governess or companion—all of which accorded a doubtful social position and made for a dingy life. Betty felt that an awful lot of girls got married with no love coming into the equation at all.[19]

Helen Archdale indignantly urged another world view. She used to come up with her great friend Margaret Rhondda and Betty was conscious of, and embarrassed by, the fact that they always made a nuisance of themselves. It was all quite friendly, Betty observed, but they used to speak out about the school, suggesting it should be pushing the girls more.[20] Elizabeth Hake recalled these occasions. 'Her [Helen's] physical appearance was extremely strange, she was very large and rather sort of loose and lots and lots of chins—she was a very big woman who'd rather gone saggy—I do remember her speaking at Senior meetings—she was always up on her hind legs talking, usually above my head, I must say—but you see she was very much at the beginning of women's suffrage—and she went to gaol with Mrs Pankhurst—and she was very proud of it—so would I be, if I had, too.'

Helen first met Margaret Thomas, as she was then called, when they were girls at St Leonard's school. But it wasn't until they had both grown into intellectual and independent women that they were drawn into an affectionate partnership. Margaret's father, David Thomas, was a Welsh coal owner, financier and politician, the Liberal MP for Merthyr Tydfil. During the war he was sent to the USA to negotiate the supply of munitions to Britain. His success led to a peerage and he became the first Viscount Rhondda. Later in the war he became the minister responsible for wartime food rationing.[21]

After leaving school Margaret studied briefly at Somerville College in the days before women were allowed to take degrees at Oxford. She seemed to conform to social expectations when she married a neighbour of hers in Wales, Humphrey Mackworth, who belonged to the Conservative Party and was master of the Llongibby hounds. But Margaret was restless and dissatisfied with the expectations of women in society. Within four months of her marriage she had joined the Women's Social and Political Union. And as with other intelligent women, she experienced a release of energy, a sense of usefulness, adventure and excitement.[22]

The movement forced Margaret to educate herself on feminism, current history and the politics of the day. She was drawn to the weekly reviews because they made her pause and think and gave her something approaching a considered opinion. She was enormously interested when in 1913 the *New Statesman* was born and the militant movement led Margaret to writing. Helen Archdale too had gathered organisational and journalistic skills through the movement, and both had shared a fairly liberal upbringing. Most importantly, they admired each other's work for the cause.

During the suffrage agitations, Margaret's conservative husband took what must often have been an uncommonly irritating situation amazingly well. On occasion he even went so far as to bring the car and a thermos flask full of hot soup in to Newport, to meet special excursion trains which came down after the great Albert Hall meetings and arrived at three in the morning. His only request of Margaret was that she not go to prison, to which she laughingly agreed. It was a promise she later felt induced to break, to the detriment of their marriage. Compelled by the militants to relinquish self to the cause, she was arrested for trying to put chemical bomb letters inside a postbox. After hunger striking she was released.[23]

Not only was Margaret vitalised by the militant suffrage movement, but during the war an opportunity came her way which altered her life irrevocably. Her father, when a minister, was looking for someone who could be a cross between a confidential secretary and a right-hand man whom he could completely trust. His wife advised him to try his own daughter and in February 1918 she was offered the post. Margaret accepted it and asked her friend Helen Archdale to join her in this work. With Margaret's father's death in the same year, his peerage passed by special remainder to her, and she became Viscountess Rhondda.[24]

These experiences and independent positions took their toll on her marriage and it was dissolved. 'I always remember we went somewhere down in Wales where her husband was, and it was a very friendly but rather sad do,' said Betty. 'They agreed to part because Margaret obviously wanted to stay in London and keep on and he being a Welsh landlord, well he wanted as a wife a woman who would stay there and take up the social whatnot. But I remember feeling very sad about it because he was very good about it and she was too, but they just realised that this wasn't a goer—there was no sort of animosity or accusations of not doing the right thing.'[25]

Eventually Sir Humphrey married a nice country woman, but in those days many people considered divorce an absolute disgrace and a lot of Margaret's friends ostracised her. Hurt and distressed by the public attitude, she desperately needed someone she could confide in. Helen Archdale, newly widowed, her respected colleague both in the suffrage movement and in the Ministry of National Service, was ready to provide both comfort and support. 'She took to mother because mother was a very sort of stable, sound woman who had good advice and a good sense of values,' said Betty.[26]

At this time the government, acknowledging that 'the women were splendid' in their work during the war, introduced legislation allowing them to vote, but only after they were 30 years old, and specified some fantastic domiciliary differences. The former suffragettes thought this wasn't enough and Margaret Rhondda began welding together the women's movement in Britain by initiating the Six Point Group to lobby for better conditions for women. With the motto 'Equality First', it limited its objective to six definite points, all attainable through legislation, to bring about changes such as equal pay, retaining one's nationality on marriage, and admission to various professions. Whenever an aim was achieved, a new sixth point would be added to the list.[27]

A mixed bag socially, the Six Point Group was part of a little group that was the left wing of the women's movement. They weren't regarded as being respectable (like the National Council of Women) but they were more effective. They joined with the National Union of Women Teachers at a time when women teachers did not get equal pay and were sacked when they got married, the Federation of University Women, and the St Joan Social and Political Alliance, a Roman Catholic group. They cooperated with the Equal Rights Committee.[28]

'For seven or eight years we worked away at a heap of niggling little laws that needed altering,' said Margaret Rhondda. 'Finally the Equal Rights Committee tackled the only big purely legal inequality that still existed—the Franchise Acts—and at last, when in 1928 the vote came on equal terms, one felt free to drop the business.'[29] This wonderful win was not without a history of emotions heightened by repeated failed promises and inaction on the government's part.

Helen Archdale wrote: 'the postponement to 1928 of the introduction of the Bill promised in 1927 roused to white heat the indignation which had been simmering since 1918. All organisations of women, even many only most remotely political in aim, spoke together. Threats of militancy were made. The Six Point Group was not backward in expressing its wrath. I believed then and do so still, that it was fundamentally the fear of the renewal of militancy which finally quickened the pace and brought success. The words of Mrs Drummond, that dauntless fighter, publicly spoken in 1914 when war was declared and militancy dropped, were remembered by all. "Yes," she had said, "we have buried the hatchet but we have marked the spot." The militants who threatened and who knew just where the hatchet was buried awoke a fear in Government circles of its reappearance.'[30] However, for Helen, with the passion born of militancy, that equality was not enough. 'Our nation, in spite of having taken sex out of the franchise, was still a poor place for an independent woman and I threw myself into all sorts of attempts to alleviate her position.'[31]

So did Margaret Rhondda. Possibly empowered by her business skills, on top of her suffrage activities before the war, her wealth and her new status as a viscountess, she was in a position to excite other women to recognise their strengths. Soon after establishing the Six Point Group and several years before the 1928 *Franchise Act*, Margaret turned her attention to a weekly review. The journal Margaret had in mind was to be a feminist forum ranging over the whole spectrum of human interests in the arts, politics and industry. In it, newly enfranchised women could use their minds and their new-found influence in an attempt to raise society's consciousness.[32] She drew together a team of women which included Helen Archdale.

A weekly review had never been started by a woman and Margaret was wildly enthusiastic about it. There was nothing in this world, she exclaimed, that compared with the joy of finding something to do that one believes to be absolutely worthwhile and then doing it. She wanted to find people who were worth hearing, and make sure that they were heard, if not by the multitude, at least by that inner group of people who ultimately directed that multitude.

Helen Archdale was in the thick of it. Having echoed her mother in raising alone two sons and a daughter, she now emulated her father's career in journalism when in 1920 she became the first editor of *Time and Tide*. Margaret Rhondda, who was in bad health for some years and also had other business responsibilities, did not take over the editorship until 1927.[33]

The reformist zeal of Alexander Russel seems to have surfaced in his daughter. Helen's six years as its editor are generally regarded as the time when *Time and Tide* was most strongly feminist and left-wing and gave political organisation and pressure the highest priority.[34]

But although Helen occupied the editor's chair, Margaret, who was insistent on a non-party principle that would leave the weekly free to judge political behaviour, probably hovered over each issue. If something she disapproved of slipped in while she was away or ill, she very soon detected the offending item and wanted to know the reason for its inclusion. 'Editing a weekly paper was in one sense only a means to an end,' said Anthony Lejeune when describing Margaret Rhondda.

'That end was the championing of the ideas in which she believed: the absolute value of freedom, the necessity of fearlessly opposing all tyranny and, perhaps her deepest belief, that every human being should be treated as an individual with an immortal soul not as a cog in an administrative or social machine. With all this, she was a pragmatist, changing not indeed her beliefs but the direction of her fire as new enemies hove into sight.'[35]

There is no doubt that the paper was Margaret's baby, and it was her name alone which became synonymous with *Time and Tide* for the 38 years until her death. She expected those involved to put *Time and Tide* first in their lives as it was first in hers. She was a shy person and not at ease with strangers, though few of them realised it, but in the interest of the paper she was prepared to do whatever seemed necessary and to be quite ruthless.[36] She was urgent in her need to convince women of their own worth, their own point of view and the importance of women's issues. Only then would they be able to agitate to change the Victorian mores that prevented them from taking full advantage of the freer atmosphere of the postwar period.

With women's franchise in sight, at last, the journal's urgent task was to apply pressure. Shirley Eoff, Margaret Rhondda's biographer, noted the first volume 'carried comments on the plight workers, a none-too-generous assessment of male parliamentarians' recent performances, and a critical exegesis of the pending Bastardry Bill'. The arts were included and non-political issues, but the thrust was clearly feminist. 'Broad ranging, trenchant, and critical, this first issue set the pattern that *Time and Tide* followed until the mid-1930s.'[37]

Time and Tide also determined to educate its readers about continued legal, political, economic and social discrimination. 'Discrepancies in voting rights, pay, employment opportunities and educational training were ruthlessly exposed...The journal boldly confronted controversial issues such as double standards for ethical behaviour, birth control, marital rape and child assault, always with a view to stressing women's rights and responsibilities. It fought for parliamentary reform' and aimed 'to force politicians to be more aware of the needs and voting power of women,' wrote Eoff.[38]

The journal gained eminence by attracting contributions from and women writers of the time, as well as both conservative and radical politicians. . Among the women were Lady Astor, Vera Brittain, E.M. Delafield, Winifred Holtby, Cicely Hamilton, Rose Macaulay, Naomi Mitchison, Rebecca West, Ellen Wilkinson and Virginia Woolf. Apparently George Bernard Shaw had such a high regard for the magazine and for Margaret Rhondda that he refused to accept payment for his many contributions. Other men who were supportive included G.K. Chesterton, St John Ervine and Gilbert Murray. It became known that the journal gave a warm welcome to those whose work was boycotted elsewhere.

Margaret became known for her objectivity. In writing about her after her death, T. S. Eliot said: 'I should like to recall one instance of her fairness and tolerance. There was no paper in which I felt more assurance that any serious letter of mine was likely to be accepted than *Time and Tide*. There was one occasion on which I felt impelled to protest against an undertaking which no one had publicly questioned. I do not think that Viscountess Rhondda agreed with me; the man whom this enterprise was designed to commemorate had been her friend; nevertheless she printed my letter and told me privately that she respected my motives.'[39]

The inclusion of such famous people of both sexes and the tolerance of divergent opinions lent credibility to the review and prevented it from being regarded as a purely feminist propaganda organ. In the early 1920s it reached between 12,000 and 15,000 readers.[40]

Working together so closely, Helen Archdale and Margaret Rhondda soon developed a symbiotic relationship. Helen supported Margaret emotionally, and it seems Margaret supported Helen and her three children financially by sharing accommodation. The Archdales left the Horseferry Road house and moved into a flat under Margaret Rhondda's in Chelsea. It was more convenient and was very nice, said Betty, overlooking the river. As the Archdale children were at boarding school, they only spent the beginning and end of their holidays in the flat because they mainly stayed in the country, first at Chart Cottage and then at the larger Stonepitts, houses that Helen and Margaret shared in Kent.

Helen and Margaret settled into a permanent relationship. In letters to the American feminist Doris Stevens, Lady Rhondda admitted that she cared deeply for Helen and frequently expressed admiration for her contributions to the cause. Biographer, Shirley Eoff, believes that isolated references indicate that the very close and mutually supportive friendship between Helen and Margaret had romantic overtones.[41]

However, Betty wasn't comfortable with this allusion. 'Oh no there was nothing, uh oh!' she said. 'Neither of them ever looked at being lesbian. There was certainly no physical relationship at all.' She explained that it was the first time there was a real move out of the home for women and believes Margaret and Helen were experimenting in living arrangements that were different from the prescribed marital and spinster patterns of the time. 'I think women, especially the first generation to go out of the home, had very good friendships with other women—but certainly none of that crowd would have been lesbians—ooh!,' laughter.[42]

As *Time and Tide* tapped a more fruitful and independent cross-section of British intellectual life, the people who were associated with it were drawn into an expanding coterie of friends around Margaret and Helen. When the children were home from school on holidays and staying at Stonepitts, they were exposed to a range of people who were regarded as the intelligentsia of the day. With both wealth and position and now influence, Margaret relished being a hostess to them all.

It was at Stonepitts that Betty remembers meeting George Bernard Shaw, who once wrote that Margaret Rhondda was one of his 'most valued friends'. 'I can remember he spoke at a lunch there—he was quite nice,' said Betty with reservation. 'I didn't approve of his views—he wasn't very good on women, oddly enough, but he was a perfectly decent man and very clever of course and the advantage was he didn't care who approved of what he said.'[43]

Betty also remembered Winifred Holtby and Vera Brittain: 'They shared a flat or a house. They were close to Margaret Rhondda and mother too. For some reason we all liked Winifred Holtby but we didn't like Vera Brittain—probably quite wrong but you get these things when you are children. I think Winifred Holtby was more interested in other people and Vera Brittain was more interested in getting her views across … They were very fine. Winifred was more human—you felt you could go to Winifred and discuss things with her but not Vera.'[44] In fact, according to the Eoff biography, Margaret had an intense friendship with Winifred Holtby, who became an indispensable member of the staff of *Time and Tide*.[45]

Helen and Margaret had a friendship with Lillian Baylis, manager of the Old Vic, which under her became a joint home of Shakespeare and opera. And they were both friendly with Winifred Cullis, the first female professor of physiology in London University. Opposite Stonepitts lived Henry Ainley, who was regarded as the leading actor in England at the time. He was later influential in establishing Betty's brother Alec in his acting career. St John Ervine, playwright and critic, used to visit, as did Algernon Blackwood and Rebecca West. 'I liked Rebecca West, she was difficult,' said Betty. 'We used to play a game on the lawn, lawn-tennis with quoits and Rebecca used to be very rude about the dance of the elephants on the grass—because mother was a fair size and so was Margaret. She [Rebecca] was very outspoken, you know the sincere type, she wasn't easy—she was a character—but she had a lot of courage—she was honest.'[46]

Betty said the crowd of friends were all the sort of women and men who thought women could do what ever they wanted to if they chose. They were intelligent and pleasant to talk to. She believed her mother was the kind of person who was always generous to those in need of help and they often had people stay who for some reason or other had nowhere else to go.

The social gatherings really centred round *Time and Tide*. Margaret Rhondda loved meeting people and entertaining them and she became renowned as a hostess. She was generous, funny, shrewd, never cruel, though she saw no reason why she should not intimate that a fool was a fool and a rogue a rogue. In spite of her worldly experience she was shy, so she understood the anxieties of others and came halfway to meet them. Nobody was ever left out at her parties. Also she chose her friends for their qualities, not for their achievements or worldly fame. For her, people existed for what they were, not for what they had done or what the world thought of them. At her house people from all walks of life, the world famous and the quite unknown, met on an equality of friendship.[47]

Living with Margaret at Stonepitts and in the Chelsea flat in London, Betty could not fail to be influenced by the headiness of Margaret's idealism and rigorous integrity, her massive mind, her lack of pettiness, her hatred of shams, her colourful involvement with people, and more particularly, her resolve not to take no for an answer from fate. In this environment it seems that Betty unconsciously adopted the role of an undemanding observer, rather than a participator, in the emotional life and causes that Margaret and Helen espoused. In this way she absorbed their mode of interaction and for the rest of her life Betty, like her strong female models, eschewed small talk and only felt interested in, and was at her happiest when discussing, larger world issues.

When the friendship between Helen and Margaret was at its height, these two imposing women took Betty away on holidays with her school friend, Diana Ashcroft. Diana said she didn't think Betty particularly hankered for close friends so she was immensely flattered to be asked to join her on a fortnight's motor tour around Scotland in the summer holidays. They were sixteen years old. But the trip was far from what Diana had envisaged. Every day it rained and Betty and Diana sat in the dicky seat and got soaked—and Helen Archdale and Lady Rhondda sat under cover in front and didn't notice. They went from Edinburgh to Lairg, right up to John O'Groats, to Betty Hill and Dunnet's Head. There were a few fine days, but not many.

Diana's mother had insisted she take two new pretty dresses to change into for dinner. But she never used them because Helen Archdale made no effort to dress Betty. When it came to changing in the evening, Betty hadn't anything to change into, so Diana didn't change either, she wore the old tennis dress she had been wearing all day. Every evening she and Betty appeared looking like nothing on earth and nobody paid any attention to them, she recalled.

'We weren't paid any attention to by the adult world who were very politically minded and very suffragette,' said Diana. 'They were very much votes for women all the time—and they were always talking about H.S.—he was an editor of something or other—they were arguing about him, the fors and against of different things. It was probably all to do with women's suffrage … They used to talk about this over meals but I think Betty and I were rather silent. When we arrived at places we used to go off on our own and do things, then we used to appear at dinnertime and hear them talking politics—we had to sort of more or less be quiet and listen to those political discussions. They weren't really warm to Betty, they weren't cold either. She was treated much more as an adult than we ever were at home—we were children till we left school, but Betty was not really treated as a child.'

By the time the party reached Oban and were contemplating another week on the Isle of Mull, Diana was feeling homesick and wanted the rest of the holiday with her family, so they put her on a train and she went back to Yorkshire. 'But I think that Margaret Rhondda was very much more human a person than Helen Archdale actually,' said Diana. 'I really had not much more use for Helen Archdale than I had for Alec, which is very little, I have to admit. Now Lady Rhondda was a very different cup of tea, she was a much more intelligent woman—yes a highly intelligent woman I should think.'[48]

It is interesting to recognise that while the Archdales cohabited with Margaret Rhondda, of the three children it was only Betty who formed an attachment to her. Nick by this time was striking an independent path at university and in his earliest job with a publisher. Alec was also at university. But more than that, it seems that neither of the boys deigned to share Betty's unqualified admiration for Margaret. And Margaret didn't get on with Alec, especially after she caught him rudely laughing at her missing the ball at golf.[49]

But there is no doubt that a warm relationship developed between Betty and Margaret. They were photographed walking along a path at Stonepitts arm in arm. Margaret with a broad smile on her attractive square face. Betty, a tall schoolgirl, looking more wary. Throughout the rest of Margaret's life Betty asked for Margaret's counsel on work decisions. She also sought her praise of articles she submitted to *Time and Tide*. They wrote to each other and Betty went walking with Margaret at Pen-Ithon, commenting in her diary of 1934 that they had talked well together. What is more, Margaret accorded Betty the honour of allocating her the best guest room. 'I was very close to her,' reflected Betty.[50]

Often Betty credited her secondary school with having a marked influence on her and her life's work. She would harken back to her St Leonard's days as if they provided her with the most spontaneously happy times of her youth. And her experiences there led her to say later that she'd like to see every child do a year or two at boarding school. Living always at home was a mistake. She thought it was valuable living in a shared situation, learning tolerance, understanding each other's weaknesses.

She believed the school had a strong influence in setting almost heroic Grecian standards which were good not only for a small group of girls in Scotland but for the world in general. They were standards of honesty; the need to stand up for what you believed in; the need for tolerance of others' views; being kind to people you defeated and accepting defeat yourself; courage, always owning up. 'I was always in trouble,' said Betty, 'but we were never dishonest about it, you told the truth.'[51]

'I think Christianity was a stronger force in England and Scotland then than it is now,' Betty said in the 1990s. 'There were certain principles that we lived by—I get the feeling that they don't now. Our life was much simpler. It was quite clear what was good and bad, and it wasn't just the churches [who recognised this] but the ordinary people. The children we went to school with all had the same ideas—you didn't lie, you didn't cheat, and you didn't steal—you were kind to people.'[52]

The girls left St Leonard's with a strong sense of responsibility to other people and an obligation to serve the community. A contemporary said she thought, on reflection, that school had put so much emphasis on doing things for others that the girls almost forgot to do things for themselves.[53] For Betty, the main gain was that, however she performed in work or sport, the school bolstered her morale.

But despite these strong idealistic views, whenever Betty was asked whether she was more influenced by her home or schooling, she said the home won every time. 'My mother was a very strong influence … she wasn't a dictatorial, dogmatic person … She must have had a very odd life because she wasn't expecting it, I don't think. In her days when you married that was that, and then to have to cope with three children. She and her friend Cicely Hamilton [author of *Marriage as a Trade*] and Lady Rhondda had an effect on us as children—they had far more influence than the school.'[54]

7

MCGILL AND AMERICAN FEMINISTS

When Betty left school she decided to abjure the familiarity of Britain and go to university in Canada, where Alec was studying forestry at McGill University in Montreal. At the end of two years he came back, as a hand on a cattle boat, for a vacation and Betty thought it would be interesting to go back with him. It was partly the whiff of adventure that attracted Betty, but also the desire to be with Alec, the person with whom she had had the greatest intimacy.

With both Helen and Margaret absorbed in journalism and other political agitations, Betty decided to study economics and political science at McGill. She and Alec travelled to Canada by ship. On board, both brother and sister performed jauntily before the camera. In a dark cloche hat, a large loose-fitting overcoat with a broad fur collar, woollen gloves, stockings and strapped, sensible high-heel shoes, Betty has an ingenuous smile, an uninhibited pleasure in her new departure.

Fortuitously at her table was Charles Herbert, a genial friend of Alec's and the nephew of a prominent MP. He was studying Arts at McGill. His intelligence and sense of humour drew Betty and they remained close throughout her time at university. When they arrived in Montreal Alec, whose major achievement at university to date was being hailed as a rising young amateur actor, settled into lodgings with his sister. He was president of the McGill Players, on the committee of the

St James Players and also on that of the McGill Red and White Revue, a big annual event that played for a week in Montreal's biggest theatre. Grandly, he introduced Betty to his friends.[1]

Because she had taken the Senior Matric Betty went into second year of a four-year course. But despite the fact that she was lured to McGill because of Alec, their time there together was very short. 'One Friday evening … I was having a cup of coffee with the President of the Student's Union,' recalled Alec. 'During our talk, out of the blue he said, "You know Alec, I wonder you don't go on the stage professionally". An age later I think I said "what?" And I can remember no more of that conversation. I rushed round to the apartment and told Betty that this was "it". This was what I must do, now, go back to England and attack the professional stage. Betty presented no objections and we set about the operation immediately. Packing, passage, the installation of Betty in the resident Women's College, the few goodbyes were all completed in what seemed a moment, and I sailed on Tuesday morning.'[2]

Left on her own, Betty settled down well in the Royal Victoria College. The only other girl studying economics was Ida Greaves from Barbados and they became great friends, doing everything together.

Betty said she learnt a lot from university in Canada. She sensed a certain freedom there which at the time she hadn't experienced in England. 'I was an ordinary, fairly conservative, English schoolgirl—quite convinced that in Britain we did everything better than anyone else and anyone different from us, well it was their bad luck. It was terribly good to go to a country like Canada which was very much the same—it wasn't different enough to jar you and Montreal was French speaking. To realise things could be different and yet just as good—different didn't mean second rate and this has stood me in very good stead, especially when I came out here [Australia].'[3]

At McGill, Betty's professor in political science was the quixotic Stephen Leacock, who was more widely known as a humorous writer. Politically, he was on the right. Despite his august position, Betty found him broad minded and great fun. While he gave the students all the facts, he was never didactic and although he wasn't regarded as a brilliant economist he lectured well and held the students' interest.

Betty performed very well at university, receiving firsts in all tests. Not that her whole attention was taken up with studies. After the gruelling discipline of sport at St Leonard's, it remained a driving force in Canada. In a letter to her mother in October 1928 she wrote: 'It has been an energetic week. Both Sports practice and Basketball. On Thursday I went to a Sports practice from 12–1, played field Hockey from 2–3 and Basketball from 5–6. The Sports were on Friday. It snowed in the morning and was so cold the thing was a farce. I was second in the Javelin and Baseball. The winner in the Javelin only threw 53.9in., while I threw 53.4in. My record is 79.71/2 in. so you can guess how cold it was.'[4]

She also started writing for the student paper, *The Daily*, and agitated strenuously for women to be regarded equally on the student paper after the men who controlled it dismissed the woman editor because of a controversial story. Betty was frustrated when other female journalists didn't take a stand for fear of causing unpleasantness or antagonism. 'I do not know how you ever got suffrage if other women are as apathetic and afraid of offending the men as they are here,' she wrote to her mother, seeking approval.[5]

Betty proudly reported that she had managed to get equal rights on the agenda of the House of Commons Club's meeting on peace and that she was due to give a paper on feminism at one of the meetings. Such actions on Betty's part must have warmed Helen's heart. Apart from working with *Time and Tide*, the Six Point Group and the Equal Rights Committee, Helen Archdale was orchestrating a new campaign, which was led by Margaret Rhondda, to obtain admission of women peers to their own House. Betty was kept constantly informed of all these developments and couldn't help but be influenced by them.[6]

Student life suited Betty very well—groups of boys and girls mucking around together without too many emotional demands, working in summer resorts for the next year's university fees, going skiing, and horse-riding. Often university days are a time of emotional and sexual awakening, and Betty was not immune to enthusiasms. When, in several interviews in later life, she said she fell in love with a lad in Canada whom she might have married, it was to Charles Herbert that she was referring.

They used to write essays on various topics and exchange them.

At one stage both Charles and Betty had been reading Montaigne so they decided it would be fun, as self-discipline, to make themselves put their thoughts down in words. Forty-six years later Betty still had a whole book of these essays at her home.[7] On returning to England after leaving university Betty kept up correspondence with Charles, and they stayed friends but nothing more developed.

Although she said she never had any shortage of male companions, Betty never worried about marriage. She was always too busy thinking about what she was learning or what she was doing. She thought she was shy—for no real reason—and although it was her instinct to like people, nothing sexual came into it.[8] But Betty had a lurking feeling of being a lesser person because of her disinterest in sexuality and marriage. Years later she wondered how much her lack of interest in marriage was her mother's influence: 'I think probably the suffragettes that went to gaol—it would be very hard to avoid having a certain hostility [towards men] wouldn't it?'

Betty didn't have a role model of men and women together. Her father was a nice person but of little significance to her, dying when she was eleven. She had grown up in a nest of feminists and the women she admired most, her mother and Margaret Rhondda, were very happy as single women. They found fulfilment within the community of women, a level of intimacy and satisfaction lacking in relationships with the men in their lives. There was never any suggestion from Helen that Betty should look out for a young man and get married. In the social set-up her mother inhabited it wasn't done to make yourself attractive to men.

In fact Helen wrote passionately on just this subject: 'Both men and women have to clear from their minds the ideals of the harem. Until we, the women, can do so, we shall find ourselves always outside, peculiar, judged for our lesser rather than our finer qualities. We must not ourselves use the appeal of sex and we must reject demands for its use when made by others. If everyone of us, when painting ourselves, when hanging on our person jewels, beads, skins, furs and feathers, were to pause and ask ourselves "Why am I putting on this particular thing?" would we not find ourselves still in the harem, preoccupied in becoming or remaining the favourite? The harem or the market place, they are ours to choose, but we must not, we cannot mix them.'

Helen railed against her society for its remarkable concentration on sex. To her, men and women, old and young, seemed able to write, and to talk, to draw, and to paint, to chisel, to compose, only sex. 'I, who am much bored with sex, cheer myself with the hope that like an abscess it has burst and we are covered with its contents. When that is finished all will be sane again.'[9]

But despite Helen's fervently written, strident views, she too had her vulnerabilities. While Betty was at McGill, her mother suffered a great trauma. Margaret Rhondda and Helen, who had been inseparable, sharing domestic and working and social lives for at least seven years, parted bitterly from each other.

It seems that Margaret, who had been in poor health and preoccupied with outside business interests, refocused her energies on *Time and Tide*, undermining Helen's editorial role and changing the emphasis of the review by broadening its subject matter. Helen, who was increasingly involved in international feminist movements, could well have seen Margaret's lack of stress of the feminist cause as a betrayal. The resentments and backbiting from the workplace poisoned the personal relationship. Margaret's biographer says there may also have been an element of jealousy involved. Helen apparently resented the time Margaret was spending on the journal, claiming that 'at present *Time and Tide* is all and everything for her and I am excluded from that entirely.'[10]

Helen, distressed, came to Canada to see her daughter. The break-up must have shocked Betty, but just as she never explored with her mother the relationship with her father, she didn't like to ask her mother the details of what had happened between her and Margaret. She understood it was some disagreement about *Time and Tide*, but also felt that their friend Professor Winifred Cullis had somehow been involved in the split. Whatever the cause, Betty felt it was a great pity. And she very much admired her mother for not preventing Betty from having a continuing relationship with Margaret.[11]

It seems extraordinarily controlled of Helen not to discuss with her daughter the reasons for the disintegration of this central, intense relationship. The same control is evident in her autobiography. Helen never refers to the falling out with Margaret, nor to the pain she must have experienced at no longer being involved with *Time and Tide* and all the stimulating people associated with it. Having been its editor for its first seven years, it was to a certain extent her baby as well.

Margaret Rhondda in her autobiography also excludes any reference to Helen Archdale, apart from what seems to be a prompted footnote near the end which acknowledges of *Time and Tide* that 'although I am its editor today, it was not I, but my friend Mrs Helen Archdale, who was its first editor'.[12]

However, both women felt the separation keenly. Margaret developed health problems and went on a Mediterranean cruise to gather emotional and physical strength. Among her travelling companions was Theodora Bosanquet, permanent secretary for the International Federation of University Women (IFUW).[13] According to Betty, Theodora was an aesthete, a literary person, who was capable of being a devoted and serving companion. Years earlier she had been Henry James's scribe, to whom he dictated several of his novels.[14] She became Margaret's live-in companion, her confidante, and preserver of everything that Margaret wrote, until Margaret's death 25 years later.

Margaret decided to sell Stonepitts, so Helen bought a little house called Stilestone in Crouch, Kent. Margaret also found a new home in London, saying to friends that 'while she would miss the lovely flat she had shared with Archdale, a clean break with the past was necessary if the new relationship were to work. "I suppose the truth is," she admitted, "I do hate being alone."'[15]

As for Helen, after helping win equal franchise in her own country, she threw herself into women's issues in both Canada and America. Immediately she became indignant about the fact that while Canadian women voted on the same terms as Canadian men, the provincial vote was still denied to women in Quebec, where they might not own property, their own earnings or their own savings, and where they might not practice law, etc. She was astounded at the dissension among the women's organisations and befriended the single-aimed suffragists, proudly counting their leader Idola St Jean, a magnificent and selfless fighter, as her friend.[16]

After a few weeks in Montreal, and when Betty had finished her end of term examinations, mother and daughter accepted the invitation

1. Mervyn Archdale (Betty's cousin) and the ruins of Castle Archdale, Enniskillen, Northern Ireland. (Photograph by Deirdre Macpherson)

2. Helen Russel in Shetland before her marriage in 1901. (H.E. Archdale papers)

3. Theodore Archdale (standing fourth from left, resting on the gun, his wedding ringed hand seen through the spokes of the wheel), with the 66 Battery, Jhansi, India, November 1904. (H.E. Archdale papers)

4. Suffragettes Dr Garrett Anderson (*left*) and Mrs Emmeline Pankhurst outside the House of Commons on Black Friday, 18 November 1910. (Central News photograph — the London Museum)

5. A member of the Women's Social and Political Union being taken to a Police Station on 'Black Friday'—the day of the Suffragette Raid, 18 November 1910. (Central News photograph — originally published in *The Daily Sketch*, 19 November 1910)

6. Arrested Suffragettes wait outside Bow Street Police Station the morning after the Suffragette Raid. (Central News photograph — H.E. Archdale papers)

7. Betty dancing on the Isle of Man. (H.E. Archdale papers)

8. Adela Pankhurst in retreat from the suffrage movement, holidaying with the Archdales at Wemyss Bay in 1912. (H.E. Archdale papers)

9. Helen Archdale (right) boxing with Adela Pankhurst at Studley Horticultural College. (H.E. Archdale papers)

10. Annie Kenney when with the Archdale family in Locarno, Switzerland, 1913, before going to Paris to meet with the exiled leaders of the suffrage movement. (H.E. Archdale papers)

11. Three boys? Betty, Alec and Nick at La Corbière, 1914. (H.E. Archdale papers)

12. Nick (*top*), Alec and Betty on the steps of their horse-drawn caravan at Rye. (H.E Archdale papers)

13. Betty at St Leonard's School, Scotland. (H.E. Archdale papers)

14. Miss J.K. Stewart, housemistress of Bishopshall East, St Leonard's. (H.E. Archdale Papers)

15. Cricket nets, St Leonard's School. (Courtesy St Leonard's School)

16. Hockey team with the influential sportmistresses Miss Strathairn *(middle row, third from left)* and Miss Andrews (known as 'Bill'), and to her right, Betty Snowball, who became vice-captain of the first English women's cricket team and one of the finest wicket-keepers in the world. (H.E. Archdale papers)

17. On holiday at Dunnet Head in Scotland — Betty *(left)* with Viscountess Margaret Rhondda and her mother Helen Archdale. (H.E. Archdale papers)

of the National Women's Party of the USA to be their guests in Washington. According to Betty, the party was very much the equivalent of the Six Point Group in the UK; they were the left wing end of the women's movement and neither was as respectable as the big groups.

While in the US, Helen and Betty had the unforgettable experience of seeing a Republican Convention for the selection of their candidate for the presidency. It took place in Kansas City in the middle of a hot summer and the National Women's Party had a stall in the biggest hotel. From this, for ten days, Helen and Betty were able to watch the lobbying machinery of a party convention. As a centre where all must pass, the hotel lobbies became a perfect jam of humanity. Every now and then a group of twelve or twenty men would enter, in seeming fancy dress, stand in the centre of the jam and sing the praises of their candidates.

In the huge convention hall where speeches were delivered, there was singing and processions of rattles, trumpets and drums to accentuate applause. As it was obvious that Hoover was to be the chosen candidate, Helen asked why the convention nevertheless continued for ten days. She was told that the state delegations had come long distances, the election only happened once in four years, the town had been promised ten days of occupation and the thing had to be kept going for at least that time. While in Kansas City Helen attended many lunches and dinners in private houses and country clubs. In none did she take part in the mass movement of hosts and guests down mysterious stairs and through mysterious doors, but she noticed an increased cheerfulness on their return. Prohibition was the law in the United States in those days.[17]

All through the turmoil the National Women's Party remained steadfastly at work, trying to influence party officials to include among official promises a commitment to insert a new clause in the United States Constitution by which all inequalities based upon sex would be abolished.

It was on this trip that Betty met Alice Paul, the US suffrage leader who introduced the first equal rights amendment campaign. While doing graduate work in England in about 1908, Alice Paul joined the British suffragettes, participating in militant action and receiving three gaol sentences. It was then that she and Helen Archdale met.

Returning to the United States, she advocated the use of militant tactics to publicise the need for federal suffrage amendment. As chairman of the Congressional Union for Woman's Suffrage, later the National Woman's Party, Alice Paul organised marches, White House protests and rallies.

Betty admired Alice Paul, finding her to be wonderfully active, very left wing and dominant—you agreed with her or else you got out of the room. It was she who organised the World Women's Party in 1938. After days in the mountains Helen and Betty went back to Washington and did some work in the Congressional Library. Stimulated and proud of her work, Helen wrote to the St Leonard's School *Gazette*, urging participation from old girls. 'At present I am sidetracked in the United States by the most amazing development of feminism,' she noted.

Helen described the 1928 Sixth Pan American Conference held in Havana where feminists from the United States, led by Doris Stevens, Chairman of the Committee on International Action of the American National Women's Party, convinced the Conference to appoint an Inter-American Commission of Women. Its first stage was a study of the laws of the 21 republics. 'It is in this [study] that this particular Senior spends long, very hot but happy hours in the glorious Congressional Library in Washington,' wrote Helen, who by now was also a member of the Committee on International Action, American National Women's Party. 'The second Senior, Elizabeth Archdale, is spending her vacation from McGill buried deep in the labour laws of the same 21 Republics.'[18]

When Betty returned to McGill for her final year, Helen moved about, giving lectures on equality between the sexes, her theme being that the education women had struggled to win had produced an awareness of the injustices and limitations imposed on them by those who were possessive of their power and feared competition. Intelligent women could then do no other than revolt.

The ultimate aim of international feminists was an Equal Rights treaty. They had aimed at equality in national affairs but now the whole world was swept by international law-making, and so they also had to turn to that field. Helen learnt much about the possibilities of international feminism when she attended The Hague in the summer of 1929. Here the International Commission of Jurists for Codification of International Law, appointed by the League of Nations, met with 'nationality' on its agenda. Feminists believed that the lot of a married woman struggling with her nationality was an unhappy one. Owing to the variety of national laws in regard to her husband, a woman found herself sometimes deprived of any nationality, sometimes burdened with two, and always without personal choice. She was an appendage, not an individual.

The women from many countries who gathered at The Hague decided to form a new international organisation, stripped of the programs of all existing organisations, which then embraced every injustice under the sun. The Equal Rights International thus came into being with the single object of obtaining an international agreement that would give men and women equal rights. Helen Archdale, who was instrumental in its formation, accepted the office of its first Chairman.[19]

While Helen spread her interests internationally, Betty finished her degree in 1929 with dramatic results. She and her friend Ida Greaves had both gained first-class honours, Betty winning the Governor's Graduate Fellowship in Economics and Political Science, and Ida the Montreal Manufacturer's Graduate Fellowship.[20] The quandary that faced Betty now was whether to take up the scholarship or return to England to study international law. She twice telegraphed her mother, uncertain as to whether she may regret not taking the scholarship worth $800, even though it meant studying economics when she wanted law.[21] Helen, who saw value in either option, replied by cable on 25 May: 'following your own considered inclinations also great myself feel too ignorant to give valuable advice Margaret concurs if you have time ask Alice Paul. Mother.'

Eventually, Betty decided against staying in Canada. 'I don't know why, I just felt an interest in law and I thought it would have been useful,' she said. 'I think I must still have been thinking of all sorts of discrimination against women and the need for the law side to be improved ... I think it would be easier to improve law, whereas to improve the economic set-up ... heaven help you!'[22]

Ida Greaves decided against accepting her scholarship as well, so the two of them went to see Professor Leacock. At the time economics was not considered a suitable subject for women to study. And although the professor had had women in his lectures before, and had never shown any discrimination, Betty felt he had been rocked by two women doing honours and topping the course: 'The sigh of relief when he realised we were both going, so that male students could get the postgraduate scholarships, was incredible. Dear we laughed. Obviously the businessmen of Montreal wanted their money to go to boys not girls, but still they were very good to us, we couldn't complain, we had a very good time. Stephen Leacock said, "Of course you two are going to teach" and we both said "No!" in one burst—the one thing we weren't going to do, we knew this, was teach. I think because in that generation, teaching was virtually the only thing you could do. We became the generation that said that the last thing we were going to do was teach.'[23]

8

LONDON LAW

Re-entering London in 1929, Betty realised that her years in parochial Quebec had been a restful time-out from the reality of world issues. In London, with its proximity to Europe and vibrant diversity of thinking, she felt she was in the centre of things. Yet there was disturbing evidence of the Depression. Far too many unemployed were walking around the streets, some forming little groups playing instruments. And the fathers and brothers of her friends were having a hard time.

Betty was still very much in training, so personally she wasn't as affected. She constructed an energetic social life, mixing legal studies, feminist agitation and sport. She decided to study law at London University at a time when everyone in Europe and certainly Great Britain was interested in peace and how to prevent another war. Convinced that international law offered the only permanent fundamental hope for real peace, she undertook her LLB and then the LLM, specialising in international law. Because of the many unresolved women's issues, mass unemployment and the general indications for reform, her other strand was constitutional law.[1]

The law faculty was distributed among University College, King's and the London School of Economics. There were very few women in the faculty but with friends Betty trailed around to all three colleges according to subject, without experiencing any sexual discrimination—until she later sought admission to the Bar. While the university courses attracted a variety of people, socially and economically, the Bar had always been conservative. In those days to qualify one had to keep nine terms at one of the Inns of Court and keep a term by eating three dinners. Betty approached Grays Inn, with Margaret Rhondda acting as a referee and providing surety.[2]

The dinners, run by students, were full of etiquette in relation to toasting and asking permission to smoke—but not when it came to the inclusion of women. At the first dinner Betty attended there was a certain amount of hostility to the women present. A senior student called Betty out front and ridiculed her for wearing brown under her academic gown instead of navy blue or black. Everyone present laughed. Betty laughed too, she had to, despite inwardly being very annoyed.[3] For someone who had met with leading feminists in Washington and agitated for world-wide changes for women's conditions, the petty hostility of these young Englishmen must have seemed ludicrous.

For a year or so Betty was secretary to the Six Point Group. Margaret Rhondda was chairman and, despite the breakdown of Margaret's partnership with Helen, she remained very close to Betty. Sometimes Betty stayed with Margaret at her family home, Pen-Ithon. It was unusual for Betty to recognise or describe her feelings, yet after one weekend she wrote in her diary that she had walked and talked with Margaret and that on her return to London she had 'a sort of homesick feeling for Llanwern'.[4]

Helen Archdale was still involved with the Six Point Group too, but more as a roving ambassador. Betty spent weekends with Helen in her bungalow in Kent, but increasingly Helen was away in Geneva, working to obtain an Equal Rights Treaty at the League of Nations. Betty visited Geneva too, as a representative of the Six Point Group, whenever the Assembly of the League met. With her colleagues she would interview delegates to stress the need for a better deal for women. Here Betty met a lot of women from other countries, including the feminist Jessie Street from Australia.

Betty's academic and political life was balanced by her other passion, sport, and she had lyrically happy times playing cricket and hockey and making good friends.

In 1926 a group of women, all hockey and lacrosse players, had formed the Women's Cricket Association (WCA). Mrs Heron Maxwell was the first chairman and her friend, Miss Cox, was secretary. Together they lived (with a browbeaten Mr Heron Maxwell) in Kent where they developed their own cricket ground and started the Comp Cricket Club.[5]

At the time, Mrs Heron Maxwell and Miss Cox were venerable old-fashioned ladies who seemed to be in their eighties. They farmed and their staff mowed and cared for the ground, which was surrounded by Jersey cows and orchards. When a visiting eleven came to play, the tea was a real social event with fresh bread and butter, lettuce from the garden, cakes and a basket of cherries picked by the farmer's daughter. The standard of fielding after tea was said to show a marked deterioration.[6] The patrons' stern gentlewomanliness frowned on competitions, cups, aggressive or self-congratulatory behaviour. The women played because they liked to play. 'That's why we hark back to those days—we laughed a lot. The days of Comp we look back on as golden days,' said Felicity Charles, a friend of Betty's.[7]

Betty did the legal work for the WCA, drawing up the constitution. She was familiar with all the women's cricketing hierarchy. Miss 'Bill' Andrews, her former sports mistress at St Leonard's, became great friends with Miss Cox, so much so that Miss Cox went up to live with her after Mrs Heron Maxwell died.

Another institution which evolved at this time was cricket week, started by Mrs Scott Bowden and her husband who ran the Park Hotel at Colwall—a little village near Malvern. They began by inviting enough women for two teams to stay at the hotel and other digs for a week and play cricket on the Elms (a local school). As the popularity of cricket week grew, three other grounds were involved. It was light-hearted and fun and there was always an 'entertainment'.[8] But while the cricketing fraternity grew enthusiastically in the 1930s, women cricketers were far from accepted. Betty remembers getting off a train in London and the engine driver thought her carrying her cricket bat was the funniest thing he'd ever seen.[9]

In stark contrast to those halcyon days, the social malaise associated with the Depression increasingly concerned Betty. With the capitalist system seeming close to collapse, and the USSR boasting of substantial improvement in man's condition, Betty and others were curious to discover if any lessons could be learnt by Great Britain. So with her flatmate Dorothea Vaughan, Dorothea's brother, Arthur, and Mildred Welts-Smith they booked an Intourist tour and in July 1932 sailed on a small boat called *Co-Operation* through the Baltic Sea to Leningrad. Before sailing Betty wrote to her mother, telling her of her LLB results and her comments on a draft resolution for international law in relation to nationality.

On board, Betty assiduously tried to read Marx's *Capital* and Trotsky's *History of the Revolution* and to master the Russian alphabet. From Leningrad the foursome went to Novgorod, to Ivanovo-Vosnesensk and then back to Leningrad, which they found rather sad and forlorn. Betty and her friends were ordered about by their guide and weren't given any choice but to see anti-Tsarist propaganda. Frustrated, they insisted on seeing factories and schools.[10]

They next travelled to Moscow, but although it was crowded and seemed more prosperous, their stay in the once-fashionable New Moscow Hotel was disheartening. The shared rooms on the seventh floor were meant for one person. On top of this the water hardly ever seemed to rise so high.

One hot night they were taken to a cinema to see an indistinct propaganda film, *One Against All*, depicting Russia's struggle during Revolution and Civil War. They went to a rubber factory which had poor ventilation and girls eating at their benches without having washed. They saw a workers' flat—three rooms with three families—all very clean and tidy but with no bath or gas. And a creche which seemed quite nice except that there were flies 'all over everything as usual'. The group went to a Park of Culture and Rest. Whenever Betty had asked about women's sport she had been assured there was plenty, but when she only saw twelve women doing some very elementary machinery exercises and one or two playing tennis she realised the boast was an exaggeration.[11]

There was a large peace demonstration being staged, with speeches and a band. 'They are absolutely convinced that the capitalist countries are going to make war on them and they are fully prepared,' noted Betty, who later wrote that the only thing that really impressed her was the stress on removing exploitation. At that time the Russians wanted no-one to be in the position of being able to exploit the labour of another.[12]

While she preferred communism to capitalism, Betty recognised that Russia had had to endure a lot of suffering to bring about change. And that despite the Revolution the country had a low standard of living and was choked by inefficiency and red tape. Nor was Russia doing as well as Britain, which had better pay, better working conditions and a better deal for the working class. So Betty never joined the Communist Party, but the appalling conditions of the Depression in England in the early 1930s gave her a lifelong tendency to vote Labour.[13]

When she returned to London Betty resumed her active life of sport, started studies for her LLM, went to the theatre, and mixed with friends and her brothers and their wives. She was intrigued that although her mother was a small-l liberal, Nick was 'so conservative you wouldn't believe it', as was Alec in many ways. They both believed women were not as good as men and Betty was the only one of the Archdale children who followed her mother's line. She wondered if her brothers' reaction was due to the rather forceful suffragettes they knew. 'I suppose it was a result of having been dominated by a woman,' Betty suggested, 'although she wasn't domineering at all. But they were very conservative.'[14]

On leaving Oxford, Nick went into publishing, then teaching in Kent. While there he met and married Sheila, the adopted daughter of Sir Tom and Lady Callender. 'He was lazy, full of life—always sport of course,' Sheila said. 'That was me too, playing cricket, playing hockey … I was more interested in sport than anything else.'[15] Nick was invited to become the headmaster of a private school, Ashbury College, in Ottawa, where he worked for many years. They had three children, Patricia, Elizabeth and Audley. As a family they seem to have been detached from Helen, Betty and Alec, while Betty's diary entries indicate that she didn't get on easily with Nick. In fact she and Alec had the impression that Sheila had to put up with a great deal from their brother.

Alec married Pat, daughter of Sir William Wolseley, member of the Executive Council of British Guiana. She had been on the stage too. Together they had two sons, Dominic and Anthony. 'Pat must have had

an awful time I think,' said Betty. 'But Alec was great fun, he was very nice
and kind and that sort of thing, not the sort of reliable type. I think stage
people often aren't.'[16] Betty remembered that Helen Archdale gave them all
a capital sum at some point and Alec blew all his in about a week: 'He had
no idea of saving or thinking for the future at all, which is quite a good trait.
One can worry too much about what one is going to do next.'

In the early days of their marriages, the two brothers and their
wives occasionally dined with Betty and saw plays with her. In 1934 she
and Pat went to Alec's first night in *Men in White*, and as they emerged
from the theatre they met Sybil Thorndike.

The plays may have been amusing, but Betty's reading matter
wasn't. She was studying for her LLM and every few days she was required
to read a dense book. Between the 2 and 21 February 1934 she consumed
G. V. Portus's *Studies in the Australian Constitution*, the second and third
volumes of Spender's *Life of Asquith*, Morley's *Life of Gladstone*, Garvin's
Life of Joseph Chamberlain, *Memoirs of Sir George Foster* by W. Stewart Wallace,
and W. A. Rohan's *Justice and Administrative Law*.[17]

In fact Betty's greatest satisfaction was serious discussion of serious
topics, as is indicated in her diary entries. 'Tea with Phyllis Lovell and
Mime Frankestein from Germany—interesting discussion on equal pay
and intelligence test—she is well educated and economist'; 'Mr and Mrs
Somerset came to dinner—quite good talk on International Law. March
6 listened to Margaret [Rhondda] in "Whither Britain"—her voice came
over very well—good especially on heart and mind re pacifism but
nothing very original or daring—went round to Somersets to meet a
French barrister—a royalist—very interesting talk on the future of France.'
She also maintained a dynamic correspondence with Alice Paul in Canada.

When not reading and discussing social issues, Betty spent time
with sporting friends, particularly Kathleen ('Rosie') Doman, who had
been at St Leonard's and was one of the founders of the Women's Cricket
Association. When in Scotland on a hockey tour on 5 April Betty sent a
postcard to 'KD' with 'what's the use of a perfect day if you can't have a
perfect night?' on it: '(a joke)—had hysterics in PO when sending it off.',
she noted in her diary. Betty usually referred to Kathleen in her diary as
'Doman' and it could be that the use of surnames for women colleagues

in sport reflected the same tensions the new class of professional women, such as Margaret Rhondda and Helen Archdale, found themselves experiencing. They were forced to imitate male values, including emotional distancing, to prove themselves in a man's world.

In fact Betty didn't seem to get very involved in the intimacies of their lives. One day she jotted: 'met Privey at tea—she is being psychoanalysed—has evidently been mental but has recovered—very warm day, walked along Mall after supper—letter from Mother and Evans—surprised that Mother thinks my T&T letter "excellent".'

By March 1934 life in London had taken on a comfortable if busy rhythm when out of the blue came a letter from Miss Cox. Writing as secretary to the Women's Cricket Association, she asked, unofficially, whether Betty would go to Australia. The initiative came from the Australian Women's Cricket Council (AWCC), which had courageously issued an invitation to an English team to tour Australia. The New Zealand Association followed suit. Betty immediately responded positively.[18]

'It was the kind of thing that even though one might have had daydreams about was never really expected to happen,' Betty later wrote. 'Women's cricket was relatively new. There were only some hundred clubs in the country. We were one hundred percent amateurs. How were we going to send a team to Australia and New Zealand? Their invitation was to pay our expenses once we landed in Australia: we had to get there. We were amateur of the amateur. Without exception we were all students or in jobs … We really did play for the fun of it. We were nice people with nice manners but had no money at all. Nevertheless the invitation was accepted and the fun began. Being the first tour of its kind it aroused considerable interest both in the general public and in the press.'[19]

The proposed tour was to be a lengthy undertaking, leaving England in October 1934 and returning home in April the following year. Anyone who could afford to take six months off and who could raise the £94 10s fare (the equivalent of 43 weeks salary) sent in her name. Some teachers and secretaries had jobs kept for them, others not, and although some of the most talented players applied, the team did have a long tail. This was a concern as it was believed that women's cricket was much more advanced in Australia than in England. The

Depression was far from over and the AWCC had only 14s 6d in the bank, which made the invitation and the acceptance of the tour all the more amazing. The Australians were gambling on sufficient public support to make ends meet.

It was on 9 June that Betty was informed that she was to be captain of the touring team. Two friends from St Leonard's were also given responsibility, Betty Snowball being vice-captain and Betty Green manager.[20] As Betty was not an experienced captain, she assumed her appointment was because she was studying law and could cope with the necessary speech-making.

In fact Betty's reputation had preceded her to Australia, and on 3 September 1934 the Melbourne *Herald* quoted a Sydney woman, Mrs Linda Littlejohn, president of the Equal Rights International Committee in Geneva:

> Betty Archdale is an exceptional young woman, for apart from her career as a cricketer—or a wicketer, as Delysia would say—she has an imposing array of letters after her name.
>
> Like her mother, who was formerly president of a big Geneva International Committee, she can stand on a platform, and without a trace of self-consciousness, give tongue to her ideas and ideals on almost any subject. In fact Miss Archdale has been heard to tell her friends rather sorrowfully, that 'it is this gift for the gab that has made me the team's captain, not wholly my cricket …
>
> It is a pity Mrs Archdale cannot be persuaded to come to Australia with her distinguished daughter … as she would be one of the Centenary's most cultured visitors. Among all her other feminist activities, she recently was joint editor with Lady Rhondda of the London magazine 'Time and Tide', I am told.[21]

Apparently the decision to appoint Betty captain wasn't universally well received. Some players from Surrey emphasised that the team was not really an English representative team (that is, a team made up of the best players). They believed that one of their number, Molly Hide, should have been made captain. Betty heard the cricketer Violet Straker express how very annoyed she was that her friend Molly wasn't appointed. Molly was much younger and, according to Betty, a superior all-round player.[22]

The tour received attention from the press on both sides of the world, because cricket was a particularly emotional issue—the women's tour following closely after the 1932–33 Bodyline series. However, the press also seemed to be in disarray, uncertain as to how to describe the female players. One minute they wrote of their looks, the next in terms of equivalent, better known male cricketers. However, on 11 June 1934 the Melbourne *Herald* gave a thumbnail sketch of each player:

I am informed that the team of English women cricketers which will visit Australia at the end of the year will consist of girls with much more than an average sprinkling of beauty.

They will be a well-balanced side in more senses than one, and should be one of the most popular teams that ever visited Australia.

E. Archdale, the captain, is a solicitor, a strong, forcing batsman. She makes a century every season, and is a good slipfield and reserve wicketkeeper.

S. Snowball, a games mistress, is the Oldfield of the women 'keepers, and a stylish opening bat.

H.E. Green is a games mistress, and a capable actress of the Ruth Draper type, a beautiful field near the wicket.

M.S. Burlston is studying to be a games mistress, and is an all-rounder.

M. Hide, a University student, is the finest all-rounder in England. She scored 51 yesterday in 20 minutes, and took half the wickets. She throws in like a man.

M. Maclagan is of independent means. The team's Woodfull, she is practically unbowlable. She is also a fine squash player.

G.A. Morgan, a civil servant, and another reserve wicketkeeper. A careful bat.

J.E. Partridge, games mistress, a fine slipfield and a good bat.

M.F. Spear is studying to be a games mistress. She is a good length bowler.

M.E. Richards, a games mistress, is a good bat, a slow bowler, and an excellent field.

C. Valentine, of independent means, is sister of the captain of the Kent county team. She does not share her brother's batting talent, but is a fast medium bowler. Of small build, she is a good lacrosse player.

M. Child, a games mistress, is a strong forcing No. 4 bat, and a wicketkeeper.

D.M. Turner, a clerk, is the Larwood of the team. She takes a long run, and bowls at express speed for four overs.

J. Liebert is an art student, an all-rounder.[23]

Before she sailed to Australia Betty had to complete her LLM exams in three subjects. To free herself from the distractions of mounting excitement for the trip, she went to Switzerland to study. Her efforts were well worthwhile, because four days before she sailed she found out that she had passed, and was third out of six in constitutional law and first in international law.[24] She celebrated by having tea with her mother.

The day after finding out her results Betty went to see her lecturers, one of whom, Jennings, was 'rude as usual'. Whether Jennings was rude or not, there is no doubt what her teachers thought of her. H. Lauterpacht, her lecturer in international law at the London School of Economics and Political Science, wrote not only of Betty's knowledge of the subject but of her general ability and of the thoroughness and conscientiousness with which she did her work. He said she was never content to rely exclusively on the lectures or standard textbooks, but read widely on her own initiative in the field of both English and foreign literature: 'As to her personal character and bearing, I share unreservedly the very high opinion which all my colleagues formed about her. I venture to think that she is a first class candidate for any work in some way connected with her studies and requiring steady and independent judgement, reliability and unfailing tact.'[25]

But Betty had little time to relish her academic success. She was to sail in three days and on 18 October, the eve of her departure, she was interviewed by the *Express* and *Mail* and went to dinner at Belgravia and a reception at Caxton Hall. Her speech was well received and there were 'tons of photographers'. Mrs Heron Maxwell gave the dinner and when Betty asked her if she did not wish she were coming too, she replied she didn't like travelling and she didn't like meeting people. 'Yet she was generosity and hospitality itself in her own home,' said Betty, 'and although we were terrified of her we also admired her greatly and treated her with a warm and affectionate manner.'[26]

'Where have these women gone?' Betty later reflected, 'independent in the sense of having married or inherited income, and not having to work from 9–5. They were honest, outspoken and independent in the best sense. And if they had standards; standards of honesty, of thought for others, of integrity; above all standards about which they were quite certain. It was not as if they lived in easy times. The Boer War, the First World War, the Depression, the Russian Revolution, did not lead to their world being calm and certain, far from it. Yet they kept their standards and passed them on to the next generation. I think it was my generation that began the doubting period—doubts about the future, about standards and about what the world was all about.'[27]

It was just as well Betty's core values were intact, because she was about to become a media personality. *The Star* described her as 'sturdy, tweed clad, with hair cropped as close as a boy's and with more centuries to her credit than any other woman cricketer'.[28]

On 19 October Betty lunched with her brother Nick and drove to St Pancras station. Here she found great crowds and photographers. Sheila, Nick's wife, Alec and Pat Archdale, Dorothea Vaughan, Mildred, Helen Archdale, a legal friend, Ali and Miss Cox, all came to farewell her and the team.[29] 'Got to Tilbury about 4.30,' noted Betty, in the same manner as her late father Theodore, 'and sailed about 6.30. Very comfortable cabin, wrote 16 letters thanking for wires.'[30]

9

CRICKET
IN THE ANTIPODES

The morning after setting sail Betty asked the purser about nets for cricket practice. Two days later the girls, some still fragile from seasickness, were on deck, bowling for an hour after lunch.

They were second-class passengers, but being the first women's cricket team to go on such a tour they were inevitably a centre of interest. Almost daily they played deck cricket against the ship's officers and passengers to keep their eye in. A pail of water was kept near the bowler to keep the string ball wet and hard so that it stung the fielders' hands good and proper, and at the fancy dress party Betty, Betty Green and Grace Morgan bandaged themselves up and went as deck cricket after playing with the officers.[1]

The touring team's first proper cricket game was at Colombo on 11 November. A crowd was attracted to the game because of its novelty but stayed on to enjoy the play and, according to the local press, marvel at the excellence of Miss Snowball's batting, the speed of Miss Hide's deliveries and the brilliant fielding of all.[2]

At the luncheon in the Galle Face Hotel, Betty, as usual, was at the top of the table. Carol Valentine was in the team and as her brother had frequently played in Colombo she knew several of the locals. At one stage a note was passed to Betty which was definitely not intended for her but for Carol. The note asked if Betty was as like Hitler in manner as in looks. Betty, who had short hair and a forelock, made an appropriate answer and had a good laugh.[3] For a while, however, the nickname Hitler hovered. 'I was a bit dictatorial—you do as I say or else,' Betty recalled. 'I'd never been in that sort of position—I'd been captain of school teams—but it was a joke. I don't remember minding at all. Yes, I was called Hitler—isn't it terrible?'[4]

As captain, Betty had a good deal of authority that nowadays would belong to the manager and the players had to consult her before making independent plans. But Betty got on well with the team members and had to exercise very little discipline. There were no rules and regulations, just the understanding that if they didn't behave they weren't chosen again. The girls had great fun on board and most of them fell in love—but not the team captain, who kept a wary eye on them all.

As the touring party approached Australia the sense of excitement grew daily. They had never seen Australian women play and the Australians had never seen them. Despite the limitations of practising on board, the trip out had given them a feeling of confidence in their ability. They were a mixed group from varying schools, homes, jobs and regions, but their common interest in cricket and four weeks on board ship welded them into a unit which 24 hours in a plane would certainly not have done.[5]

The bonding was no accident. Betty encouraged teamwork in their daily practice at the nets. Avoiding the development of cliques was another ploy. Whenever they travelled on trains or stayed in hotels Betty required them to draw lots as to whom they were to room with. Betty mixed with them herself, so no-one ever thought that she was favouring anybody.[6]

On 20 November the team arrived in Fremantle, where they were met by a large crowd including the press. Everyone was friendly and the Australian cricketers burst into a welcoming song. They were quickly whisked off to Perth and a round of receptions, lunch at a Perth Hotel and practice at 3 p.m. with a large crowd watching. For a group of very ordinary people to be treated as celebrities was a heady business and needed a good sense of humour.

The *West Australian* said: 'After only two practices the Englishwomen's cricket team have opened the eyes of followers of the game. Until recently, mention of a woman handling a cricket bat or bowling a ball brought a smile, almost of contempt, to the face of the average male cricketer, but those who have seen the visitors at the net have changed their minds. That does not mean that the West Australian women play a poor class of cricket; it has taken the first visit of a combined team from England to awaken interest in the game as played by women. As a result of considerable practice and matchplay, the Englishwomen view their cricket seriously, but happily not too seriously.'[7]

In fact Betty was very much aware that her team had come only a year after the controversial men's Bodyline series with its legacy of tension between the nations. Keen to establish a fresh and healing tone to the tour, she said to the press that they had come to Australia to play the game for the game's sake, and there was no talk of taking back the 'Ashes'.[8]

The Englishwomen had new uniforms. Instead of the usual white pique frock which was apt to split longitudinally, they wore what must have been divided skirts, which came to the top of the knee, with a white shirt. In spite of the long white stockings their uniform was a tremendous advance in comfort and respectability. Betty's team was rather pleased when it found most Australian teams were playing in long skirts, halfway down the calf. This gave the English players a pleasant feeling of one-upmanship. West Australia, however, was one up on them, playing in long white slacks.[9]

The game was to be played according to MCC rules with only minor amendments, the boundary line set at 60 yards and a five-ounce ball instead of the large one used by men's clubs. Although some manufacturers made special women's bats, most of the women found that these were best avoided. Betty happily and successfully used a full-sized man's bat. Not only that but it was thoroughly saturated with linseed oil. 'What the bats must have weighed, I hate to think,' she laughed.[10]

In the nets of the WACA oval at Perth the Englishwomen became rather pensive and waited for the match against Western Australia with mixed feelings. If the women cricketers were as good as they appeared to be in the west, what were they like in the east, where they were reputed to be so much better? The Western Australians ran up to the wicket and bowled with free and easy actions. The balls looked fast and straight and the batsmen hit them hard.

On the morning of the opening match Betty woke up at about seven with a sinking feeling, wondering what the matter was. Then she remembered. The toss won, Maclagan and Snowball started off, both obviously nervous. 'Gradually, as it became apparent that the bowling was not so good as it had looked in the nets my inside returned and by the tea interval all was well,' said Betty. 'At 4.05 our innings was declared closed. Score 201 for 3. Hide 100; a beautiful innings that gave the tour a splendid start.'[11]

It was clear from the very first that the tour would be a success. The two-day match against Western Australia, which ended in a draw, attracted record crowds of 3500. The Englishwomen realised at once that a Test match against an Australian team was going to need several days. Initially they had laughed when they received their itinerary, which allocated three days for each of the three Tests, and they wondered how they could make a match last that long. In England 90 percent of their matches were club games played from two to six on Saturday afternoons. Some were from six to nine on weekdays after work. Once or twice a year they might have played a whole-day match. In England they had been used to greater moisture in the air and softer wickets. But the drier and harder Australian wickets were truer and matches lasted longer.

The friendliness and hospitality of the locals, as well as the unaccustomed glare of publicity, were tremendous fun but also exhausting. The tourists fell onto the ship *Balranald* to go to South Australia. As they crossed the Bight, many of them tired and seasick, a passing ship, the *Bendigo*, sent a note to the cricketers: 'The English team of bellringers, who have been touring Australia and are now returning home, send you cordial greetings and wish you every success.'

The cricketers did not play in South Australia, but were welcomed and entertained, and a leader in a South Australian newspaper, reporting on the number of English sportswomen in the country, including tennis players and golfers, remarked: 'Women are certainly invading fields where they would have been regarded as trespassers less than 20 years ago'.[12]

However, it became clear that some journalists had difficulty in classifying their subjects—as women or as sportsmen. To the team's delight the more social press described Betty as 'a brunette, with dark straight hair, Eton cropped, and big brown eyes,' while Marjorie Richards was 'a well built girl, with fair hair and arresting blue eyes'. Doris Turner 'looked attractive in a brown and white ensemble. Her hat was trimmed with field flowers, which are so popular in Adelaide at present.'[13] The tourists thought that such writing was hilariously funny. No-one in England cared what they looked like or what they wore, far less the colour of their eyes. Betty decided that the fuss about their apparel was one of the penalties that women paid in this not yet liberated world.

Meanwhile, the pace of the tour was strenuous. On the day of their arrival in Victoria the team was given an official reception by the Victorian Cricket Association, a civic reception at the Melbourne Town Hall, and an afternoon tea at Parliament House as guests of the Speaker. A highlight was the day the women cricketers were taken to the Melbourne Cricket Ground. 'I can still remember the thrill of being in the stand of the VCA and walking on the hallowed ground,' said Betty. 'Years later, in 1976, when Lord's allowed a women's match to be played there, I was pleased to be able to say that some 40 years before we had played at the ovals in Melbourne, Sydney and Old Trafford so what was the fuss about?'[14]

As well as their dress, the papers commented frequently on the English team's use of surnames. In England, men frequently addressed each other by surname and the women followed their example. It was an unconscious effort to be sensible and to keep out emotion or anything frilly and feminine. Another difference was the almost complete absence of make-up. The Melbourne *Age* commented: 'All the English Women cricketers touring Australia are single, and declare themselves far more interested in their game than menfolk.' In response, a poem printed in *The Bulletin* began:

> They're set on conquest, but it isn't misters
> They aim at captivating with their smiles;
> It's just to wallop their Australian sisters
> With batting artistry and bowling wiles,
> With cunning cuts and devastating twisters,
> The maids have travelled all these thousand miles.
> To men, mere men, their thoughts will never stray—
> Not till the tour is over, anyway.[15]

The English team had several practice sessions before the match against Victoria. Arthur Biddicombe, the coach of the Victorian women's team, noted that the straightness with which the Englishwomen held their bats could only have come from much competition and tuition. 'The English girls generally are quicker in their movements than the loose-limbed and free-shouldered Victorians,' he wrote, but he believed that what the Australian girls lacked in orthodoxy of play was counterbalanced by their virility, which they employed to advantage.[16] Betty admitted that her girls had had plenty of coaching from well-known male cricketers, and used indoor nets in winter. The comment on the Victorians was also interesting for another reason. In England the women had been brought up on the idea that Australians were tall, large, loose-limbed people. Loose-limbed they were, but to their surprise the British women were nearly always the taller and larger team.[17]

Already the tour was arousing widespread interest. At the Melbourne Cricket Ground nearly 5000 people, many prompted by curiosity, saw 'novel and entertaining' cricket. 'Judged by any standard short of a first class men's match the play was a revelation,' wrote C. H. Gardiner for the *Sun News Pictorial*:

> Scoffers who went to criticise remained to watch silently, or alternatively to cheer some special piece of work which showed a keen insight to the game. The English girls had never previously played on such a wicket. The pace of it at times completely baffled them, but at the start there was a touch of nervousness in both the batting and fielding. The most attractive innings was played by Molly Hide, who made a century in the first game in Perth. She only stayed 12 minutes to make 12 runs, but she batted in business-like style, and one hard cut, square of the wicket, was worthy of any first class players. Her personality captivated the crowds, which was sorry to see her depart. Myrtle Maclagan made 21 in 40 minutes with two leg boundaries. She had no mercy on any loose balls.
>
> Just when the innings might have collapsed Joy Partridge and Betty Archdale, the captain, stayed together for 42 minutes to add 22 runs and changed the aspect of the game. The best stroke of the innings was Miss Archdale's cover drive for three. It was the only real forcing shot played in front of the wicket.[18]

The Victorian match ended in a draw, one of the reasons for which,

Betty explained, was the 1.15 p.m. starting time. After their experience of Australian wickets in Perth, Betty had asked for longer hours to give the teams time to complete four innings. However, the Australian Women's Cricket Council knocked the request back without giving the Englishwomen the courtesy of a meeting. Betty admitted she then lost her temper and threatened not to take the team on the field. Eventually the hours were altered. It was a small row, more of a growing pain really— neither side having any experience in international tours—though it resulted in some ongoing resentments.

Betty said she was abysmally ignorant of interstate tensions and rivalries in Australia. It seemed Victoria was on the English team's side and wanted the longer hours, while NSW wanted the short hours. When one official suggested that they wanted the state games to be drawn so as to arouse more interest in the Tests, Betty made it clear that they had not come 12,000 miles to play a lot of drawn games. She wrote a long firm letter to the members of the AWCC and they all ended up friends. Luckily the press didn't get hold of the row.[19]

The AWCC had organised for the visitors to visit country towns to play matches against local teams, thereby generating a greater interest in women's cricket and enabling the tourists to see more of Australia. In busses the Englishwomen traversed corrugated roads, red soil and saw gum trees for miles on end. They were overwhelmed by the size of the country and the horror of using primitive toilets was counterbalanced by the thrill of chasing kangaroos in cars across the uneven paddocks.

In honour of the Englishwomen, both Deniliquin and Junee declared the day of the cricket match against the local team a public holiday. There was a plague of grasshoppers in Deniliquin at the time and swarms of them rose as fielders ran after the ball. In the grandstand crowds of small boys shrieked each time a run was made. But it was a peaceful day. Eleven white English cricketers appeared on the ground in the morning; eleven red ones returned at night to their hotel. Clouds of red dust had effected this transformation.[20]

From Deniliquin the team went to Sydney by train, arriving to a wonderful reception on 12 December. The row over hours of play hovered in the background, but that was soon settled at a round-table conference, as Betty believed it should have been in the first place.

A list of people at the official reception given by the NSWWCA at the Hotel Australia included academics, judges, a newspaper proprietor and famous sportsmen such as the Test cricketer Bert Oldfield. The whole team felt that they were being spoiled and they revelled in the sun and warmth of Palm Beach, where they surfed for the first time. However, not all the press sang a chorus of praise. Brian Penton, writing as The Sydney Spy, lampooned Betty for her feminist background and for her participation in a 'male sport':

A woman cricketer. Surely a contradiction in terms. There are women and there are cricketers—two quite different things.

Women laugh at cricketers. It has no effect on a woman whatever to say, 'That's not cricket'. She just sniffs and goes on doing it.

Therefore, although it proves, perhaps, that I have a debased, Oriental, a pre-Pankhurst mind, I cannot conceive a Bradman in skirts. Not seriously.

So I went to see these women cricketers, to ask them to explain themselves …

Needless to say, I was received coldly. The sporting ladies to whom I applied for an introduction to the English visitors sent me to all the places where they weren't, and when at last I managed to ferret them out after much more patient sleuthing than I would have to spend in ferreting out the Prime Minister they greeted me like a chicken-pox suspect.

Miss Betty Archdale (the captain) took me in hand. It was plain from the start that she was not going to make any statement which could be used in evidence against her.

Training and heredity well equipped her for the job of putting me down. Her mother was a suffragette and she is a lawyer.

'Why do you play cricket?' I asked

She looked me over hostilely. 'Because I like it.'

'A lot of nonsense is talked about the good sport does for women. Makes them healthy and all that,' I said trying the approach provocative. 'Of course, this is quite untenable. Athletes are notoriously unhealthy people. See how fat they become. They get heart diseases and chest complaints and always suffer from indigestion. Even Bradman has appendicitis. You can't believe that athletics are good for women's health?'

'I didn't say so,' Miss Archdale replied.

'Then you agree?'

'Quite.'

After that we had a long, long silence.

I tried flattery then.

'One has to admit though—you English women are wonderful. Twice as manly—I mean twice as much alive as the men. Don't you think?

'Do you think so?'

'Don't you?'

'I haven't thought about it.'

Another cold—oh, very cold silence.

I thought something might be done with the toreadorical method.

'Anyway,' I said, 'I think a woman's place is in the home.'

No response.

I observed that in my opinion a woman is much better occupied tatting and sewing on buttons than in chasing a ball round the cricket field.

'How very interesting,' Miss Archdale remarked, though for a moment, as her eye lighted with a kind of incredulous outrage I thought I was going to get a run out of it. But, no, she tossed her head and simmered out into the garden. In fact we both simmered, for this kind of thing is very irritating to an interviewer.

'Anyhow,' I said, trying what a bit of arrogantly masculine disparagement would do, 'women's emancipation doesn't amount to much. She's only got what the men don't want any longer … you will agree with me there.'

Miss Archdale smiled pityingly—very, very pityingly. I repeated it all, but Miss Archdale only continued to smile and to watch me with a stonewall eye.

'Besides,' I said, 'There's no doubt women are only what men make them. As Lawrence said, they want a pattern. Man makes the pattern and they live up to it …

'A man invented even women's rights, women's emancipation, women's equality—Goodwin and Shelley did it. So the emancipated woman, the sportswoman, the non-home-loving, business-efficient woman is just a figment of masculine imagination. I see that we agree on that, anyway.'

'Oh,' Miss Archdale said.

'Well?'

'I hadn't thought of it. Really.'

I tried my last googlie. A deceitful, underhand, uncricket-like, but wholly feminine subterfuge.

'Is it true, what people say, that cricket makes women thick in the legs?'

'Well it doesn't worry me, anyway,' Miss Archdale retorted.

Ah a bite at last.

But no—she took a deep breath and smiled.

'It was a good try on his part,' Betty wrote years later, 'and I hardly think it did us any harm.'[21]

The first game in Sydney was a two-day match against NSW on 14–15 December. Although they were allowed to use the Sydney Cricket Ground and were thrilled to do so as it was sacred ground to them, they were not allowed to use the men's dressing rooms. Instead they used the Sheridan Stand and entered the ground from there.

After two days of play England beat the home side by seven wickets in an exciting match which held the crowd until the final over. It was in that over, before a crowd of 5000, that England secured its first victory of the tour. In fact NSW could have played for a draw, but their captain, Margaret Peden, sportingly declared at 5.05 p.m., giving the English girls 36 minutes in which to score 57 runs. This kind of decision was quite common in the cricket the Englishwomen played in those days. With no competitions, no cups, no points, the aim was to have an exciting game with a good finish. They relished hair's-breadth escapes and wins. 'I am sure one of the reasons for our popularity was our lightheartedness compared to that men's series,' Betty said.

There was also praise from the Hill—the grassy rise at the eastern end of the SCG where gathered the least couth, the most vociferous of spectators. As the *Sydney Morning Herald* noted:

A remarkable thing happened at the Sydney Cricket Ground on Saturday. The Hillites, who have earned for themselves an unfavourable reputation for their unruly behaviour and indiscriminate bellowing at important cricket matches, were satisfied and conquered … Most of the 'know-alls' of cricket were present, including 'Yabba' and many of his big throated mates, and, of course, the well-known inebriates, whose continual and unprovoked bellowing of nasty epithets proved so unpleasant to the ears and the temperament of the English Test players on the ground last year. But on Saturday the behaviour of the Hillites was perfect. They were enthusiastic, sympathetic, and tolerant because they were genuinely aston-ished at the girls' knowledge of the game, and at their smartness, courage, and sportsmanship in the field …

When there was a slight delay in the women players coming onto the field, the Hillites called out, 'Shake it up with the powder puff in there girls … We know you like to look pretty, but have a little consideration for us men.'

The barrackers were quick in learning the identity and names of the players. Many referred to them by their Christian names, but as they found this difficult on account of three having Mary for their name, three Mollie and three Betty, they gave them nicknames of 'Bradman', 'Hobbs', 'Larwood', etc.

Cries such as 'Bradman could not do better than that,' 'Girls, you are wonderful,' 'Look at Duckworth there. She can certainly take them,' were heard when balls were returned with remarkable rapidity from the boundary right on to the stumps …

'Hey, Yabba, why ain't yer growling?'

'Why should I, the ladies are playing all right for me. This is cricket, this is. Leave the girls alone.' …

When drinks were brought out, and the two English girls walked over to the batswomen with refreshments, the crowd thought it was a wonderful gesture. 'That is sportsmanship,' they muttered. 'Yes,' added someone, 'It is a knock to men's international cricket, all right. Imagine Larwood and Bradman helping one another to drinks.'[22]

The cheerful spirit of the game was infectious and when England needed only a few runs to win the barrackers were worked up to a high pitch of excitement. They cheered and applauded every run.

The following Monday a coffee party was held at Women's College at the University of Sydney. It went quite well, noted Betty in her diary, adding, 'feeling seems to be getting better'. The 'feeling' was the tension over the change in time for the commencement of the matches. The next day they drove to Wollongong and Betty noted 'got on better with Peden'. Margaret Peden, the captain of the Australian side, was Betty's equal in strength of will and determination. Her face was wide, square-jawed, her smile broad, and her look very straight. Her dark brown hair was cut high, and on the field was mostly pushed under a practical broad-brimmed canvas hat. It was not common for women in the early 1930s to have university qualifications and a profession, but Margaret was a social worker, and her sister Barbara an architect. Both girls had attended Abbotsleigh, a private Church of England girls school on Sydney's upper north shore where the girls played cricket. Coached by former Test players, the girls' enthusiasm was so patent that their father, Sir John Peden, had a Bulli soil wicket laid on the side lawn of his house.

Margaret Peden founded the Australian Women's Cricket Council, the NSW Women's Cricket Association and the University Women's Cricket Club. She was responsible for the Test arrangements and the match advertisements, placed under her name in the local press, which announced special trams to the ground. Accompanying this determination, Margaret had a puckish sense of humour which would have greatly appealed to Betty. In fact Betty felt for Margaret because the interstate rivalry was very high and the Victorians felt they should have had the captain.

Although Betty didn't get to know Barbara Peden until the Second Test, when she joined the Australian side, it is not surprising that she recognised both Margaret and Barbara as kindred spirits. Regarded as pioneering women, they not only became lifelong friends of Betty's, but they twice helped determine the course of her career.

After a day of cricket at Wollongong, the English players went to Brisbane, playing at Newcastle on the way. When in Queensland a paper referred to the Bodyline controversy once more, Betty responded: 'The trouble with men is that they take their cricket too seriously!' The terrible controversies that turned the rest of the cricket world upside down left the women cricketers quite unperturbed, she said, adding that the Australian women cricketers were great sports. Every match was played in an amicable spirit and the visitors made many fine friends among their opponents.[23]

One hundred and twenty-five points of rain fell at the Exhibition Grounds on 22 December, the opening day of the match against Queensland. When the covers were removed from the wicket it was found that although both ends were dry the centre of the pitch was soft. Rather than disappoint the public, the members of the Queensland and English teams took to the field in the rain and played on a pitch which had been cut out, rolled and prepared in twenty minutes. Players had inglorious slides, one ending on her back in mud amid yells of encouragement.

Everyone cheered and clapped when Betty went in to bat. 'Gee she's a ball of muscle!' a lad on the hill called. Although a storm threatened, few of the crowd left until the end of play at six o'clock. The visitors won the match by 201 runs and as the players left the field the spectators gave them a roaring cheer to show appreciation of an afternoon's bright sport under dull conditions.[24]

In Brisbane the AWCC emulated the Englishwomen by introducing a new type of divided skirt for their players, less full and less noticeably divided.

On Boxing Day, the New South Wales and Victorian members of the Australian XI came by train to Brisbane for the first of three scheduled Test matches. Not only were the opposing teams of different nationality, they were of a different socioeconomic mix. The members of the English team represented the leisured classes and had the luxury of learning their cricket at famous English schools. The Australian women cricketers were of a rather different type. They were educated and very sporty, but unlike the Peden sisters most of them worked in factories and did not start playing cricket until they had left school.[25] The average age of the Australian side was 20, rather younger than the English average of 24.

Betty was conscious that it was the first time members of the Australian XI had travelled together or played together. And she was fully aware of the extent of interstate rivalry in Australia and the grizzling about how many players from each state were in the team. In fact they were more a collection of state players than an integrated or united Australian team. So Betty rallied her team and with cricket bats raised formed a guard of honour to the accompaniment of three hearty cheers as the Australians left the South Brisbane railway platform.

The Brisbane welcome seemed to cure any vestigial distancing between the rival captains. Betty made a small note in her diary that night that Peden and Preddey came round after dinner to see her and her team, 'all very friendly'.

On the eve of the first England versus Australia Test match in Brisbane, from 28 to 31 December, the papers quoted Betty's emphasis on the non-competitive element. Even so, she and the other players were all conscious that this was an historic occasion, that their play and behaviour were under close scrutiny, and that the match meant much to the standing of women's cricket. The press also underlined the importance of the event, the *Telegraph* noting: 'It was the first occasion on which the women of Australia were able to emulate the example of the men by contending with a visiting English team for mythical "ashes" ... and Brisbane was singularly favoured in being made the scene of this first encounter.'[26]

In perfect weather conditions, and on a dry pitch though the outfield was slow due to recent rain, the Australian opening pair of Hazel Pritchard and Ruby Monaghan took to the field. At 1.20 p.m. Pritchard faced the slow bowler Myrtle Maclagan and with a straight bat blocked the good length ball. And if both players were relieved to get the very first Test match under way, after the next delivery Pritchard was even more relieved because her snick through the slips was a chance that Joy Partridge missed.

The nervous tension of the occasion had communicated itself to the members of both teams. But the Englishwomen had two advantages—they had travelled together halfway around the world and were in top form, having already played several matches as a team. Their other advantage was that by now they were more used to the interest of the press, which for the Australian team was new and unnerving. So on the first day of play the British rattled the Australians out for 47.[27]

The public had taken such a peculiar interest in the game that for the first two days there had been an attendance of over 7000 and the receipts totalled approximately £300.[28] Australia rallied in the second innings with 138, but at 4.25 on the afternoon of the third day the Englishwomen defeated Australia by nine wickets. While commentators said that the Englishwomen thoroughly deserved to win, the Australian women fought with such determination that it was predicted they would give the visitors a harder battle in the remaining two Tests.

When the game was over the umpires gave each of the Englishwomen a card with the only reference to them made by the press inscribed inside: 'The only persons out of place, but not position, were male umpires, V.R. Castles and D. Given—they looked incongruous in an extremely feminine setting.'[29]

Marjorie Pollard, an English journalist, cabled Betty's analysis of the game to an audience which was vividly interested in the team's progress. England won because of the rock-steadiness of its bowling. Australia's batting was very strong, but the side suffered from nerves. 'It is obvious that we at home must concentrate on spin-bowling for a while. We are rather apt to be just "up and downers"—with only a light variation of pace.'[30]

Australian wickets presented a selection problem for Betty and she wasn't able to play Carol Valentine, who was unable to gain the same movement in the air as she did in England, because of the difference in climate. While Carol was good about it, some of her friends who were influential in the cricketing hierarchy in England were vocal in their annoyance.[31] Despite her concern, Betty said of her girls in a letter to Marjorie Pollard how pleased she was with the grand team spirit, and the readiness to back each other up.

The Second Test, held at the Sydney Cricket Ground on 4, 7 and 8 January 1935, attracted an average of 4500 spectators over the three days. Rain prevented play on the Saturday so there were two rest days in the match. An unusual feature was the fact that the Australian team included two pairs of sisters, Margaret and Barbara Peden and Essie and Rene Shevill.

The playing conditions were perfect. Betty Snowball and Myrtle Maclagan made a century opening partnership in fewer than 90 minutes and the rate of scoring was maintained throughout the day. 'Miss Maclagan when 97, did not scratch about nervously,' wrote Test cricketer Arthur Mailey in the *Sun*. 'On the contrary, she stepped out with Bradmanish confidence and sent the ball crashing to the off-side boundary and brought the century opposite her name [the first century in international women's cricket] in 157 minutes—not a bad performance for a girl on a large ground and on a second-hand wicket which produced an occasional shooter.'[32] England won the Test match by eight wickets, giving the team the rubber.

'A Male' in the *Sydney Morning Herald* commented on the general air of enjoyment which pervaded the match. He noted that the girls did not lose sight of the fact that they were playing a game and always appeared to appreciate good work on the part of their opponent.[33]

Betty later described her requirements for good sportsmanship throughout the tour. The best team should win, according to the play and the luck of the game on the day, by playing hard to win but with good feeling towards the other team, and by not showing your joy when disaster befell your opponents or triumph came your way, nor taking an unfair advantage of your opponent. It meant not hurting another's feelings, and never questioning the decisions of the umpire, although 'Many's the time I was sure the umpire was wrong and sent seething back to the pavilion, but I tried (not always 100 percent successfully) to hide what I felt, and so did we all.'[34]

With each match being described in detail in the press, the visitors became so well known that when Betty Snowball and Myrtle Maclagan were strolling in the Blue Mountains two men working on a ditch came up and asked, 'How did the batting end up yesterday?'[35]

The tourists played one-day matches in country towns, the organisers having prepared a hectic itinerary of cricket, touring and entertainment. Even when travelling on a train, it would sometimes stop somewhere in the middle of the night and the platform would be full of people ready to greet them. Everywhere they went there were speeches galore. However small the township, the expectation for speeches remained the same. On their return to England Betty Green, the team manager and a marvellous raconteur, wrote: 'Archdale and I usually took it in turns to reply; often we were both required. When second, one had hectically to wrack her brains for anything the first had left unsaid. The most glorious moment was when a veritable eulogy on NSW was delivered accidentally in Queensland! Our record day was at Junee, where, with the temperature between 90 and 100 degrees, we sat in the Town Hall in our cricket things amongst row upon row of bottles and listened to twenty-one speeches of welcome before the match started.'[36]

As the Australians hadn't toured themselves, or organized an earlier tour, they didn't know how demanding it could be. In the evenings the visitors had to wash their whites as well as attend numerous functions, and if they didn't all turn up there was a bit of a fuss. In this the organisers lacked understanding and both Betty and Myrtle Maclagan could vividly recall their exhaustion.

Then they were back in Melbourne for the third and last Test, to be held at the Melbourne Cricket Ground on 18–20 January. For the first time the English team won the toss and elected to bat. The public was intrigued. The novelty of seeing women playing the game, in beautiful weather, over three days might have accounted for an aggregate attendance of 13,905 spectators, who paid £485 9s 6d for the right of seeing the pageant.

However, the English team suffered its first collapse in the series when four of their leading bats were dismissed for 48. The match ended in a draw, though greatly in favour of the visitors. Myrtle Maclagan was the star of the English team, gaining her third consecutive fifty and a bowling analysis of 7-60. It was believed that, had time not intervened, the English team would have won because of its superior understanding of the science of the game, its correctness in batting and in placing the field.[37]

So ended the Australian tour, with the girls from England not losing a match. 'It was very nice to stamp our superiority,' admitted Betty, 'but we were a bit lucky. We were a united team from the word go, whereas the Australians were sort of divided... They had as good or better players—we had the experience and teamwork.'[38]

Significantly, Betty had met and become good friends with Australian women of her own ilk, who were spearheading the path for women in sport and the professions—'independent types', she called them. Apart from the Peden sisters, they included Kath Commins, journalist with the *Sydney Morning Herald*, and Peg Telfer who later became the registrar of the University of Sydney.

When the cricket was over, the visitors were given a great send-off by the Australians. In her farewell speech Betty expressed the hope that the tour would mark the beginning of a regular interchange of visits between the women's cricket teams of England and Australia. In fact the English WCA had already issued an invitation to the Australians, but because of slow communication Betty was unaware of it. 'We do not like the idea of leaving Sydney at all,' said Betty. 'Everywhere we have found friendliness and sportsmanship. There is such a nice spirit existing among women cricketers in Australia.'[39]

The team then sailed away to New Zealand, where they were greeted with the same enthusiasm as in Australia. They played matches in Auckland and Wanganui, winning with ease, but the excitement of the tour was catching up on the group and they were tired. As ever on the tour, they were constantly asked what they thought of Australia or New Zealand. Years later Betty wrote:

I am sure all of us were overwhelmed by the scenery, the enthusiasm, the climate and the friendliness of both countries. But comparisons are odious and we tried to avoid making them—at least in public. My recollection is that some of the team reacted not very well to the rawness, bustling competitiveness and gaucheness that showed in some Australians and were impressed by the more 'English' atmosphere in New Zealand, while others, of which I was one, accepted the exuberance of Australians and found New Zealand slightly provincial, but still lovely.

There was slight, but unconscious, class bias in our reaction. Women's cricket in England was predominantly middle and upper middle class. There were many working class factory teams but the leadership came from the middle and upper class. When we reached Australia we found that until we reached NSW not only the players, but the organisers were predominantly working and lower middle class. This was excellent and we made good friends but some of our team found it difficult to relate to people who did not speak the same language. The Australian accent was also a bit of a shock. But by and large any criticisms were obviously superficial and trivial. The overwhelming fact was that thanks to a mere handful of women in Australia and New Zealand, the 15 of us were having the time of our lives.[40]

In Christchurch they played their only Test against New Zealand. The English were the stronger side and the match finished early. Betty can remember being annoyed at being asked to play on to amuse the crowd. Being tired, she refused ungraciously. And so home the team went, aboard the SS *Rotorua*, across the Pacific and Atlantic, completing a round the world trip. During the tour they had remained unbeaten. As if to force themselves back to reality on the voyage home, they helped to paint the ship, wash down the deck, and sew canvas.

There was great excitement on their return to England on 4 April and they were welcomed at Tilbury not only by relatives and friends but by the now inevitable press. Cedric Belfrage wrote in the *Daily Express*: 'Eleven sturdy British maids with eleven bats came back to London last night … For half a year they have swept Australia and New Zealand in turn with their bats… It's the cue for our male cricketers to blush a lovely crimson.'[41]

The only dampener was a group in Surrey who were a little 'toffee nosed' and who 'stressed the fact we weren't really an English team, THE English team,' remembered Betty, 'we weren't selected on merit. They were absolutely right—so that you find in any English history on this we were a sort of touring team and the first real selected English team, selected on merit, regardless of whether you could pay, was after the war.'[42] Nevertheless, the detraction was disappointing and over 50 years later Myrtle Maclagan said Betty didn't get the kudos in England that she deserved. 'But it was a very successful tour. When Betty was captain there was never a cross word, I never knew of any disagreement. Throughout the time she managed our team magnificently … It's very important in a touring team that the captain should be good off the field as well as on the field in controlling and understanding her team.'[43]

Critics aside, no-one could deny that Betty had led an adventurous band of women cricketers to the other side of the earth and put womanhood on world view in an unfamiliar sporting setting. Throughout the six-month tour she maintained a cohesive and successful unit. For that courage and daring she earned herself a lifelong reputation for initiative and strength.

She was pursued to her doorstep by a journalist from the *Sydney Morning Herald*. In her flat in St Peter's Square, Hammersmith, with its canary yellow stairs, simple furniture, many books and carefree bohemian atmosphere, a bronzed Betty was busy unpacking souvenirs of Australia. They included slippers made from kangaroo hide, gum-nut toys, koalas, boomerangs, Maori headdress, scores of photographs and a cricket ball (a gift) which was used in the last Test match of the 1911–12 MCC tour of Australia. Betty said that she had been tremendously impressed by the spontaneous friendship shown by perfect strangers. On one occasion, as she was leaving the grounds at Sydney, a man handed her a parcel. Later, when she opened it, she found it contained fifteen brooches—one for each member of the team—in the form of a cricket bat and ball, worked in silver.

Not surprisingly, Betty confessed that she did not feel inclined to settle down to work again after the wonderful time she had had in the Commonwealth.[44]

10

THE ROAD
FROM JARROW

It was through Helen Archdale's network of friends that Betty aligned herself with another remarkable woman, and found herself involved in an extraordinary event.

While reading for the Bar, Betty was employed as secretary to Ellen Wilkinson, a Labour MP. Ellen Wilkinson had bright red hair, was vivacious, interesting, great fun, and very small … at her full height she was 4 feet 10 inches. But she had great generosity of mind and her tiny frame and large personality evoked waves of protective masculine sympathy and attracted many distinctive epithets from 'Elfin Fury' to 'Fiery Particle'. In the Attlee administration, 'Red Ellen' became a Privy Councillor and Minister for Education.[1]

For Betty, Ellen came to represent the ideal politician, constantly abandoning her private needs to protest against poverty and inequality. 'She was marvellous—full of life and loved everybody—didn't mind whether you were Conservative or Labour or what have you, if she liked you, she liked you—she wasn't party tied,' said Betty. 'She was a convinced socialist but she got on very well with the other side too. She didn't think that anyone who wasn't a socialist was evil necessarily.'[2]

In the lead-up to the 1935 elections the Conservatives promised to help distressed areas by generating new industries. But once in power they ignored their pledges. It was in these elections that Ellen won the seat of Jarrow, on England's north coast. Jarrow's single industry was shipbuilding, but because of reduced demand the shipyards were closed and a 40-year ban on reusing the site for shipbuilding imposed on the purchasers. Living conditions in Jarrow quickly deteriorated, the incidence of death from malnutrition and from tuberculosis being amongst the highest in the country, according to Ellen's biographer, Betty Verson. When three young male workers died in swift succession from malnutrition the local vicar described them as 'looking like eggshells— all right outside but when faced with an infection in winter they had cracked'.[3]

Ellen Wilkinson immersed herself in Jarrow's problems. She visited the townspeople in their homes and so identified with her constituents they called her 'Our Ellen'.[3] To draw attention to Jarrow's plight, a hunger march was organised to London. It became known as 'The Crusade'. On 5 October 1936, the Jarrow contingent of 200 men, each medically checked and equipped with a kitbag, was given an official send-off.

Although Ellen did not, as rumoured, walk all the way from Jarrow to London, 'she did cover much of the journey on foot, and spoke nightly at public meetings organised en route. Her participation had its disadvantages because of her short stature'—one marcher recalled her taking 'three steps to every one of ours which upset the rhythm of the marchers'. Nevertheless her courageous toughness was a great incentive; all too often she was seen walking 'almost unconscious on her feet',[4] wrote Vernon. Betty drove slowly alongside her, trying to inveigle her into the car to prevent her walking the whole 440 miles or so to London.

At each town they passed through at nightfall the local members of the Labour Party organised sleeping quarters and provided food. At one stage 200 pairs of underpants and grey flannels were given to the marchers, and cobblers of the Leicester Co-Operative Society worked through the night to repair their shoes. Ellen observed that so many motorists along the route raised their hats to them that they began to feel like monuments.

On the last day of October, in pouring rain, the men finally reached London. They looked so ramshackle and weary the waiting journalists dubbed them the picture of a walking distressed area. Their appearance made a lasting impression on many observers, including Eleanor Goodrich, a lifelong socialist who could recall at the age of 90 the marchers' arrival in London. 'I remember seeing Ellen at their head and the sight of that procession moved me so deeply that when I reached home I cried desperately.'[5] But the government refused to meet the marchers. Betty said the men demonstrated outside Parliament House and gained a lot of publicity, but received little else. There were, after all, other marches too.

Working at Ellen's side, Betty became known as 'The Office' because of her efficiency, particularly in election campaigns. She was in awe of Ellen not only because of her views but also because of her spirit and will to work. Ellen had a similarly high regard for Betty, and so did the whole Wilkinson family who affectionately nicknamed her 'Rumble'. And she is remembered as playing the Toreadors' song on the accelerator of Ellen's car while waiting for her.[6]

There is no doubt that Betty's responsibilities were varied. At the time of the Coronation, a columnist in Newcastle's *Sunday Sun* reported on 16 May 1937:

> Bridge Street, Westminster, 11 a.m. Wednesday. Well, I don't know about Durham and Jarrow, but the Empire's all right. I have sat here for two hours and watched the representatives of the far-flung outpost ride past in state to the Abbey which is just around the corner.
>
> And everybody now feels proud they have been born British—and no doubt, the Germans and the Japanese and the Americans wish they had been too. At least that is what we are thinking at this tremendous moment while we sit and wait for the Sovereign to ride through our cheers.
>
> I saw folks staking their kerb claims at 7 o'clock last night. They have now been standing, sitting and fainting for 16 hours … I have been fortunate. Betty Archdale, who captained England's first women's cricket team to play Test matches in Australia, ran us down to the House of Commons, where we breakfasted with Ellen Wilkinson, looking anything but Ellenish in the so-sweet veil the Earl Marshal had ordered for Abbey wear…
>
> This is indeed a wondrous land. Ellen is red-haired and once met Lenin, man to woman so to speak, as a fully fledged Communist delegate, but here in the mother land of the Empire where the sun never sets, Ellen is a close friend of duchesses and millionaires. Lord Spencer's green coach was on the road to the Abbey too.[7]

Betty would have felt at home not only in the world of Ellen's political and social agitations, but also in her involvement with Margaret Rhondda and *Time and Tide*. Throughout the 1930s Ellen contributed to the radical liberal weekly, which was taking a refreshingly unstuffy, non-establishment stand. She wrote features, criticism and leaders, under her own name and pseudonyms, and was acerbic in her political assessments, particularly of Chamberlain's foreign policy. 'In these days of shame … the present negotiations between Britain, Germany and Czechoslovakia are aimed at making Hitler's path easy for him. [They] read like a chapter in a new Gibbon, The Decline and Fall of the British Moral Empire,' Ellen wrote.[8] Neither Margaret Rhondda nor Ellen, who met weekly for editorial board meetings at the Ivy restaurant in London, pretended to believe in anything they did not hold to be true.

Despite being on the fringe, Betty wasn't lured into the political arena herself. She wasn't sufficiently tied to one party. But the despair of the masses in the 1930s influenced her election behaviour. Meanwhile, she maintained her enthusiasm for hockey and cricket. In this she had a kindred spirit, the Australian Barbara Peden, who had come to England to work as an architect. Once in England Barbara met and married a Scotsman, Colin Munro. Barbara Peden was a bit more light-hearted than her older sister Margaret. She became a very close friend of Betty's and joined her cricket club in Kent.

One evening on the way back to London after a match at Comp, Barbara Peden, who was driving, knocked down a man on a pedestrian crossing. The old man had walked out without looking, but according to the law Barbara was automatically guilty. The case was heard in a magistrate's court and Betty, who knew how a magistrate would react if three women cricketers turned up in his court with no hats and wearing skirts with shirt and tie, insisted that they dressed for the occasion. They all turned up with hats and wearing ladylike frocks. This paid dividends, since the magistrate remarked favourably on the character of the witnesses. He had to convict but made it clear the offence was technical.[9]

Egging each other on, in 1936 Betty and Barbara Peden overthrew the requirement of the Women's Cricket Association to wear stockings with their accompanying, inconvenient suspender belts. Betty persuaded club members to change to wearing knee-high hose (legally still stockings) while Mrs Heron Maxwell and Miss Cox were away for the summer holidays. The women returned to a fait accompli. The furious elders reacted as if Betty and Barbara Peden were ruining the whole image of cricket.[10] On the other side of the world the *Perth Daily News* reported on the stocking furore, as did the Melbourne *Herald*. Their interest in the issue was because an Australian cricket team was preparing for a tour of England.[11]

Betty's work with Ellen Wilkinson was cited as an excuse not to include her in the English team which was to play the touring Australians in 1937. Molly Hide was the new England captain of a team that included Myrtle Maclagan, Betty Snowball, Mollie Child and Mary Taylor from the previous touring team. Amongst the touring Australians were the familiar Margaret Peden, again as captain, Peggy Antonio, Amy Hudson, Marie Jegust, Nell McLarty, Barbara Peden, Hazel Pritchard and Kathleen Smith. Having previously attracted glory as the first touring captain, to not be in the team at all must have been a remarkably hurtful fall from grace for Betty. But she was silent.

The First Test was held at Northampton on 12, 14 and 15 June. Australia won by 31 runs. The Second Test was in Blackpool at Stanley Park Cricket Ground on 26, 28 and 29 June. England won by 25 runs. When Betty attended the Blackpool match as a spectator she suffered a further humiliation when talking to the Australian visitors at the afternoon break. Molly Hide prevented Betty moving in with them to have tea, saying only the teams were allowed to participate. A cricketing friend, Felicity Charles, said it was the only time that Betty was annoyed. Yet before the end of the match Betty learnt that she was to be included in the team for the final Test.[12]

The Third Test was held at Kennington, London, on The Oval on 10, 12, and 13 July. Audrey Collins was also selected and batted with Betty. 'Betty was so much older and respected because she was intelligent and independent,' said Audrey. 'My recollection of that match was that we both enjoyed ourselves enormously—because I think I went in number 8 and Betty had been in for a little while. Molly said, "I want quick runs so that I can declare". So we were scampering up and down the pitch … I was lucky to be able to be making runs and she [Betty] was established there and got her eye in. We put on 54 in half an hour so we didn't do too badly.'[13] The game ended in a draw.

At the time Betty sought to be called to the Bar. While the Bar exams were relatively easy, finding a place in chambers for the required year was much more difficult for a woman. To Betty's delight her reputation as a cricketer gained her a place at Gray's Inn.

Not only did Betty now enjoy the friendship of Barbara Peden in England, but she found her circle of friends expanded with other Australian friends of the Pedens who began to arrive in London. Nancy Lord was one, Janna Bruce another. Both of them had, like the Peden girls, been schooled at Abbotsleigh. Intriguingly, Nancy Lord had decided in Australia, after reading Vera Brittain's *Testament of Youth*, that she wanted to work for Lady Rhondda on *Time and Tide*. On arriving in England she asked for a job and became a member of the secretarial staff. It was an extraordinary feat for a young Australian woman with no qualifications whatsoever.

Betty said that Nancy wasn't a very bright girl—a key measure for Betty—but it seems she made a point of getting on with the right people. 'She used to have a fearful enthusiasm for things and she couldn't think of anything else, an absolute bee in her bonnet about it,' said Janna Bruce. 'She was very interested in archaeology and she spent her time rushing out to Jericho and back again. It was very exciting to her. None of it involved any men, like Betty. There were no men anywhere—I seemed to be the only one who had boyfriends—they didn't.'[14]

To Betty's chagrin, she found that Nancy Lord developed a very close friendship with Margaret Rhondda, with whom Betty felt she had a special relationship. Just as Betty had done, Nancy would often go with Margaret to her country residence, Pen-Ithon, in Wales. There they would go for a ritual walk up the hill to a high lake and listen for the curlews, the long-billed wading bird with a throbbing, musical cry.

At the time Margaret Rhondda was living with Theodora Bosanquet, who was tall, thin and dry as a bone. Nancy Lord found her to be a forbidding character who judged people and found them wanting. She was an intellectual snob and she used to print everything Margaret wrote.[15] Although Nancy Lord met Helen Archdale, whom she found to be enormously tall, amusing and a feminist in a very large way—more feminist than the others—Helen was no longer in Margaret Rhondda's inner circle. 'Margaret always spoke very much against Helen Archdale so you knew there had been some serious quarrel,' said Nancy. 'But Margaret and Betty were great friends. Betty was very fond of Margaret but she didn't say much about it [the quarrel]. She was never critical of her … She had no illusions about Margaret and that helped her keep quiet about the great row whatever it was.'[16]

Janna Bruce was an artist who through Nancy Lord was asked to do some illustrations for *Time and Tide*. When Janna first met Betty she was in awe of her because she was working with Ellen Wilkinson. But 'she was exactly as she is now—she hasn't changed at all, Betty,' Janna said in 1991. 'The thing that's odd about Betty is that she is completely and utterly cerebral and has no visual sense whatever about anything, about architecture or people, landscape or anything. She never makes a comment that suggests that she's in any way involved visually—very, very strange because she's a friend of mine, but I'm only interested in visual things.'

Betty struck Janna Bruce as someone who was self-sufficient emotionally. At that time, Betty lived alone. 'I don't know who she had a particular friendship with at all,' said Janna, looking back from her eighties. 'I never heard of anyone being very close to her… I don't think she was interested in us as human beings—it was only what we were doing. I don't know whether it's shyness or whether she just hasn't got what it takes. She hasn't enough sensitivity for the other person's concerns…She's a very unusual woman and you wonder why she has achieved what she has—what makes people put her in the positions she's had.'[17]

Nancy Lord said that Barbara Peden and Betty were very close, close but entirely unsentimental. Barbara was very amusing and they did a lot together and had fun, and of course they had their cricket to talk about, but her friends saw Betty as being afraid to lose herself to someone else in a relationship. Nancy conjectured that Barbara might have been a safe person for Betty to have as a friend, not only because she was a cheerful companion but she was more of a nurturer, and, more significantly, she accepted Betty as she was, she didn't ask intrusive questions. But although Barbara didn't exactly resent it, Nancy Lord believes she was sorry that Betty was quite so inhibited because she would have liked to have known a lot more about her—she would have thought it was more natural, and Barbara was always very natural. 'I don't think she [Betty] had any closer relationship than the one she had with Barbara Peden,' said Nancy. 'It seems she didn't have any love relationships … Barbara was very fond of her, full of admiration for her like everyone else is. Nobody says anything nasty about Betty. I've never heard any word of criticism from anybody about her.'[18]

To have understood Betty would have required recognising the impact on her of the insistent drumming of Helen Archdale and her preoccupation with women's rights. While Betty might have appeared to have a larrikin streak, she was always mindful of the importance of her mother's work. Helen Archdale made sure of that.

In 1934 Helen had only recently returned to England, seeking a well-earned rest. She had spent four years in Geneva working for equality for women on an international scale. Her first opportunity was the Conference for the Codification of International Law at The Hague in 1929. There she became aware that women scarcely counted at all, their only access to the conference was through their representatives. The utter exclusion of women from participation in world affairs, she decided, justified all revolt, whether expressed in militancy, or persistent lobbying, pursued into private lives.

It was obvious that work for an international agreement which gave men and women equal rights should begin at once. When Equal Rights International came into being in 1930, Helen Archdale was its first chairman.[19] She moved to Geneva to carry out her work amongst delegates to the League of Nations, then only ten years old. During this time she lived in a comfortable flat close to the League Secretariat and to the lake. She later counted those four years as the happiest of her life. It was the joy of having a clear aim, and having that aim understood by statesmen of unassailably high reputation gave her new life, new courage.

With little money and few members, Helen and her fellow

equalitarians began working in Geneva by interviewing delegates. They asked directly that they introduce to the League an Equal Rights Treaty by which women's rights should become indistinguishable from men's rights. Helen made some of her colleagues nervous and hesitant by seeming to rush for interviews without gaining permission from higher authorities or following standard League procedures. She was reproved by some women who had worked in the League. 'One Britisher protested "You cannot fling an Equal Rights Treaty in the face of a startled world", but we insisted that we could and we did,' boasted Helen, who believed a big advance was made in those first few years.[20]

The first interview in Geneva was with Eduard Benes of Czechoslovakia, an eminent statesman and one of the builders of the League of Nations. Helen's voice seemed to tremble and be almost inaudible, but Benes said to the women, 'Certainly, you are quite right and I will help you'. Later, he said, 'You will succeed because the current of history is on your side. The only uncertainty is the date of your victory.'

With only one exception, all who were interviewed that first year gave the women encouragement and renewed their faith. During this time Helen also supported the Open Door Council, formed to end discrimination against women in employment legislation. She was part of a successful thrust for freeing professional women from the restriction of the Night Work for Women Convention and she agitated for the replacement of the word 'mankind' in resolutions including both women and men. She summarised the story of the women's movement towards equality to be used by the Academy of Historical Science as a basis for inclusion in history texts.

Helen found the slow changing of the situation in women's equality was intensely interesting to watch and to take part in. A sudden advance, such as the 1932 decision to give equal status to women in collaborating in the work of the League of Nations, seemed like a miracle.

With further advances in the wind, and the end of her three-year term of office, Helen, aged 59, returned to England. She had been active in the movement for 25 years. It had been a time of enormous personal growth for Helen. If she had experienced any timidity in her earlier feminist initiatives, it had now evaporated. Large of mind and body and forthrightness, Helen had evolved into an archetypal leader of a new social order. She had won a reputation for her truthfulness and straight dealing. She had developed powerful official contacts and many new friendships. She had read avidly the newly published books in the libraries of the League. Fearlessly she had walked with a knapsack on her back in the Jura to the north of Geneva, on the shores of the lake, and in Savoy to the south. She had wintered in Majorca, Yugoslavia and Greece, often making contact with 'splendid individual feminists'.[21]

On her return to England Helen decided to withdraw from active participation in feminism, and settle in Stilestone. The bungalow, in which photographs of the Pankhurst family were scattered, was set in an orchard in a tiny village in Kent, called Crouch. She only left the comforts of home to visit her eldest son in Ottawa in 1936, later attending a Pan-American Conference for Women in Lima. An adventuress, she returned via Valparaiso and Santiago, and by train across wide pampas to reach Buenos Aires. Her only contact with feminism was as a co-opted member of the Liaison Committee of Women's International Organisations. However, she was lured back to Geneva in 1937 to be its honorary secretary for twelve months and thoroughly enjoyed herself.[22]

Betty not only noted, but acted upon, her mother's reformist behaviour. She worked for Mrs Wintringham, the first woman who actually took a seat in the House. And at a rally for the MP Sir Edward Mosley, who was not only a staunch supporter of Hitler but also bad about women, Betty unfurled a flag which said, 'Don't Vote Mosley—Down With Fascism—Anti-Nazi'. An innocent Nancy Lord, who Betty had dragged along, held up one end of the banner. To Nancy's astonishment, both she and Betty were rapidly removed from Albert Hall.[23]

Although Betty's intention was to go to the Bar, she put it to one side because she had another tempting offer. A cricket tour was being planned to Australia in 1939 and she had been selected once again as captain of the team. But the war broke out only weeks before the team was to sail. So that ended that, said Betty pragmatically, and the abandoned tour's blazer hung in her cupboard for the rest of her life.

11

WRENS IN THE TROPICS

As World War II loomed, Betty and Barbara Peden decided they must enlist in one of the services, so they went to a recruiting evening with the Women's Army. As an architect and a barrister they were rather cocky and felt certain the army would embrace them. But when they were asked whether they could cook or type they both lied and said 'No'. The Army noted 'no qualifications' and wrote them off as useless.[1]

When war broke out Betty joined the Women's Royal Naval Service (WRNS), largely because its director (D.WRNS) Mrs (later Dame) Vera Laughton Matthews was a friend of Helen Archdale.[2] While the army and the air force accepted all fit applicants, the navy tended to be selective. It was generally thought that the Wrens were of a different calibre from women in the other forces; they tended to be more independent in their thinking. Initially it was a bit insular, according to Betty, the first intakes often being from naval families.[3]

At 32, having been raised to be freewheeling in her reasoning, Betty initially chafed against the regimentation of the WRNS. She was in the second batch of women to undergo the officer training course. At its conclusion, in an interview with D.WRNS and other seniors, Betty was asked whether she had learnt anything. With characteristic bluntness she said no, she hadn't really learnt anything at all (partly because the WRNS weren't certain what their officers were going to do) and that she didn't think the course was what was needed for the training of an officer. So she was sent home for a month to learn a bit more sense.[4] Nonetheless, Betty was given her commission straight away, which was unusual, because very soon every Wren had to join first as a rating and then work her way up the ranks. She was sent to Yarmouth, where Wrens were being trained in the receipt and deciphering of signals.

After about a year, one of the weekly Admiralty Fleet Orders came saying that Wrens were wanted to go overseas, it didn't say where. 'We were all faintly interested,' said Betty. 'It just happened that D.WRNS came to Yarmouth. The officers (three of us) had tea in our board room and I said, I thought very reasonably, that I was interested but where was overseas? "Archdale, if you volunteer to go overseas you volunteer to go anywhere," D.WRNS snorted. Quite right because, security-wise, the fact that you were going overseas would have meant something to somebody—and I laughed like a train, so I said, "Yes Ma'am, sent my name in" and was horrified by Singapore.'[5]

The other selected Wrens reacted much the same way, expressing their disappointment because there was no war over there. But D.WRNS phoned Betty on 2 January 1941 asking her to lead the twenty Wrens for special work. They were the first Wrens to go abroad and Betty accepted, saying that it should be an interesting job and anyway she'd be able to see a part of the world that she had not seen before.[6] Betty, who was the only officer invited, wondered with her ever present modesty if she had been chosen because of her experience as captain of the touring English women's cricket team seven years earlier, or because of Laughton Matthews's friendship with Helen Archdale. But D.WRNS was also shrewd and would have seen Betty as a good naval person and a barrister and with sufficient good sense to be a leader.

Before she left England Betty had dinner at the Ritz grill with Margaret Rhondda and Ellen Wilkinson, her two mentors, and Theodora Bosanquet. She spent the night with her friend Nancy Lord.[7] A farewell party had been planned to take place at WRNS Headquarters at the Admiralty with their Patron, Her Royal Highness the Duchess of Kent, attending to wish them 'God speed'. Just before the party the Wrens' tropical uniform arrived. To their horror it consisted of a thick white industrial overall, white cotton stockings, white canvas shoes and a larger than normal version of the sea-ranger hat with a removable crown. The outfit was shapeless, and they were told they resembled a bunch of hermaphrodites. They managed to have the bodices reshaped in time for the party.[8]

In March the Wrens went to Glasgow and embarked on a small vessel, HMS *Nestor*, with Captain Power at its helm. They were Second Officer Betty Archdale, Sister L. Young, Chief Wrens, Elizabeth (Dusty) Miller, Joyce Allingham, Monica Armstrong, Joan Barber, May Blood, (Bunch) Burrows, Betty Dart, Jean Epps, Margarete Finch, Marjorie Finlay, Lily Gadd, Gwen Heap, Margaret Hodgson, Phil Holmes, (Jackie) Jackson, Henrietta Marshall, Enid Monson, Eileen Moorley, Rene Skip and Joan Sprinks.[9]

The *Nestor* set sail at 2 a.m. on 7 March and when the Wrens went on deck later in the morning there were ships as far as the eye could see, and to their astonishment they were steaming north. The next day at about four o'clock a number of Focke-Wulf 200 Condors swooped out of the sky and dropped their bombs amongst the ships. Hastily donning lifejackets and tin helmets, the Wrens got to points of vantage as the destroyers raced about, rounding up the convoy like collies herding sheep, as was the tactic at the time. Later, the policy was to scatter. One plane dropped six bombs. Round and round raced the destroyers and frigates, firing all the time. It was at this point that a ship's officer noticed the Wrens and sternly ordered them below. There were no hits.

The next morning the *Nestor* was on its own and steaming south. The rest of the convoy was bound for America and the Wrens felt rather lonely and unprotected.[10] 'Off we went,' said Betty, 'We went round by South Africa, the Mediterranean was in German hands. We had a very nice trip—it was very interesting—because I found that in the air raids in England and Kent I felt quite certain that every bomb was coming straight for one—and yet at sea I thought no-one will get hit outside here—I never felt any sort of worry. Quite wrong, the next lot of Wrens that went three weeks after us—they went to Gibraltar and they were sunk hook, line and sinker, not one survived.'[11]

Right from the start Betty went into bat for her charges. She had them treated as second-class passengers, not as third-class as was the ship's wont. She developed a routine for the women of physical exercises, telegraphy and instruction in Malay. The trip bound the Wrens together and they nicknamed Betty 'Big-Hearted Popsie'. There were mostly men on board and they gravitated towards the Wrens, but Betty took her role seriously. She wrote to Helen Archdale, 'I am getting to know the Wrens very well and feel I can trust them alright'.[12]

After seven weeks at sea they arrived in Singapore in late April. Singapore looked green and beautiful. The women filed off the ship and lined up in two ranks to be presented to Rear Admiral Drew and Mrs Drew and Lieutenant Commander James McClelland, who was in charge of the Civilian Shore Wireless Station. In a temperature of 90 degrees, the small group stood to attention in their white, shapeless and seemingly air-tight uniforms. Mrs Drew's smile froze after her first incredulous look at their cotton stockings. She led Betty aside and there was no doubt that their uniforms were under discussion. The Wrens soon learned that the admiral's wife had condemned the dresses as being quite unsuitable and advised Betty to have new ones made in lighter material … and with more style to them. The stockings should be scrapped and ankle socks substituted.

The Wrens were taken to Kranji, over an hour's drive inland, and about 200 feet above sea level, where they settled in bungalows raised high above the ground. To Betty's delight she had a bungalow to herself. At Kranji there was nothing except the station, which was perched in a clearing. It had grand views over the jungle. Rain fell every day, the annual average being 95 inches. The whole station was covered with drains and when it rained they became streams in a few minutes.

Men from both the army and the navy, plus some civilians, kept watch at Kranji and they were wildly excited over the Wrens' arrival. They organised a dance for the Saturday night and, looking upon the women as their own, did not send any invitations to the other establishments. However, the news soon got around and more than a score of personnel from the naval bases and Seletar RAF station managed to crash the gates. Consequently, while each dance was in progress, there were knots of glowering males on the sidelines just waiting their chance.

'The next morning, Sunday, we were told not to go ashore [leave

the station] until we'd had a talk from the Master-at-Arms,' wrote
Elizabeth Miller:

> I believe the authorities were terrified at the responsibility of having us,
> and expected us to be raped and ravaged in the first week. They had even
> made an attempt at planting a bamboo hedge round our living quarters, a
> source of much ribald laughter. This feeble hedge would have been no bar
> to a fairly robust infant, and the station dogs passed in and out of it with
> ease.
>
> Miss Archdale wasn't worried at all. She knew us. I think we could
> have been described as innocent toughs, with a burning zeal for the hon-
> our of our Service. If we suspected any smearing of the name of 'Wren'
> we were furious. I think it was this which drove us together, and knit us
> into an almost perfect 'Sisterhood'. Whoever hurt one, hurt all.
>
> The Master-at-Arms was a tough hard-bitten Australian Cobber. His
> shorts reached to his calves, and we always spoke of him as 'long-pants'.
> We assembled in our recreation room to hear his talk on the dangers
> which beset young girls.
>
> Twenty pairs of innocent eyes were turned upon him, and he started
> to stammer.
>
> 'Now I ain't 'ere to upsurp yore Orficer,' he began. 'The last thing I
> want to do is upsurp 'er.'
>
> There was a delighted gasp, and we settled down to enjoy this, but
> what with his accent, and his stammering and stumbling, very few of us
> knew what he was driving at. He withdrew in a mystified silence.[13]

On 1 May, the Wrens started work. They were divided into four
watches, five Wrens to a watch. The wireless office, the bahru, was
completely sealed for air-conditioning but the air-conditioning plant
had three times been lost in the Atlantic. The office was originally intended
to accommodate four operators, but there were always about a dozen
people on watch. The temperature in the bahru was seldom under 98
degrees and electric fans simply moved the hot air about. The women
took a small towel on duty with them to mop their hands and arms,
otherwise the writing paper stuck to them. Every time they came off
watch they needed a complete change of clothing.

The Wrens were taught Japanese morse code, using American
machines invented for the purpose. Throughout the hot nights they
struggled against sleep, listening for signals, usually of one or two seconds,

from Japanese submarines before they dived into obscurity once more. Immediately the Wren on watch would raise her hand and tell the officer in charge, who would track the submarine down and alert waiting aircraft and ships. 'So it's likely we killed a few of the blighters,' said Phyll Puttick.[14]

A Tamil sweeper used to come to the bahru every morning about six o'clock, just as it was getting light. Two operators would take the contents of the waste-paper baskets and burn them in the incinerator while the sweeper was busy inside. Elizabeth Miller was always pleased to be given this duty of disposing of the waste paper. It was like escaping from the black hole of Calcutta, like being re-born after dying, for the morning was always beautiful, the green landscape, the wooded hills, the rubber trees looking like silver birches, and under-foot the trailing heavenly blue morning glories, wide open at dawn.

Betty had worked quickly to create new uniforms and by 20 May they were ready. She sent a photograph of her girls in their new apparel to D.WRNS, writing on the back, 'Don't we look good?' As the Wrens settled into their extraordinary routine Betty found McClelland very easy to deal with and the Wrens started to make their presence felt on the island. In July the *Singapore Free Press* wrote: 'Since their arrival in Singapore some two or three months ago, the Wrens have become familiar figures about town in their white tropical uniforms … When we see the Wrens, dancing at Raffles, at the pictures or at any of the various Service Dances they are very much off duty and enjoying themselves, and, like all hard workers, getting a big kick out of it.'[15]

Betty encouraged her Wrens to play sport, forming cricket and hockey teams to play those of the YWCA and of ships that came into the harbour. When commenting on the women's final hockey trial at the Girls Sports Club ground, the *Singapore Free Press* said Betty Archdale was again the outstanding player.[16]

Betty's main social life was with the Drews and McClellands, shopping with their wives and other civilian women, occasionally going to the pictures with men. In November, the Governor, Sir Shenton Thomas, asked her to a dinner at Government House to meet Sir Archibald Wavell, Supreme Commander of the Allied Command, Far East. She found herself in a party of 34 including admirals and generals, but as the only officer with the Wrens she was aware of a certain loneliness. In October she wrote to her mother: 'I saw our Sister in hospital yesterday—we get on all right on the surface but have nothing in common really—she is a nice little thing but her ideas and mine are not the same. There is no-one here alas with whom I can discuss things which is sometimes rather a strain, but on the whole things have gone very well—it is the feeling that I can never relax that is so tiring but I hope the war will not last forever.'[17]

It was in her almost daily correspondence with Helen Archdale, which she posted in batches every Monday, that Betty found some solace from her isolation.

The difficulties she faced were various. She had to have an officer reprimanded for making slanderous statements about the Wrens. At another time there was a great water shortage, and no toilet paper despite repeated requests. After about seven weeks it materialised and in such quantities that the Wrens had difficulty in finding room to stow it. Betty fought on behalf of the Wrens for their acceptance in the social life of the community. When the civilian women, who tended to believe they belonged to a superior social bracket, made sure the Wrens could not join the Golf Club or the Singapore Club, Betty went to McClelland, who persuaded the clubs to let the Wrens in.

Then there was the problem of morale. The extreme conditions had an eroding effect on the Wrens and after seven months some of them became fractious, complaining about the food and other things. So Betty mustered them and gave them a blast which seemed to have a salutary effect. The women were never very pleased when told that Lady So-and-So or Lord Such-and-Such was coming to inspect them. They felt that it was simply a day out for their lordships and a day in for them, because shore leave was cancelled until they'd gone. 'One day a young Duchess was scheduled to arrive at half-past-one,' remembered Elizabeth Miller.

> We hung about in the mess-block, starched and blanched, not daring to sit down for fear of creasing our dresses. At two-thirty her car was sighted, and we, very disgruntled by this time, formed two rather mutinous ranks underneath the bungalow.
> The Duchess was inclined to be gushing, but we weren't in the mood.

She passed slowly along the ranks asking, 'Tell me, do you like Singapore?', 'Tell me, is your work interesting?' Then she stopped in front of Moorely and said, 'Tell me, what was the worst thing about the London air-raids?' Moorely, in her Derbyshire accent replied, 'The high explosives'. That set us off. Miss Archdale, sensing that morale was at breaking point, hurried the visitors out to the kitchen, signalling me to dismiss the squad as she went.

They expected to be brought to attention, right-turned and dismissed, instead of which I looked wearily at them and muttered 'sugar off'.[18]

Betty also had to summon wisdom in fielding the perplexities of romance, which hung heavily in the tropical air. Its presence was hardly surprising as, on the island, there were 20,000 men to each Wren. 'We played the field, didn't we. Oh boy!' said Phyll Puttick. The Wrens were often entertained at the three large dance halls in Singapore known as 'The Worlds'—the New World, the Happy World and the Great World. By August Betty told her mother, 'Another Wren has just been in to say she is engaged to an Army Captain [she met] on the ship coming out—that makes four already and several others heading that way.'[19]

While understanding, Betty demonstrated a certain naivety. When she was told that a woman, not of the Wren party, was pregnant she said, 'She can't be, she's not married!' But she was very good to Eileen Crompton, allowing her to live out of quarters after her marriage to an RAF staff sergeant at Seletar. Eileen came to work every day in her own little car. As for her own heart, Phyll Puttick said Betty was more like one of the boys than anything else. 'I've never seen her even look at anybody as though she were interested. She was always busy, though most of us found time. I'm afraid each of us were distracted there. She could have done as well.'[20]

Whether it was Betty's sense of duty which compelled her to place the interests of her charges before any possible romance of her own, the Wrens weren't sure, but they noticed she never attempted to make herself look attractive and her hair was always cut very short. Betty usually had all her meals alone in her bungalow, and while it was a relief not to have to worry about anyone else, she recognised that it would be nice not to be so entirely on her own.

Not that Betty failed to enjoy her role. Through her sporting prowess she tasted, savoured and then came to expect leadership roles. 'I assumed I was pretty good. I assumed I could succeed better than others,' she admitted in her 88th year. Her intelligence, physical presence and ability to enthuse those over whom she had authority meant that she was usually able to keep this group of women cheerful, whatever the circumstance. But if her arrangements were disturbed or overruled, Betty tended to be tetchy. In this sense she was autocratic, but because of her purity of purpose she somehow got away with it.

While reflecting a fierce loyalty to her Wrens, Betty's letters reveal that she didn't really have a close connection with those in her charge. She talks of having fun on outings, or of good food, but events and people and sport are all spoken of in the same tone, as if they were equal in importance to her. She is more emotive when writing about puppies born in a cupboard in the empty bungalow opposite, or inquiring about the plants at her mother's cottage. It's as if her ability for intimacy was deeply inhibited.

In answer to those people who in later years speculated that Betty's single status might be due to lesbian tendencies, there is no hint of it in the five years of correspondence, when she was in her early thirties and living exclusively with women. This is even more remarkable when one takes into account what happens in wartime. Relationships between men and women are quickened and intensified by the sense that lives might be lost. And yet in spite of this atmosphere of making love while you could, which affected all ranks, Betty was unmoved. She didn't link up with other women. She didn't link up with other men.

Phyll Puttick said Betty was 'chummy with everybody—men and women—without sentiment. We all thought the world of her because she was such a super leader and we trusted her and we liked her.' They didn't question her leadership and Puttick noted that Betty had the capacity to listen to other people's point of view and was always there if they wanted her. 'That was important to us … but thinking back down the years I always felt she was rather remote from us and it wasn't just because she was an officer and we were chief Wrens. You got a feeling of a solitary person anyway, and a rather shy person.'[21]

Betty's leadership seemed to be appreciated by the WRNS

hierarchy and Vera Laughton Matthews wrote to Helen Archdale: 'She seems to be managing everything in a splendid way and we hear excellent reports of her from the powers that be.'[22]

It appears that Betty's personality was well suited to the environment in which she was raised. She was influenced by the thought and actions of the suffragettes because they elicited a response from some part of Betty herself. While her brothers reacted against the movement and lived another life in another world, Betty appears not to have disagreed with her mother. So it is not surprising that in Singapore, while accepting their kindnesses, she became 'sick to death' of those civilian women she met there who defined themselves by their husbands' status and spent their time socialising.[23] In contrast, she valued correspondence with Ellen Wilkinson, Doris Stevens (the American feminist), Margaret Rhondda and Barbara Munro who was now married and living in Australia with her little son, Colin, Betty's godson.

But clearly it was Betty's brain rather than the play of her emotions that determined what she did each day. Her mother catered for her intellectual needs by sending a steady supply of news of her feminist activities and acquaintances, of the suicide of Virginia Woolf, and many publications including *Time and Tide*, *Hansard*, the *Kent Messenger* (for local news) and a wonderful array of books including C. S. Lewis's *The Screwtape Letters*, H. G. Wells's *Phoenix*, Viscount Cecil's *Great Experiment* and a good book on the Czechoslovakian leader Eduard Benes.

In a spirit of discussion enjoyed by them both, Betty wrote to her mother about the international fracas. 'Although a world run by GB and USA would be far from ideal,' she noted in October, 'I am not sure that it would not be a step towards a real world government and if it put a stop to these interminable wars would be something to be thankful for … it will only work if GB and USA play a predominant part instead of hanging back as they did with the League of Nations.'[24] But Betty was unsuspecting of Japanese interest in the area and in July she reported: 'There is much speculation here as to whether Japan is going to take any action but on the whole people seem to doubt it—our air raid shelters are just about finished but I hope we never have to use them.'[25]

However, in the early hours of Sunday, 7 December, the Japanese attacked Pearl Harbor and the island of Singapore was awakened by wave after wave of aircraft passing overhead. 'We went to the verandah to stare up at them,' said Elizabeth Miller. 'They were in V formations of nines. Searchlights picked them up and tracer bullets could be seen flying around. We were surprised as we hadn't known there were so many Allied aircraft in the Peninsula. We thought it was a jolly good show and went back to bed quite cheerfully. Later in the morning we learned that what we'd taken to be manoeuvres were Japs.'[26] The Wrens now knew they were in the thick of war and the outlook was gloomy. The only comfort was the knowledge that the United States of America was at last actively involved.

On 8 December the Japanese landed at Patani and Kota Bahru on the east coast of Malaya. While the invasion set off a stream of evacuations, including civilian English women and children, the Wrens were kept in Singapore longer than most. Phyll Puttick recalled: 'We were there till the last minute—we just got on with our job and we hoped that somebody would remember us in time to get us away. But it was amazing, the atmosphere, it was just like one big happy family—we never had quarrels—in the most appalling circumstances—working and living and raids—never heard a quarrel between anyone and I think it must have been due to Betty Archdale to a very large degree.'[27]

The feeling of unease on the island increased with the growing recognition that there was nobody to help. Churchill hadn't the planes to send to their rescue, and the guns of Singapore pointed out to the surrounding waters, anticipating attack by sea. But there were rumours that the Royal Navy's newest warships, the *Prince of Wales* and *Repulse*, were in the vicinity and on 8 December they boldly showed themselves at Singapore. Their presence did much to hearten the inhabitants, who cheered them madly. When the sailors came ashore and a film show was arranged for them it was decided that the two watches of Wrens who were off-duty should hand out programs and talk to them. 'The men were delighted to see us,' said Elizabeth Miller, 'but being the target for about two thousand pairs of appraising eyes was distinctly daunting. We tried to spread ourselves as far as possible, and I found myself in the middle of a row with a dozen or so cherub-faced boys.'[28]

Two days later, five Wrens were on watch when the Japanese

newsagency announced, in English, that the *Prince of Wales* and the *Repulse* had been sunk. 'And of course we all said, "wishful thinking",' said Phyll Puttick, 'they'd like that wouldn't they?… And it was true.'[29] The news rocked the island and beyond. Elizabeth Miller wept when she thought of her 'cherubs' struggling in the oily, shark-infested waters, and being strafed again and again.

Over a thousand men were lost, but 50 of the survivors were drafted to the Wrens to help shore up the defences. The reinforcements, however, were so shaken by their terrible experience that they were liable to shoot at any moving shadow and the Wrens felt nervous about going on watch after dark. So they started shouting 'Wrens going on watch' or 'Wrens coming off watch' as soon as they left the bungalows or the bahru and they kept shouting until they were safely under cover again.

With the Wrens relegated permanently to their base and the mounting fear of the advancing Japanese, pressure on the various romantic relationships of the Wrens intensified. An airman from Changi had been the constant companion to one of the girls and he frequently flew over the station sending flashlight messages in morse. They didn't see the boy for some days after the Japanese entry into the war, but they knew that he and his plane must be fully occupied. Then one evening they heard him circling round. On looking up they read his message, 'I love you Joan'. She wasn't there, so several Wrens got out torches and signalled 'R' for 'received'. Then they sent X's for kisses until he was out of sight. He never returned.

On Christmas Eve Betty wrote to her mother, 'There is another Wren getting married on the 30th to an Army Captain and two more planning to get married. It is hard to blame them with things so uncertain, but it is not much of a married life.'[30] At the end of December, three Wrens married in successive days. Betty, who was totally understanding, was asked to all services and sometimes drove the bride in a little car she had acquired.

After raids the Wrens often found shrapnel lying on their beds when they returned from the shelters. Confined to the station, Betty relieved the tedium by organising a five-hole golf course to be constructed around the dormitory block of what had been quickly christened the

Wrennery. But as the situation grew worse the Wrens were not allowed to show themselves in the open more than was necessary. Elizabeth Miller arranged whist drives in their mess-lounge and invited the sailors to attend. However, they could only play cards during the first dog watch (4–6 p.m.) because when night fell they were unable to black-out properly. The Wrens whitened the edges of the steeply stepped path, but were sternly ordered to obliterate their handiwork in case it was spotted from the air. Consequently they sustained many twisted ankles and barked shins as they blindly groped about from place to place.

As they could not leave the station on Christmas Day the Wrens asked if the padre would come from the base to administer Holy Communion. They had no chapel but in the rec-space they fashioned an altar from beer-crates covered with a Union Jack. About 40 of them made communion. As soon as the first five had celebrated they hurried off to relieve those on watch till everyone had been to the table. That day, Hong Kong fell to the Japanese.

The Wrens' work had increased tenfold and there was never a moment's relaxation in the bahru. But they did manage to pick up Churchill addressing the Canadian parliament in Ottawa. He mentioned that a Vichy general had predicted that England would have her neck wrung like a chicken's. Then, after a pause, he remarked, 'Some chicken—some neck!' The Wrens had their first laugh in weeks.[31]

Every day the news was monotonously the same. 'Our troops have successfully withdrawn to more southerly positions.' The Wrens knew this could not go on for long. Penang was only 340 miles from Singapore and by the middle of January, with the Japanese only a 100 miles away, it became obvious that the work of naval intelligence could no longer be carried out at Singapore and it was decided that all personnel thus employed were to be evacuated.

The *Evening Standard* printed the story: 'When a squad of Wrens left England last May for service abroad they said regretfully we're going too far from the war. Now they are in the front line of the war in the Pacific. They are the 30 young women who, headed by Second Officer Betty Archdale, ex-captain of the women's cricket team which toured New Zealand and Australia in 1934–35, had been working in Singapore for seven months as wireless telegraphists and were the first to receive the news of the loss of the "Prince of Wales" and the "Repulse". The Wrens were almost the only women remaining in the island fortress of Singapore.'[32]

On Sunday, 4 January 1942, Betty called a muster and Lieutenant Commander Sandwith came to say goodbye. The Wrens packed their possessions and Eileen Crompton and Elizabeth Miller were sent to the dock early in the morning with a lorry-load of baggage. The 'bodies' were not going on board till after dusk. They had just arrived at Keppel Harbour when a wave of Japanese planes attacked, dropping bombs and machine-gunning everything in sight. Elizabeth, who could see the pilots' faces quite plainly, was very frightened to be looking into the eyes of the enemy at such a close range.

Just outside the gates of the wireless station were two huge oil containers like gasometers and there was a good deal of anxiety lest they be hit before the Wrens got away. The Wrens conjectured that the Japanese purposely missed them as they intended to use the oil themselves, but the British dynamited them before the surrender.

Eileen Crompton telephoned her husband Tom at Seletar, telling him of her imminent departure. He managed to come over and was deeply upset because the Wrens didn't know where they were going. It was likely that he would soon have to fight his way out too, and he couldn't at this moment see any way of getting in touch again. When Tom came out of Eileen's room he said to Elizabeth Miller, 'Look after her for me, Dusty.' Elizabeth said she'd do her best. Before long their home of only a few months was reduced to rubble, along with most of their wedding presents.

The amahs were crying bitterly when the Wrens said goodbye and the women felt dreadful at deserting them. The coach took them to the docks and they arrived there about the same time as the contingent from the naval base. Elizabeth pointed out their ship to Betty. It was the *Devonshire*, belonging to the British India Line. Conscious of the trauma for the four freshly married Wrens leaving husbands behind, and for the others leaving boyfriends, Betty told Elizabeth Miller to draw up the women in two ranks and march them on board in good order. She, in accordance with tradition, would come aboard last. 'We went forward with our heads up, hands swinging shoulder high, and furtively licking in the tears which were pouring down our cheeks,' wrote Elizabeth. 'I looked back over the land but very little could be seen through the thick pall of smoke which hung over the city. Then we were ordered below for safety.'[33]

The *Devonshire* moved off shortly afterwards, at 11.30 p.m., and was provided with a destroyer escort. As soon as they sailed the Wrens turned into their bunks and slept for fourteen hours. During the past four weeks they had never had more than two consecutive hours of unbroken rest, and were exhausted.

The *Devonshire* ran south, skirting the coast of Sumatra, which was well within the range of Japanese planes and submarines. The ship was considered vulnerable until it had passed through the Sunda Strait and into the Indian Ocean. Then their destroyer, *Scout*, turned back again. She was later sunk.

At sea, Betty wrote to her mother: 'Well here we are again—off on another 1000 mile trek. It was very sad to have to leave Kranji, especially under such circumstances—the organisation for which the Wrens work is moving, so we had to go too, but we hope to move back in a few months … the Japs coming steadily nearer all the time was not very nice. I have a horrid feeling Singapore will fall, but we should get it back all right in a few months. The people I am sorry for are those who have left husbands behind.'[34]

After they'd been at sea for ten days they were told that they were nearing Ceylon, so at last they knew their destination. They could smell the island before they saw it. There was a fragrance of flowers and spices blowing from the land. On 14 January 1942, the Wrens were taken ashore to their new quarters at Colombo. Their place of work, the Pembroke Academy, was about ten minutes walk away and they all trooped round there on the morning after arrival. The equipment which they had brought from Singapore was unpacked and soon in service again, and they were back in watches as quickly as possible. It was Sunday and they were kept busy till about eight in the evening helping to decode messages which had piled up while they were on the water.

The arrival of the Wrens caused a bit of a flutter on the island and invitations to social functions poured in. Waiting for Betty in Colombo was a letter from the Deputy Director of the WRNS. 'I thought isn't this nice, she's written to say she's glad we're out of that mess without having been killed,' Betty recalled. 'But far from it—it was a letter saying "What did Second Officer Archdale think she's doing altering the uniform, the only person who can do so is the King".'[35] Betty was touched when Admiral Drew, on his return to England, told D.WRNS that it was he and his wife who had decided on the changes in uniform. Although she rationalised that it really didn't matter two pins to her what the authorities thought, Betty relayed the criticism to her mother: 'They have no idea what it is like out here.'[36]

Betty was quickly involved in enhancing the working and living conditions for the Wrens. Once again each Wren had a toilet of her own, and no toilet paper. But while in Kranji the naval people had been friendly, here in Colombo the Wrens didn't belong to anyone. Without help or advice, Betty felt strained, alone in her responsibilities. Still, the small band of women settled down with some sense of security. They felt a long way from the Japanese. But soon thousands of evacuees arrived from Singapore.

By the end of January the British had lost Malaya and the battle for Singapore began. The first infiltration by the Japanese was up Kranji creek, the Wrens' old camping-ground. On 15 February, Singapore fell and 75,000 troops, not counting those killed or captured previously, were out of the war. Sister Young still had no news of her husband, but he survived and they met again after the war. Others were not so lucky. Eileen Crompton went to the RAF Headquarters in Colombo almost every day to see if they could tell her where her husband was. There was never any news. Eventually one of the Kranji sailors, who had been rescued after his ship had been sunk, gave her a letter from Tom but it was so stained with sea water as to be almost indecipherable. Eileen often puzzled over it with a magnifying glass. It wasn't until four years later she found out that her husband had been killed.[37]

Soon after Betty had arrived in Colombo, the padre started to call on her. He obligingly tracked down a wireless set for the Wrens, and asked Betty to accompany him to a cricket match. While they may have been drawn to each other, he also met a particular need in Betty by providing her with books on Christianity. Although she had kept to the Christian Scientist regimen espoused by her mother, it was during the war that she was compelled—partly due to fear—to explore a broader spectrum of religious thought.

Betty's charges also appeared to be taking a similar interest and someone remarked to Betty how marvellous it was to see so many Wrens in church. Betty didn't disillusion them by telling them the real reason that most of them allowed themselves to be bussed some distance to church was to shop at a naval store close by, where they could indulge in favourite foods. 'People thought they were such good girls, which they weren't,' laughed Betty.[38]

There were more marriages amongst the Wrens, often with receptions held in the Wren quarters. In April Betty wrote to her mother pragmatically: 'Another one was married today and there is another wedding (the seventh) on Thursday. That ends most of the present romances I think.'[39] But Betty was impressed with the women in love, commenting that all but one had been extremely good about it and not let anything interfere with their work. Once again, she was humane, and allowed the newlyweds to live 'ashore' together.

In Colombo, Betty had the pleasure of being recognised and welcomed by people who remembered her from the cricket tour in 1934, and others who recalled her playing on all sorts of unlikely grounds in England—grounds where she hadn't realised there had been any spectators at all. She was made an honorary member of the Cricket Club, and often played in matches for them. The club allowed the Wrens to use their nets for practice, which Betty urged them to do each morning. In April the *Ceylon Daily News* reported:

> A thoroughly enjoyable game of cricket was provided last afternoon by women players in the SSC Ground when Miss Betty Archdale's XI just succeeded in beating a Ceylonese team got together by Mr Henry de Silva.
>
> Miss Archdale, herself, opened her team's bid for runs and so monopo-lised the play that she remained 75 not out … Her batting was in a class by

itself and her effort was all the more creditable as it was made against some very keen bowling and fielding by the local side as a whole.[40]

Betty was also asked to speak on radio about cricket and hockey. And she gave the inaugural address at the YWCA Luncheon Club, talking about life in the WRNS. 'Though the work is hard, the hours long, the difficulties innumerable, not a single Wren Officer or Wren will ever willingly leave the service,' said Second Officer Betty Archdale.[41]

The Wrens' work went on as usual, but a feeling of unrest was sensed everywhere. By Good Friday Betty was arranging the mounting of blackout shades and on Easter Sunday, 5 April, there was an air-raid warning. Many planes flew overhead and there was heavy gunfire. The air force brought down about 57 enemy aircraft but one of the Wrens' husbands was amongst those killed when the *Hermes* was sunk.[42]

As the air raids persisted, the people of Ceylon were unnerved and it soon became apparent that Colombo would not be suitable as a naval base. The harbour was too small to contain and protect the fleet and ships were being torpedoed as they lay outside at night. It was obvious that the Wrens, as part of the communication branch, would have to be in closer touch with the Far Eastern Fleet (which was based on a small atoll in the Indian Ocean some 600 miles west of Ceylon), so they were told to pack up and were once more on the move. On 23 April they were conveyed to the docks and boarded the HMS *Alaunia*, an armed merchantman. The Wrens were thrilled to be travelling in one of His Majesty's ships and were most punctilious about saluting the quarterdeck as they stepped on board. They sailed the next day.

'We had no idea in the whole wide world where we were going from Colombo,' said Phyll Puttick. 'People were guessing, is it the States or even Australia—or would we turn round and go back? In fact it was Mombasa—it never occurred to us in a thousand years—Kilindini was the base there.'[43] After the Seychelles the Fleet turned south to Madagascar to stand by in support of the allied landings at Diego Suarez. The *Alaunia* was left to steam alone the last thousand miles to Mombasa.

Eventually the Wrens sighted the coast of Kenya. The *Alaunia* entered Mombasa harbour on 3 May. Hoists of flags were being run up and down every ship in the harbour, bugles were blowing and the people lining the shore were cheering. For the first time the uniformed Wrens stood lining the upper deck, alongside matelots and marines, properly at ease. 'We were crying with pride and excitement at being in the Navy,' said Elizabeth Miller. 'It was amusing to see the reactions of the crews of other boats; they'd give us a casual glance, half turn away and then the head would snap back, the eyes would pop and the mouths would sag open as if to say, "Blimey—Women!"'[44]

Their new quarters comprised a floor of the Spanish-style Lotus Hotel. Mrs Johnson, the proprietress, and her pet mongoose were on the steps to meet them. It wasn't until seven months later that the Wrens moved into quarters that had been especially built for them, with consultation from Betty, called HMS *Tama*.

The male wireless operators had remained in Ceylon to carry on working until the Wrens had established the new station. It was a gratifying responsibility for the women, who remembered how reluctantly they'd been accepted at first. They commenced watches at Aladini, a former school. Because of the heat the walls had many openings. At night the lights attracted mosquitoes, flying ants, and preying mantises which watched the Wrens with bulging eyes.

Malaria was said to be rife so the women had to order long-sleeved uniforms and boots or leggings for evening wear. But they didn't deter the Wrens from playing hard. Phyll Puttick gleefully confessed:

> We would say 'goodnight' at the Lotus Hotel in Mombasa and go to our various rooms, wait a suitable time and then climb out of windows and get out—or run 'ashore' as we called it, with our boyfriends. We were always wearing these ghastly canvas leggings and long arm things against mosquitoes—[we'd] take them off just before we got in. One night I'd been out with another friend, I think it was Renee Stitt, we came in through our usual way, through our own lavatory window—put a leg through the window onto the shoulder of, it turned out afterwards, but I didn't know at the time, Betty Archdale—who without even seeing me said, 'Report to my room at 9 o'clock tomorrow morning please Holmes!'
>
>   God knows how she knew it was me—I think she must have checked out the bedrooms and of course I got a blasting the next morning but in the nicest possible way. She was such a tremendously good sport and we

trusted her implicitly—that was the chief thing—she knew what blighters we were but she also realised that a lot of them had been through a very bad time in Singapore, and we were evacuated again from Colombo …

We all thought the world of her because she was such a super leader and we trusted her and we liked her, which is more important. I think that the powers that be at home thought she was much too lenient with us—she spoilt us—but I don't think she did. She knew that they'd had a very bad time.[45]

However, Betty's tolerance in the belief of a broader good was to be critically assessed by those with a greater rigidity of thought.

Elizabeth Miller, her deputy, was recalled home to be commissioned. It was now evident that this small number of pioneers had proved that Wrens could successfully be employed on overseas service, and Elizabeth was to be put in charge of a small unit which she would take to South Africa. That reactionary forces were on the way was evident to Elizabeth Miller when she stopped at Durban on the journey home. At a servicewomen's hostel, about a dozen third officer ciphers were taken aback when she walked in. Elizabeth was only too conscious of the fact that they were thoroughly observing her rather unorthodox uniform. After the first stunned silence the senior officer told Elizabeth that she and her crew were on their way to Mombasa. 'I could have shrieked with laughter every time I thought what was in store for the unsuspecting gang I'd left behind me,' she wrote. 'As far as I could count there would be more officers than ratings and the poor souls would be perpetually at the salute.'[46]

In Mombasa, Betty was expecting some new Wrens, but on 28 July First Officer Robinson, who had flown in, rang and asked to be collected. 'It was clear it was going to be a big base and quite rightly they sent out a chief officer [of the WRNS]. She appeared and no more Wrens, so it was all very awkward,' explained Betty. 'I only had twenty Wrens and she was going to have about two thousand—so that it needed someone—but unfortunately she arrived much too early.'[47]

On the first day Robinson made it known that she took a dim view of the Wrens' discipline. She was determined to make her presence felt. Two days later she and the chief Wrens went off to base to be inspected by the Duke of Gloucester. Betty, who had been the only officer throughout three relocations of her group of Wrens, was left behind in the hotel, 'very forlorn'. Betty then took Robinson to Allindura, the naval headquarters, where she was welcomed with open arms. They showed her around and gave her a pass. Betty was shattered. That night she wrote in her diary, 'wept and [underlined] wept in bed—wish I knew what was happening and could understand it'.

Alone in her misery, Betty wrote to her mother: 'I am evidently expected to stay as a Junior Officer and Quarters Officer neither of which I feel like doing—after 18 months in command it is not easy to be Junior. I would not mind transferring to a junior job somewhere else but I think it is asking a lot to expect me to stay on here. The Wrens are very worried—and angry too, which is why I should go, as they will settle down and be loyal to the new officer quicker without me … I am feeling terribly hurt at the moment but suppose I will get over that. I can't believe the Director has meant just to push me out without a word. On the face of it, it looks as if she was very dissatisfied, which I had had no inkling of at all—if she feels as badly about me as it looks I should have thought she'd have recalled me.'[48] In retrospect, Betty said she didn't behave well. She was understandably annoyed at being pushed aside and she let it show, but she was bewildered because up till now she had only received praise from those in the naval hierarchy.

A week after her arrival, First Officer Robinson took Betty aside for a long talk. She seemed to be more understanding. She had been through the files, was amazed to find no instruction from HQ and now realised a bit more what the job was like, and she realised why Betty's initiatives were necessary. Still, for two months Betty was seriously underemployed. Sometimes her work for the day was completed by 8.15 a.m. and she spent her time pottering around, tidying up her things. She read voraciously, including Rebecca West's *Black Lamb and Grey Falcon*, which Helen had sent her. She silently suffered, finding it difficult to sleep, crying in bed and noting in her diary that she was feeling bad, miserable, and lacking concentration. She would not have coped as well with the frustration if she hadn't been saved by Markus.

It was only just before Robinson arrived that Betty wrote to Helen saying that a man called Markus had rung her the night before. He had been at Bedales, where he said he knew Alec, and asked Betty to dinner the next night. The evening went well and Betty described his house with its many books. Markus's father was Jewish, had good taste, and was one of the first traders in Mombasa, telling marvellous stories of the early days. The family asked Betty to come to their house any time she liked and to make herself at home. Betty described Markus as an intellectual and very left and very nice. He established familiar ground by being most enthusiastic about Bedales. What is more, he offered to help Betty get into the Mombasa Golf Club.

Then followed weeks of almost daily activities with Markus. They played golf together (he had previously been a Kenyan champion), squash and bridge, went to the Mombasa Club for dinners, dances and a hilarious ball, to a play and to the cinema. He introduced Betty to interesting personalities of the region including Moses Mohammed, a wealthy Arab who spoke English, French, German, Italian and Swahili. They visited his shawba on the mainland, going by ferry which was pulled by a chain of boys who sang and stamped. After driving back Betty had dinner with Markus and, departing from her propensity to be visually unaware, she wrote in her diary, 'perfect moonlit night'.[49]

Betty needed this enthusiastic man's attentiveness, because the reality of her life in the navy was very humiliating. Two naval officers came and talked to the first officer and Betty about Betty's request for a transfer. Betty gathered that her request would probably be granted, but she felt that all three were extremely rude, discussing her as if she was not there and never once asking her what she thought. They attached a written note to her request but never showed it to her; they just passed it round amongst themselves.

Weeks passed without news of a move. Betty was not even sure whose or what staff she was now on. Lost, she seemed nobody's business. Certainly, she thought, no-one lifted a finger to help or showed the slightest bit of consideration.

No-one except Markus, that is. He took her through the old part of Mombasa in the moonlight, visiting native houses and dance halls. Another night they dined with the Chief Justice of Kenya and the American Consul. He took her round his hide and coffee godown and gave her a leopard skin which she could have made into a rug. He also found for Betty a rare and magnificent large wooden chest which would have been originally used for the trading of spices and gold from the nearby island of Lamu. 'How I am going to get it home, I don't quite know,' she told her mother, 'but it will be most imposing if I do.'[50] It is one of the few possessions Betty retained for her one, modest room in a retirement village.

Gradually, Betty found she was getting quite used to this life of leisure—although it, too, was becoming complicated. On the way home from a dance at the Railway Club, Markus kissed her. 'Did not really like it—hope he is not serious—definitely much prefer Padre,' she recorded in her diary.[51] A week or two later she noted, once again, 'Harry got sloppy and kissed—did not like it much!'[52]

This is not surprising, because a certain detachment was apparent in Betty's recording of the fun she was having. Throughout the two-month courtship she had interchanged the spelling of her suitor's name in her diary, sometimes writing it down as 'Marcus' and at others as 'Markus'. It is usual if someone is enamoured of another that details such as the spelling of the beloved's name are fastidiously observed. But what is more extraordinary was that for all this time she had been using his surname exclusively. It wasn't until she chronicled his attempts at intimacy that she referred to him as Harry.

Generally, Betty was becoming more fraught and when one night First Officer Robinson said that nothing had happened in Mombasa until she came, Betty could take it no more and 'had it out with her'. As voices were raised in the enclosed courtyard of the hotel, the upstairs bedrooms doors opened and Wrens quietly emerged to listen to the exchange. When the row below was over, Sister Young comforted Betty and gave her some pills to help her sleep.[53]

Finally on 2 September Betty received news of a transfer to Basra in the Persian Gulf. She was especially glad to be leaving as, while Harry Markus was obviously smitten by her, Betty knew she could never love Harry.

On the morning of her departure Betty went to the wedding of one of her Wrens in the cathedral. Her car, which was to take her to the docks, came at 2 p.m. In an attempt to defuse the situation, Betty had delayed telling the Wrens of her imminent departure. She did so that morning and stuck up a notice on the board which read: 'Thank you all very much indeed for being such a grand unit during the past eighteen months. You have an excellent record so carry on the good work. Goodbye and the best of luck to you all—we'll meet again at Home. H.E. Archdale 29/9/42.'[54]

It was on board that Betty wrote of the great wrench it had been parting with the unit. They in turn were shattered, while Helen Archdale, reacting to Betty's situation as any mother would, was disturbed and obviously had written to Alec about it. He tried to comfort her by saying: 'It's too bad about Betty being pushed away like that but I should think if she gets back to England she'll get some fine recognition. It is much the same all through the Navy. The bureaucracy that carries on in the middle so that the top men never really know what the rank and file are doing.'[55]

When Betty arrived in Basra she was told that the navy was attempting to build up a big show in the Persian Gulf to give the impression that the second front was going to come from the Mediterranean and not across the Channel. She understood they were all part of a diversionary operation. Once again Betty had to establish quarters for a small contingent of Wrens, yet to arrive. They were to be 'writers'. To her relief and pleasure, the Senior Naval Officer Persian Gulf (SNOP), Commodore Hammill, seemed to be very considerate of Betty. One day, when walking with her, he said that an Iraqi was coming to lunch the next day. 'He will be puzzled by you and will decide you are my concubine but will not think anything of it so it does not matter.'[56]

When the first batch of Wrens arrived on 11 November, Betty moved into the YWCA with them and soon they were hard at work. Betty was still hurt and confused by her previous experience in Mombasa but she began to feel more energetic with the cooler weather and worked 'like a slave' from eight till eight. Off duty, she played golf with a civilian woman on a course of crusted mud sprouting spiky plants which camels ate. A naval officer who was passing through also cheered Betty. He had recently seen the D. WRNS and said she had 'a hell of a moan' because Betty had been moved without informing her. It seemed that the whole incident had been a mistake and badly handled at Mombasa. Betty comforted herself that she had been ultra correct about the whole affair, but she was dying to 'spill the beans' when she got home.[57]

It was about this time that Betty had other news from home. Alec and Pat's marriage had come to an end. When the war came Alec joined the navy and Pat and the boys, Dominic and Anthony, went to the West Indies for safety. It was from there that Pat had written to Alec asking for a divorce. In explanation to his mother, Alec said that the war and separation had completely unsettled him and that he was more discouraged in himself than in any other aspect of the situation. It was another example of his ability to make mistakes. 'The only thing I appear to be able to stick to is the theatre,' he wrote.[58]

At this time Helen Archdale was toying with the idea of writing a play or screenplay about Emmeline Pankhurst. Alec encouraged her but warned her either option would require a healthy chunk of capital, which Helen didn't have. She was then working for the Ministry of Women and engaged with the pressure group for the acceptance of women peers to the House of Lords. But neither commanded a salary of any consequence. Alec and Betty were especially conscious of this and Betty was constantly sending Helen food parcels and swatches of materials for blouses, flannel for gardening trousers. Betty fretted about her mother being warm enough and before her departure for overseas had ordered carpet from the Army and Naval Store for Helen's house at Stilestone.

In Basra, Betty received unhappy letters from her former chief Wrens in Mombasa. They now had a mistress-at-arms, had to sign a book saying with whom and where they were going and had to wear hats to go on watch, 'as we apparently are a "scruffy" [underlined] lot of individuals' wrote Eileen Crompton.[59] The Wrens felt that no interest was being taken in them by either their first or second officer. 'R has made a muck of things I'm afraid,' wrote Sister Young. 'She might weather the storm, but she's made herself so unpopular that I doubt it—I take the attitude that "Well you all thought you were being clever and you just weren't—serve you b-well right". Now of course your praises are sung to the heavens above.'[60]

Betty also heard from First Officer Robinson, who asked if Betty was finding conditions trying in Basra and if she felt she could stand the summer until July–August. 'Of all the blank silly and fatuous questions—I shall have a job answering it without being rude,' Betty said to Helen, while writing in temperatures soaring over 100 degrees. Betty heard not long afterwards that Robinson had been asked to go.[61]

Two other pieces of news bucked Betty up considerably. On 3 January 1943 she was advised that the tropical rig of the WRNS had been changed along the lines she had initiated in Singapore—no stockings and blouses and skirts for working wear. When the fleet order came out, she laughed with delight.[62] The other news, relayed by Sister Young, was that Harry Markus had married. It relieved Betty's conscience, for he had been kind to her and she felt that she had treated him badly.[63]

Betty was getting fed up with all the little worries that seemed to constantly arise in her various roles and she wrote an article finishing with a doggerel poem for the WRNS newsletter. The poem ended:

So if any poor misguided mutt
Is dazzled by overseas,
Tell her the tale of the Persian Gulf
With its mud and date Palm trees
And tummy trouble, prickly heat, mosquitoes, lice and fleas.

The press officer for D. WRNS wrote in response: 'Dear Archdale, thank you for your letter of the 29th May, also for your rather amusing contribution to the "Wren Recorder". It is regretted we cannot actually publish this … as it may discourage Wrens from volunteering for overseas duty, and at the moment we are anxious to encourage them.'[64]

At Basra, Betty was aware that her job was much smaller than her last one and was dismayed that her chances of promotion seemed non-existent. Others were getting rapid promotions without having half the responsibility that she had had. Everything was starting to pall and Betty was bored. While being entertained by various social events, she was as sick to death of the type of women she met in the Gulf as she had been of the wives in Singapore and she longed to see her old friends.

When two years of foreign service had passed, Betty ached to go home. Almost every letter to her mother referred to plans for the garden at Stilestone. And just like her father Theodore, when first married, she mulled over horticultural catalogues. She had an urge to farm and she asked Helen to look out for land for sale near Stilestone. Meanwhile, she tried to divert her attention from longing with forays into the desert, to Kuwait and Ghenna. With friends she dined with a sheik, sitting on the floor and using fingers to eat meat, rice and pickled tomatoes. They later learnt that the sheik had shot his sister because there was some gossip about her. What a life for women! Betty exclaimed in her diary. They were all veiled, and existed in a harem mentality without any sign of change. Cinemas were banned for fear of their corrupting influence.

In July Betty was pleasantly surprised to find that the commodore had nominated her for a decoration on the recommendation of the Secretary of the Navy in the Persian Gulf. Betty doubted that she would get it because of the thousands being nominated, but she was happy for the endorsement and felt that it should please the Director.[65] But there was no sign of a replacement. Betty had hoped to take her original group of chief Wrens in Mombasa back home, but they had been returned in three drafts.

The first party sailed for England aboard the *Empress of Canada* and was torpedoed in the Atlantic Ocean. They were rescued after spending two nights and a day in the sea, but a lot of men who had worked at their side deciphering Japanese code died because they gave their places up for the women. The second draft sailed for the UK two months later. They had two passengers on board with typhus, so that everything they possessed had to be fumigated. The third draft had three weeks in Durban and then came home. Beryl Grace, who married on the day Betty left Mombasa, was later drowned with her husband and baby and fourteen more Wrens on their way back to Ceylon when the forces were moving east again.

Eventually Betty appealed to the visiting James McClelland (who had been the OC at Kranji). He induced the C-in-C to send the signals about Betty's relief from Mombasa. It is probable that McClelland, having known Betty in Singapore, was alarmed by her appearance. Years of worry and heat had left their mark and she was thinner and looking older. Working in the office, Betty saw the signal saying Second Officer Archdale needed a rest. She knew she had lost 'kick', she had had it.

In September Betty was informed that her relief was coming. Once more she felt it was a good thing she was leaving. A Major Mitchell, whom she had met playing cricket, had been asking her to dinners and dances and had got to the stage where he would hold her hand. 'I have told him I will turn him over to my relief as part of the job,' she told Helen pragmatically. 'Poor lad, all they want is a girl to take out and there are so few of them.'[66]

Betty left Basra on 19 October 1943 with an army and navy officer on an adventurous journey home by train, taxi and a lorry drive through biblical lands. At Port Said she boarded the *Dominion Monarch* and endured a colder and rougher voyage than any she had previously experienced. At Euston, Helen Archdale was on the station to meet her daughter. The next day, when Betty reported to headquarters, she must have looked awful, because they sent her home for a month. It seems that at some stage Betty had a chance to express her ire, because Alec wrote to Helen in November saying, 'Good for Betty letting off at WRNSHQ'.

However, not long after that Betty received a letter informing her that she was to be made a Member of the Military Division of the Order of the British Empire for her 'zeal and wholehearted devotion to duty'.[67] On 1 January 1944, Betty went to Buckingham Palace with Helen Archdale and Nancy Lord. The honour, bestowed by George VI, was given to 'Our trusty and well beloved Helen Elizabeth Archdale Second Officer in our Women's Royal Naval Service'.[68]

'I think down the years that we owed her a great debt. We were very glad when she got the MBE, all of us were delighted,' said Phyll Puttick. 'She said at the time—"I got it on behalf of you all"—she was given it for bringing us safely out of Singapore.'[69] There was also a rumour that Betty was awarded the MBE for taking an important message from London to Plymouth on a motorbike during a bombing raid, 'Still very hush hush!' said a former Wren in a dark whisper in the year 2000.

In the New Year, Betty returned to work at Greenwich at the Officer Training College at the Royal Naval College, where she was responsible for the timetable and planning. She was at last enjoying some recognition and was promoted to first officer. Alec wrote to Helen, 'I'm glad Betty has got her half-stripe, I wish I could hear about mine!' and in another letter, 'Fancy having a sister with all those letters after her name! Dear—Dear—I shall have to buck up!'[70]

12

WOMEN'S COLLEGE

When the college at Greenwich was bombed Betty moved with the staff of the WRNS training course to Framewood Manor, Buckinghamshire. She was a lecturer and responsible for organising sporting matches against other services. It seems that at this time she was the only one of Helen Archdale's children to be settled. Troubling news was coming to her from Canada about the deterioration of Nick and Sheila's marriage.

In June 1945, with the war in Europe over, Betty was playing a cricket match for the WRNS against the Women's Army Territorial Service when she was given a message to ring WRNS headquarters. She was asked would she be able to go to Australia the following Thursday? She answered, 'Yes Ma'am'.[1] Betty was to be in charge of WRNS personnel stationed there. She was very keen to get back to Australia because she had had a wonderful time there in 1934–5.

The urgency of the manoeuvre was soon diminished as the Pacific war came to an end. Betty celebrated VJ day, 14 August 1945, by having supper with Margaret Rhondda and Theodora Bosanquet. A week later she sailed for Australia. To her astonishment, when she arrived in Fremantle she was recognised by reporters, taken out to lunch, and met up with members of the West Australian cricket team.[2]

Betty commenced work with fewer than 200 Wrens in Melbourne.

Her duties were light, so she led an enjoyable life mixing with friends made on her previous tour, feminists, barely known relatives and the upper echelons of the naval hierarchy. Then one day Betty wrote to Helen Archdale telling her that Barbara Munro had alerted her to the advertised position of principal of the Women's College at the University of Sydney.[3]

Women's College existed on the perimeter of the university, along with four men's colleges of different denominations and a Catholic women's college. Unlike the Oxbridge colleges, they were mainly residential, with tutorials being supplementary to the university's teaching. They did have intimations of their English counterparts, but with a life of their own with intercollegiate drama, sport, debates, and balls—the young men and women developing a feisty, tribal behaviour. Traditions such as formal dinners with a high table at which honoured guests sat, the wearing of academic gowns, toasts to the King, provided a welcoming environment for the often mild eccentrics who came to be their principals.

Despite the prospect that Betty would be living so far from home, Helen Archdale encouraged Betty to apply for the position and clambered into the attic to gather her daughter's testimonials from Margaret Rhondda, her headmistress at St Leonard's and those who had lectured her at university.

Betty was able to assess the position more closely when she was moved to Sydney in November to take over a unit of 400 Wrens. She re-met cricketing friends and socialised with Peg Telfer, the journalists Pat Jarrett and Kath Commins, the gynaecologist and obstetrician Grace Cuthbert Browne, and Margaret Hay, who was secretary of the University of Sydney Law School. They were of Betty's ilk, for apart from the two Pedens, the women were all single and professional and charting strongly individual paths which earned them high profiles. Sydney was becoming familiar and attractive as a place to live. What is more, Betty seemed to be needed—she was also encouraged to apply to Ascham School in Sydney which was looking for an Englishwoman to be headmistress.

Before coming to Australia Betty had every intention of going to the English Bar after the war. But at 38 years of age she recognised that it would take some years before she could establish herself and earn a good living as a barrister. So she decided to pursue the Women's College position. She was also drawn by the slightly academic atmosphere of Women's College, the age group of the girls and the contrast with her university college in Canada. However, the appointment was by no means certain. She heard that Sheila McClemans, D. WRANS and a lawyer, had also applied. Betty had met her in Melbourne and liked her and was sure that she would be preferred.

The council of the Women's College requested an interview with Betty on 14 February 1946. With some theatricality, Betty, in full uniform, suggested to her naval driver, who was a friend from England, 'Look, we've got to do this properly. When we get there, you open the door and we'll salute and all this sort of nonsense.' She knew that the assembled council could see her arrival from the windows above. From that day on, Betty was called the 'Ad', short for Admiral, at Women's College.[4]

Whether her ruse tipped the balance of the council in her favour is not known, but the next day Betty wrote to tell her mother that Peg Telfer had rung to say, unofficially, that the council unanimously decided to offer her the job. She would return to England in April to be released from the navy, and then come back to Australia in August to take on her new role.[5] After the appointment was announced Betty received a large number of telegrams, cables and letters congratulating her, including one from Margaret Rhondda. Helen Archdale complained to Betty that since the announcement was broadcast on the BBC overseas news the press had contacted her.

In Sydney, Betty's public profile was launched. She was invited to address various groups, attend a Government House garden party and lunch with the Governor-General, the Duke of Gloucester, and his wife, and was asked to stand for chairman of the NSW Women's Cricket Association. Betty retained her modesty through this onrush of attention. And her modesty was real. The war had made her realise that much of what happens in life is pure luck. She had had an interesting war, but at the same time she realised she could just as well have been dead or captured by the Japanese in Singapore. 'I think I was conscious it wasn't anything to do with oneself that things happen to turn out very nicely. I didn't think that because I was a very good officer that I landed in the right place, at the right time, because I wasn't, and I think I knew I wasn't.'[6]

Freed from the WRNS, the anxieties of war, the constraints of Britain and the expectations of her mother, Betty came as a blithe spirit to Women's College.

Her buoyancy was reflected in the society in which she found herself. Australia had been shocked into action after recognising how narrowly the Japanese had been defeated in the Pacific. There was a strong resolve that the nation must become stronger, more self-sufficient, that the citizenry of seven and a half million should be increased with a populate-or-perish fervour, in order to face a foreign threat should it arise again. Coming back to Australia from England, where there were fears about the future, Betty found Australians living in a growing economy with expanding opportunities. It was one of the great attractions of Australia.

However, the new energy seen in manufacturing was not evident in the Women's College at the University of Sydney. It had been in survival mode during the war, and was stale and conservative. With a lightness of tone, the new principal was quoted as saying that during the war she was in charge of a Wrennery and now she was in charge of what she understood was called a 'haggery'.[7] Such a comment would have stirred the upper levels of Sydney society. The college, a large red-brick Victorian building with deep verandahs and a tower, stood tall, with dignity, on the fringes of the university grounds.

The principals preceding Betty had been remarkable women, from Louisa Macdonald, who campaigned for suffrage and spoke against workplace exploitation, to the anthropologist Camilla Wedgwood. However, in January 1944 Wedgwood was commissioned in the Australian Army Medical Women's Service, holding the temporary rank of lieutenant colonel (ironically, considering she was a Quaker and a pacifist). Her appointment to the Australian army, *The Times* said, was made at the wish of Sir Thomas Blamey to ensure that the best anthropological knowledge would be applied to the problem of protecting native society in Papua New Guinea from the disruptive effects of the war. Although described as Boadicean, Camilla Wedgwood was a striking Englishwoman who was somehow able to conform to the expectations of society. But despite such principals' influence there remained in the college a certain gentility. Care was taken to be ladylike so that people couldn't say the girls were awkward bluestockings.

When Wedgwood left, the acting principal was Miss Julie Fitzhardinge, who was quiet and maternal with the girls and who was from a grand old Sydney family with money. After Betty arrived, Julie Fitzhardinge remained and held sway as honorary secretary, a position too close for Betty's comfort. It seems there was a mutual hostility, with Julie respecting known patterns of behaviour (such as the daily hoisting of the flag) and Betty dismissing them as irrelevant. Throughout Betty's term the Fitzhardinge family gave gifts to the college, indeed so generously that Betty felt the council favoured Julie over her.   Betty, who had no money to her name, was effectively an outsider breaking in. She had been schooled in the behaviours of social reform, not social intercourse. She wore her naval blue suit even though it shone with age, and her black naval coat with a never-mended tear in its back. Certain people thought Betty was gauche and should be more careful of her dress. 'People who didn't know this person would look at her clumping down corridors … and think my daughter might end up like that,' explained Janet Hay (Cowper). 'Miss Archdale was the first one that came in looking different and having a man's brain really.'[8]

Betty even attracted comment from Ethel Anderson, the writer, who lived in Turramurra, on Sydney's upper north shore. She was very formal, her husband General Anderson having been the aide-de-camp to governors-general. Sitting upright with her silver ear trumpet, she asked Janet Hay's mother if she thought it right to let Janet go to the Women's College. When asked why not, she said, 'Well, I don't think Betty Archdale has a pair of long white gloves!'[9]

In those days all the girls had a pair of long white gloves which they wore to formal dances and they never went into town without their little white gloves. Many of the students had come from boarding school, others from very sheltered homes. They were 'nice' girls who would trip across to the university dressed in twin-sets, with Peter Pan collars tucked in, pearls, skirts, stockings and high heels. 'When you think of the dear—I mean her experience being in charge of women in the WRNS where you've got such a broad selection of the public—we would have been chicken feed,' said a college student from Betty's reign.

Initially, the girls found it hard to believe that Betty had been captain of the English women's cricket team when, said Margaret Ford, she shook hands as though she was holding a wet fish. And yet the Saturday after her arrival, she knocked off 126 not out and the fresher who dared to take the spoon from her coffee when she said she did not take sugar soon found out that the Ad could make it crystal clear that she would not be deprived of her spoon.[10]

Soon the girls found that Betty was a breath of fresh air. While she came across as an intellectual and authoritative person, she also had a great sense of humour, was always untidy, and gave the impression that material things didn't matter. 'Which was very right for us coming into the world,' said Jo Bastian.[11] In the first postwar year there were 89 students at Women's College—a manageable number who gathered under their motto 'Together'. It was wise to advocate solidarity because, of the whole student population (4500) at the University of Sydney, less than one-fifth were female.

Following the end of the war the university was crowded, the presence of ex-servicemen making it a very lively place. Applications far exceeded the number of vacancies at the college. Betty accepted two women who had been in the army and was very understanding with them. She had an ability to select a diverse, idiosyncratic cross-section of girls—from the country and city, those who were privileged and those who weren't, with a variety of courses of study. The 1947 freshers included those studying social studies, economics, architecture, science, medicine, veterinary science and the humanities.

Australian women were still closely tied, by ideology and practice, to women's traditional role of home-maker. In comparison with England, there were fewer women in the professions and public life, and fewer married women and mothers in the workforce. There was universal discrimination against employed women, who often received as little as 54 percent of the male wage for the same job. Here in the college Betty had girls who were among the ablest in the community, and she was keen to see them realise their potential as fully as possible.

The girls were more friendly to authority than their counterparts in England, and were more egalitarian. But although they were intelligent and were more progressive than their mothers, and willing to learn and listen to other people, they were still conventional in their outlook and tended to be conformists. Betty sensed there was terrific resistance to education generally, that people were shy of owning up to it. It was an attitude which placed educated people on the defensive. 'By education, I mean being aware of what is going on, an openness to spirit and liveliness,' Betty told a meeting of Newcastle businessmen. 'Educated people get much more fun out of living than the uneducated.'[12] Yet Betty had found that people didn't like thinking for themselves, although that was what was needed for the development of society. For many, the outcome of thinking was too uncertain.

Immediately Betty set to enhance the intellectual climate of the college. Although it was non-denominational it was Christian, with compulsory prayers on Monday evenings. To this captive audience Betty lured all kinds of speakers so that the young women could be exposed to as many different perspectives as possible. Mlle Kozubowska spoke on Polish history, Miss Marie Byles on Buddhism, Vice-Admiral Moore on the RAN, Mrs Jessie Street, who had worked with Helen Archdale in international feminism, talked on the UNO Commission on the Status of Women, and Dr Curve spoke on the Communist Party Dissolution Act. Betty admitted to being a snob about famous people—she loved meeting individualists who had shown courage, who had minds of their own, who had lived their lives differently, and she had a knack of attracting them to the college.

The pattern of the Monday evenings was the same. Girls were invited to sit at high table with Betty and the sometimes esoteric guests. Following the meal they went to coffee in her sitting room with its squeaky leather chairs and scattered copies of *Time and Tide*. The girls sat around and the Ad always sat in the same chair, with her legs over its arms. And she would encourage discussion. At this stage in her life Betty was thought not to have much flow of conversation herself. Students invited to the high table who talked well were welcome there, because

18. Helen Archdale *(left)*, editor of *Time and Tide*, preparing an edition of the magazine. (H.E. Archdale papers)

19. *Time and Tide* staff before a formal dinner in June 1925 which was attended by Mr St John Ervine, Mr John St Loe Strachey, Miss Rebecca West, and Lords Hewart, Riddell and Astor. Viscountess Margaret Rhondda on left, Helen Archdale *(back centre)*. (H.E. Archdale papers)

20. Betty, aged eighteen, walking with Viscountess Margaret Rhondda at Stonepitts. (H.E. Archdale papers)

21. Betty on board ship to Canada and McGill University, 1926. (H.E. Archdale papers)

22. Charles Herbert (*left*), Betty's university friend. (H.E. Archdale papers)

23. At the Nationality Campaign in Geneva during the 1932 Assembly, the deputation to His Excellency the bedjrond Zellaka Agguodaou, delegate from Ethiopia. *Left to right:* Miss Phyllis Lovell (England), Mme Margaret Volinsky (Yugoslavia), Miss Alice Paul (USA), Miss Madeleine Regency (Switzerland), Mr Zallaka, Dr Mila Obradovitch (Yugolavia), and Miss Betty Archdale (England). (H.E. Archdale papers)

24. Nick Archdale (*centre*) as headmaster of Ashbury College, Ottawa. (H.E. Archdale papers)

25. Publicity portrait of Alec Archdale, the actor. (H.E. Archdale papers)

26. Mrs Heron Maxwell (*left*) with Miss Cox at the private cricket ground where they started the Comp Cricket Club, Kent. (H.E. Archdale papers)

27. Betty with cricket journalist Marjorie Pollard, at a party in England on the eve of departure for the first international women's cricket Tests in Australia in 1934. (H.E. Archdale papers)

28. Captain Archdale, batsman, 1934.
(H.E. Archdale papers)

29. Women's College, 1934.
(Photograph by Betty Archdale)

30. The two captains — Betty with the Australian, Margaret Peden. (H.E. Archdale papers)

31. University of Sydney in 1934. Both photographs taken by Betty eleven years before she took up a position as principal of Women's College. (Photograph by Betty Archdale)

32. The English cricketer Molly Hide cuddling koalas in Sydney, 1934. (Photograph by Betty Archdale)

33. The English women's cricket team stranded by a puncture, on the road to Deniliquin, NSW. (H.E Archdale papers)

34. This and the preceding photograph are from Betty's Australian cricket tour album, on a page labelled 'Punctured'. (H.E. Archdale papers)

35. Proof of the first ever century scored in women's international cricket, beside the name of Maclagan, on the scoreboard for the 1st innings, Second Test, at the Sydney Cricket Ground, January 1935. Archdale out for 3. (Photograph by Betty Archdale)

36. Nancy Lord, before the war, in England. (H.E Archdale papers)

37. Barbara Peden and Colin Munro on their wedding day, London. (H.E. Archdale papers)

although Betty was a great personality she appeared to be rather passive. In fact Marie Bashir believes this style of being a catalyst rather than a dominating presence worked to Betty's advantage:

> I remember Margaret Mead, I remember Hephzibah Menuhin…quite extraordinary people, who in her presence were absolutely relaxed and frank. So they'd just feel at ease to describe some of the aspects of their life that one wouldn't read about in the newspaper or perhaps in a biography. Hephzibah Menuhin, some years previously, had left her husband, who was I think a member of the affluent Melbourne middle class, and had virtually eloped with a man who was a European … an emigré from Europe at the time of Hitler's invasion; who worked amongst the poor in England after the war, in Golders Green. So they were doing very avant-garde social work of a type that was very inspiring.
>
> So you can imagine young medical students and highly intelligent young people studying Arts and or Science sitting at the feet of these people, learning of the courageous and unconventional way they were running their lives and the enormous satisfaction that it was quite clearly giving them. There were those sources of inspiration. I daresay there had to be a sub-stratum within each of us to be inspired by it.
>
> But there was the intellectual aspect of it as well as the caring aspect of it, and I think that summarises very much Miss Archdale herself. There's this sense of love and care but also this extremely keen mind that's never maudlin. So it was always a treat to be asked to sit on High Table with her. You know the marvellous peals of laughter, the gentle humour that never ever was unkind or sarcastic.[13]

According to Marie Bashir, Betty's impact on the girls at college was immense because of the great radiance of her character, which was powerful without ever being intentionally so. 'She was essentially a very soft person, I believe, her personality, with a wonderfully strong core.' The young women came to learn the intellectual approach of looking at things for what they are and not what surrounds them. When Bertrand Russell and Malcolm Muggeridge came to Australia Betty took girls to their lectures.

Betty encouraged a climate of developing culture for the predominantly Anglo-Celtic girls in her charge whose Europeanisation was fairly minimal. Following memorable formal dinners, dressed in a long flowing floral chiffon dress beneath her black academic gown, she would swiftly change and, inviting two students, rush off to concerts by the Sydney Symphony Orchestra, on whose subscriber's committee she served for many years. She was always going to whatever theatre she could in Sydney, often wonderful theatre in small halls, or to the opera, which was scarce in 1950.

It was a wonderful period of growth because immigrants from Europe, particularly the Jewish immigrants, were contributing to the culture and intellectual life of Sydney. So the students were exposed to considerable stimulation on many fronts. Betty's attempt to broaden discussion was a reflection of the more intense debates in the community at large. It was as if the whole fabric of society had to be poked and tested. People argued about communism versus individualism, the churches versus secularism and the emergence of a 'new order'.[14]

The University of Sydney, with its concentration of good minds (it was until 1949 the only university in Sydney), frequently seeded the debates. The most controversial contributor was John Anderson, the Challis Professor of Philosophy. The archetypal Socratic questioner and debunker, his assaults on the Sydney establishment, the church, the university senate, the Communist Party and the planners and the regulators of 'the new Dark Age' were legendary. His camp followers embraced 'Andersonianism', including his libertarian stance which advocated the overthrow of sexual taboos.[15]

Betty became part of the intellectual scene and was befriended by academics and other heads of colleges including Bert Wyllie, principal of Wesley College, and his deputy, the biologist Professor Charles Birch, Dr Cumming Thom at St Andrew's, and Dr Felix Arnott at St Paul's College.

Felix Arnott was a person of great warmth and charm with a wonderful, mischievous sense of humour. He was not much taller than Betty, with dark untamed hair, round face and heavy black-rimmed glasses, with a wife, Anne, and four rather wild children who reduced his dignity. He was humane, intellectual and entertained people with spirited conversation in a high voice. He and Betty became very fond friends. They were like kindred spirits, both English born, who thought independently, without pettiness. While each of them had a presence, they had a similar leniency towards their charges, Felix being famously quoted as saying, 'I've never seen a Paul's man drunk … I always look the other way!' Together,

Betty and Felix had fun, conspiring as to how to win more money for their colleges—always for their students and never for themselves. They compared problems with their young, and because of their relationship Betty became the first woman to dine in St Paul's College dining room.

Disciplinary problems emerged with men in the surrounding colleges raiding Women's College and Betty became the champion for her girls. Charles Birch remembers one incident particularly. He had come to Wesley College as vice-master to Bert Wyllie in 1948. It was Wyllie who told him that one day Betty had rung him up to say his men had written a word, with weedkiller, in the Women's College lawn. She said her girls found it distressing although, she added, she wasn't sure why. When asked what was written she replied, nonplussed, 'Balls'. 'We thought she was innocent,' laughed Charles Birch years later, adding: 'She gave the impression of someone being in control, kind as well as authoritative. She commanded a lot of respect from students and staff.'[16]

Birch's description of Betty's headship did not include the less tangible, but more significant impact of her presence on the girls. Margaret Ford said that when Betty came to them, she 'did not openly appear to be doing much and yet I can remember so vividly the time when about twelve months after she came I was aware of what I can only describe as the college "spirit" which was abroad in the air. I wish I could articulate it … all I know is that it produced a bonding with the place and our fellow students which still remains one of my most precious memories and makes me still say that I love every brick of that old building … and somehow she injected that into the place though I do not know how.'[17]

It was a satisfying time for Betty. She was stimulated by the intellectual climate both on and off campus and she maintained her interest in international law by joining the NSW branch of the Australian Institute of International Affairs. It was through this group that her personality allowed her to make good male friends. She attended meetings with Bertrand Russell, Aldous Huxley, A. P. Herbert, and Salvador de Madriaga who spoke on the meaning of democracy and the spirit of European civilisation. Later, in a breakthrough for women, Betty became the NSW branch president and in 1959 she also served on the national council of the Institute of International Affairs.

Betty found the women's movement wasn't as organised in Australia as in England—due, she thought, to the fact that Australian women had won the vote with very little argument. There weren't left-wing groups going out into the streets to promote reform.

In Australia, however, she underwent a personal renaissance. Deciding that she wanted to appreciate music more, she took up the piano with Eileen Bursten at the Conservatorium. To the astonishment of the residents of Women's College, some of whom were music students, she started from scratch, in a heavy-handed manner, the C Major scale and the 'Rondo for Tiny Fingers'. 'She made ghastly noises on the piano. It was really charming,' Helen Buchanan recalled. 'Not many would have the courage.'[18] But Betty loved it when she was congratulated on her progress.

For the first time, she felt financially and physically comfortable. Her salary was £750 a year and she really thought she was in the money. It was the first time in her life that she didn't have to worry about buying the books she wanted. She was also fed and housed, with a bedroom and a bathroom on the first floor of the college and downstairs a drawing room which was used by staff and students—on invitation—so it wasn't very private. She also had a small study, but as she had no facilities of her own to prepare food she ate all her meals in the dining room. It was these quarters that fuelled a major concern, which loomed large in her mind.

Before she had even formally applied for the position, Betty had written to her mother saying that, if she got the job, she hoped Helen would come to Australia too. But once in situ it was clear to Betty that there was no spare room for her mother. While during vacations there would be plenty of space, she told her mother she would find her separate quarters for term time. She tried to delay Helen's arrival saying she wanted to get settled first and find accommodation for Helen and a car.[19] When Helen complained to Alec that Betty was distancing herself from her, Alec tried to prevent Helen from leaning too heavily on her daughter in her new role.[20]

Betty and Alec's letters leave no doubt that Helen was not coping as well as before. It seems that with every new initiative in Betty's life there came back a 'good, but what about me?' response. The tone of her communication echoes that of a depressed person. Unlike Margaret Rhondda, Helen had no partner, the war had scattered her children, and now two of them had marriages in tatters. Her considerable size was also affecting her health and she felt very much alone. Helen needed her children now as never before.

In 1947, within a year of Betty taking up the role as principal, Helen arrived in Australia, where she stayed for two years. It is uncertain whether Betty asked the council if her mother could live with her in college, but Barbara Munro found a flat for Helen to stay in at Collaroy, near the Peden family beach house. Looking back, the fact that she didn't fight to have her warrior mother at her side in college caused Betty strong feelings of guilt and shame. Not standing up for the suffragettes when she was six and in boarding school and not accommodating her mother in Women's College were the two things that worried her the most, despite the certainty that she had done worse.

Helen Archdale made a strong impression on all who saw her in 1940s Australian society. She was very tall and her large body was not restrained by underclothes. She wore black with a black toque on her grey white hair, but never wore make-up. 'She was a most impressive person. I was quite young at the time,' said Barbara Munro's son Colin, 'but I remember this commanding presence with a mane of white hair and this large chest, rather like a roll-top desk. The reason why I remember it is because planted firmly on this chest was a large silver thing that could have been mistaken for a brooch but in fact was an early hearing aid. It was round as I recall—it was quite large, it would have been as round as a cricket ball, which is appropriate, and it had filigree in the middle. It was in effect a microphone and we were encouraged to lean forward to this very ample chest and speak quite loudly into it.'[21]

There was no doubt Helen Archdale had a strong personality. The minute she entered the room, people were aware that here was a woman of significance. 'You felt that it would have been difficult for Betty to develop her personality to its fullest extent when in such close contact with a woman of quite an outstanding force,' said Aline Fenwick, who met her through the Australian Institute of International Affairs. 'Betty always gave me the impression of being the everlasting senior prefect. I don't think she's fully developed, the everlasting girl. When I saw the mother I understood why. Her mother's impressive personality tended to overshadow Betty, who was affectionate and dutiful. Alexander didn't seem to be fully developed either.' Although Betty was shrewd and perceptive, Aline Fenwick saw her as shy and lacking basic confidence— a product of an unusual upbringing. 'Parenting doesn't seem to be one of the gifts of the English upper middle class,' said Aline.[22]

In fact it is doubtful that Helen Archdale would have even understood the concept that it might have been difficult for Betty to develop fully as a person with such a strong parent. Elizabeth Wilkinson, who was at Women's College at the time, saw Helen Archdale as all-powerful and could easily picture her chaining herself to No. 10 Downing Street and demanding the vote. There wouldn't have ever been any question about whether she was right or wrong. Betty, however, was much more flexible in lots of ways. And though they were both powerful military types, it was hard for Elizabeth Wilkinson to gauge the extent to which this perhaps covered up for a shyness Betty didn't get from her mother.[23]

Betty made a life for her mother in Australia, presenting her as the important woman she had once been. Helen set about enjoying herself and 'clubbed up', attending the AIIA after producing her introduction from the Royal Institute of International Affairs, and the Penguin Club where she spoke on equal rights. She befriended the wives of trade union leaders and the former peace organiser, Ruby Rich, and she was often asked to speak when, in those days, it was almost unheard of to have women speakers.

Helen also contacted Adela Pankhurst, who had married Thomas Walsh but was now widowed and living quietly with her daughter Christian Quale in Sydney. The once pretty Adela was now worn in face and body. She had been interned during World War II for pro-Japanese talk but was eventually released for health reasons after staging a hunger strike. It seems Adela was erratic in her passions and her biographer, Verna Coleman, notes that her attitudes to appeasement, Japan and the Australia First Movement pleased almost nobody.

In July 1948 Helen encouraged Adela to meet with other elderly suffragettes in a tea shop in George Street in Sydney to celebrate the ninetieth anniversary of Emmeline Pankhurst's birthday. The tea party had been organised by Edith How-Martyn, who went to prison in a black maria with Adela some 40 years earlier. The women, who remembered Adela as a generous-hearted, spontaneous rebel, found her manner unchanged. She was eager, vivacious, her gaze as straight and interested as ever.

It is unlikely that Betty saw much of Adela, her former governess, for Adela was no longer accepting invitations by 1949. She died in Wahroonga at the Home of Peace Hospital in 1961. But the two women had in common mothers who were wedded to the cause of the emancipation of women. Verna Coleman wrote: 'Always in the thick of things, living for drama and excitement, often arrogant sometimes flippant, but never bored, Adela Pankhurst was largely the product of her enthusiast, activist upbringing in the melodramatic Pankhurst style. But as with her mother, there was something elemental about her. She worked in broad powerful strokes, and aroused strong reactions—of love and devotion, of cynical dismissal, of black hatred. There was a mysterious inner core of courage and experiment, a larger-than-life, excessive quality about her … Her native optimism survived to the end. "Life is nothing without enthusiasm," she said.'[24]

Many of these qualities existed in Betty, who was raised in a similar, though less extreme, emotional environment. Betty also worked 'in broad powerful strokes', attracted unswerving loyalty, resolutely backed what she saw as right, and had a similar inner core of courage and experiment, was larger than life, optimistic and enthusiastic.

However, in 1947 these traits were held in check as Betty concentrated on her mother having a good time. Betty's friends all rallied and entertained her. The wife of the headmaster of The King's School, Betty Hake, whose mother had been at St Leonard's with Helen Archdale, asked Helen to a meal at the school. She had asked a gentle Australian schoolmaster to meet her, but she remembers Helen riding over him fiercely. 'And also I remember her saying, "I came to Parramatta to see all these old houses and I can't see anything that isn't Victorian",' said Betty Hake. 'She didn't know her history very well.'[25]

When Betty took her mother to Peg Telfer's bungalow in the Blue Mountains in September 1948 Helen had a heart attack. After Helen left hospital, Betty brought her back to live in college so she could keep an eye on her. 'Which is what I should have done in the first place,' Betty said ruefully.[26] Here, even though she had fought for equal opportunity for women, in Helen Archdale's mind some women were obviously more equal than others. A maid at Women's College, who was good at her job and had been there for a number of years, almost revolted because Helen Archdale treated her so badly.[27] Even during Helen's convalescence, Betty tried to involve her in her world. On the day of Women's College sports she had her mother wheeled out in a hospital bed so that she could be distracted from her ill health. Eventually Helen improved enough to travel home to London towards the end of 1948.

The next year Helen, sensing time was running out, travelled to see Nicholas in Canada, and was again unwell. Betty was fretful about her, and then started a series of heart-rending letters, with Betty agonising over whether to bring Helen back to Australia to live with her, or to leave Women's College to live with her mother in Stilestone. Helen, although frail, appears to have been highly manipulative in her reasoning.

Betty's letters convey the rich and varied life she was leading at Women's College, and with it some anger that she might have to relinquish this new-found happiness to care for her mother. But a crisis was looming and in April 1949 Betty wrote a letter of resignation to the council, saying that she must return to England as she believed her mother could no longer live alone.[28] The council, 'in their usual ineffective manner', did nothing for about two months when they held a special meeting without Betty and appointed a subcommittee to approach her to see what could be done to make it possible for her to stay.

At the subcommittee meeting with Betty, Peg Telfer asked if it would have made any difference if Helen Archdale had been able to come into college when she and Betty arrived. Betty said she felt pretty sure it would have done and she told the council her mother might still like to return to live with her in Australia.

The council suggested that Betty take four months leave of absence to see her mother, and at the same time the college would take steps to provide extra accommodation in the principal's quarters. Peg Telfer proposed that any guest of the principal should pay a reasonable sum, to be decided upon.[29] 'That made me both cross and laugh as all Principals here have always paid for all visitors,' wrote Betty, indicating a growing antagonism between herself and the council, 'but I suppose they were wise to lay it down.'[30]

In July 1949, Betty wrote to her mother in Canada and told her she had booked a passage for England on the *Arawa*, sailing on 5 November. But Helen must have sensed her daughter's ambivalence, because Betty was compelled to send her a telegram in Canada: 'Very sorry letters not clear and upset you. Council offered four months leave which I accepted on clear understanding only return if you willing to come too. Otherwise gladly remain Stilestone permanently. Letter following. All love Betty.'[31]

In the lengthy letter that followed Betty said that in giving her leave with an uncertain outcome the council was taking a risk, but it was prepared to do so rather than lose her, which was flattering. While Betty said that the decision where they would both live was in Helen's hands, she added how happy she now was in Australia, that the job was going well, and that she felt she could do a lot in the next few years. She had made good friends and had a pleasant social life. Morally she felt that, apart from Helen's position, she should stay a few more years as she had initially told the council she would stay not less than five years and not more than ten.[32] Even though Betty wrote of the anticipated pleasure of relaxing at Stilestone and visiting London theatre, it was evident that her heart was not in it and that her life in Sydney was flourishing.

Four days later Betty wanted Helen to know that she would be making unwanted sacrifices if she lived in England permanently. But then she had to ameliorate her mother once more. 'I am sorry to have turned you into a pendulum but I have been one myself for so long— these things are so hard to decide by letter.'[33] As Helen experienced further health troubles and had to be hospitalised, Betty became resigned to the fact that she may have to stay permanently with her mother.

Not knowing whether she would return or not, the departure from Australia must have been difficult. Cricketers and friends gave Betty farewell dinners, her students put on a play lampooning college life and she went for possibly a last picnic by the sea. She left Sydney on 26 October, by air and a week earlier than she intended, on the receipt of a cable giving her news of her mother's health. Helen, still in hospital, was soon moved to Alec's flat, the Christian Scientist Hospice rejecting her because she had accepted conventional hospitalisation in Sydney when she had her heart attack.

It was obvious Helen wasn't going to live much longer, but she was comfortable with both Alec and Betty tending to her. On 8 December 1949 Betty was in the next room when her mother died, peacefully, from heart failure. 'I talked to mother before she died,' said Betty. 'I was quite certain we'd meet again in, I suppose you'd call it, a spiritual sense. She was too ill to say anything. I felt quite certain that mother was happier [in death]—I didn't feel sorry for her. She was a magnificent woman, no doubt about that—well ahead of her time—priceless! I think she was what I called a good woman—I think mother had very firm views and stuck to them.'[34]

However, Betty's account of her mother's death became domesticated by the passage of years. On the night, her response had been quite different. 'I know she was desperately upset when her mother died. It was very awkward,' said Nancy Lord. 'I was entertaining a young man I was working with. In the middle of this dinner she rang up and said that her mother had died and I said, "Stay with me—you'd better come up straight away". And she did, she came straight away and burst into tears and it went on for ever so long … I had to get rid of my visitor and spend the evening talking about Mrs Archdale. I always remember the night Betty's mother died because of the way Betty behaved—it was so unexpected to see her in floods of tears and the tears to go on and on. That was the one occasion that Betty showed great emotion.'[35] Betty later seemed to resent Nancy having seen her abandonment to grief. Nancy in turn recognised that Betty had English inhibitions in a big way. For that reason she felt Betty had a better time living in Australia because the less inhibited Australians allowed her to relate better.

The cremation of Helen Archdale was to be held at Golders Green. Feelings whorled around the occasion. Margaret Rhondda didn't want to attend and Nancy Lord and Theodora Bosanquet had to work very hard to get her to the funeral. Margaret was very annoyed she had to go and said she hadn't cared about the woman, which wasn't true, because once she did.[36] Only a few of Helen's suffragette friends attended the funeral, it was too late, they were all elderly. Alec spoke, but Nick didn't manage to come across from Canada. Alec, who felt his mother's loss deeply, was hostile to Nick for not helping Helen more.

Despite Alec being closest to their mother, Helen was realistic about his inability to conserve money. Over thirteen years before her death she left a will which set out to pay off his debts. The estate was to be divided equally amongst her three children, but Alec was only to receive the residual amount of his portion after monies borrowed from Betty had been repaid.[37] The will didn't seem to bother Betty or Alec, as after the funeral they went to Helen's house at Stilestone to spend time together.

Margaret Rhondda urged Betty to stay in England because her old school was looking for a new head. But Betty thought that, as much as she loved St Leonard's, it would be rather too conservative for her. In Australia, on the other hand, she could do more or less what she wanted.

Betty also recognised that relationships with key people in the United Kingdom had changed. She had felt almost like a daughter to Margaret Rhondda, who had given Betty loving attention. They talked the same language and had the same interests. But now Betty saw that Nancy Lord had secured that special place in Margaret's affections, and she was hurt. There is also little doubt that if Betty had stayed in England she would have had a less controversial and interesting time, and she wouldn't have become as much a public figure. The markedly smaller population of Australia allowed her outspokenness to be more apparent.

Towards the end of February 1950, Betty gathered herself and prepared to fly back to Sydney, to the familiarity of Women's College and a new academic year.

Helen Archdale's death brought about a sea change within Betty. No longer diminished by filial anxiety, she was free to put her stamp on Women's College and its occupants. She was able to relate to the girls more easily and she brought to the college a freshness and a new liberality. In this way she was an ideal principal, making the college completely different from the authoritarian schools and restricted homes of the time simply by her relaxed presence. She spoke to the students as if they were on equal terms with her and kept a very light hand on the reins.

Of course there were expectations. No alcohol was allowed on the premises, and no men. It was only after some discussion in 1952 that students could invite male friends to tea in their rooms from two to five on Saturday and Sunday afternoons. 'The Principal was asked to point out to the students that there was no question of not trusting them but that difficulties were seen as regards those students who would not be entertaining,' noted the council minutes.[38]

As principal, Betty was in loco parentis. The girls in her charge were sometimes as young as fifteen, and frequently a long way from home. If she was uncertain of a girl's whereabouts, rape, murder or, in those pre-pill days, pregnancy, must have entered her imagination in the darkness of the night. For dating there were procedures in place. The girls had to ask for permission to go out till 10 p.m., midnight twice a term and 2 a.m. once a term. It was all very formal, they had to put a note in a box saying, 'Dear Madame, I beg your permission to be absent from college'. They then had to go in and ask Betty for her permission. 'I remember I was going out with Hookey Street when I first got there,' said Liz Palmer, 'and Betty said to me, "He looks like your brother" and then put her head back and went "Hahaha"—I didn't know whether I was meant to go out with him if he looked like my brother … She used to throw her head back and that booming peal of laughter came out, and then you were allowed to apply.'[39]

The students came in at night through a little room called the mouse trap. If they were late, they then had to ring a bell to be let in, and the next morning they had to see the Ad. Despite the discipline, however, the students found that Betty exercised wisdom with just the right degree of firmness or eye-shutting. Many of them, sneaking home late after a 2 a.m. pass, furtively placing the key on the leave book, would be gently queried the next morning, 'Not too tired?' Betty's care and interest extended far beyond the students' academic difficulties or their comfort and physical security. From a sensitive and non-intrusive distance she seemed to know everything—when relationships were hurting and why—and somehow gave each of the students a feeling of strength and dignity.[40]

The students certainly felt they could confide in Betty and be understood, and she gave sensible advice, but not too much of it. Although she never discussed sex or more emotional feelings, the girls found her fair, patient, and unbelievably tolerant.

Very quickly a song evolved reflecting Betty's attitude that was sung throughout her time as principal:

I'm Happy Jack the Admiral,
As happy as can be,
And when the students come in late
I chucks them out to sea.[41]

Betty believed the girls' dress or their night life were not her main concern. She wanted them to take responsibility for their actions or lack of them, so she limited the rules so the students had to recognise their own standards to live by. Girls who had been troublesome at school because of an intolerance of authority figures now had no need to kick over the traces.

It was Betty's trust in the girls' behaviour that impressed them, that and the fact that she was not judgmental. One girl, enrolled in medicine, did absolutely nothing academically and Betty could see she was not going to get through the exams, which she didn't. She left Women's College after only one year, but instead of berating her Betty, typically, said, 'Well Margaret, you got more out of university life in one year than possibly other people in six'.[42]

For those who wished to learn, Betty increased the academic support by allocating freshers to resident tutors, who then advised them on their studies during the whole of their university course. There was a pooling of academic resources (especially for medical students) in shared tutorials with the men's colleges. To link the college more with the university, Betty invited half a dozen women of the university staff to become members of the college senior common room, sharing meals with the girls. In 1951 Betty arranged for extracurricular courses for the freshers on Australia's relations with its neighbours in the Pacific; on the treatment of Aborigines in northern Australia compared with the treatment of American Negroes; on inter-racial relationships (including Africa); on great thinkers from Australia; modern poetry; and modern developments in science. Willing university staff conducted the program.

There was room in Betty's acceptance and respect for a huge range of different personalities from different backgrounds. By the early 1950s there was a rich multicultural community within the college, including refugees from Nazism, the first American Fulbright scholars and many Colombo Plan students from South-East Asia. Inconspicuously, she drew these young women together with those of diverse socioeconomic backgrounds, city and rural, the cool sophisticate and the socially withdrawn. It seems Betty had an ability to spot the gold in a girl and to provide an opportunity for personality development. It was not a rare event for a fresher to arrive a shy, gauche, unconfident girl and to emerge three years later a quietly confident and perceptive woman.

Betty used to conduct an informal service before breakfast, including a Bible reading, a hymn and a prayer. Regardless of whether the girls belonged to any religious denomination, and in the presence of the overseas scholars, it was an ecumenical celebration before such an approach became popularised. It transcended religious boundaries and gathered the student body together in a sense of peace.

The students saw Betty as a person with massive integrity. The only things it seemed that she had no time for were cruelty, prejudice and self-destructive behaviour. If she felt students were not tapping their capacity or using their experience properly, she would gently attempt to guide them towards developing a better sense of their self and their worth. She was also enormously discreet.

Obviously Betty had a keen interest in sport and other leisure activities and she encouraged the students in their basketball, hockey and tennis. The college athletics were conducted on the front lawn, often with Betty, larger than life, in a very bright dress, sprawled in a chair. She approved of those who rowed, seeing them in a similar elevated light to cricketers. One Christmas, Heather Morgan, senior student, reported that in 1951 'we set out with lanterns and music to sing carols to the other colleges … and we returned exhausted at 11.30 pm with two lovely bunches of flowers, four suppers inside us and a telescope which Santa Claus sent for Miss Archdale.'[43] That Santa Claus was possibly Felix Arnott.

'The relationship between Betty and Felix was very warm and splendid,' said Marie Bashir. 'And of course as the students began to marry, more often than not Felix would officiate at the weddings, including mine, and of course on all our guest lists Miss Archdale would be an honoured guest … I've got a photo of Betty looking wonderful with Felix and Anne at Val Slack's [wedding] at the Hotel Australia. She looks young and pretty, she's wearing an evening dress with little straps and a little pendent necklace. People probably thought Betty had a negative view of clothing, but there was something nevertheless about her, that had a style and elegance that carried on from Edwardian England … It was not excessive or ostentatious, in fact it was sparse, but it just had a beauty of its own … She'd put on an old evening frock and the gown over it to come to dinner. Really there was something that always uplifted your spirits in seeing this and I really believe that we identified with that quality which emanated from her. And there was never even a soupçon, never one indication of snobbery.'[44]

Through her public speaking at various organisations in the city, Betty managed to put Women's College on the map. Her students felt enormously proud of their principal at a time when adolescents can be very critical of their peers and their elders. Her public speaking also brought to light another impact of Betty Archdale on the girls at college. The generation of the girls' mothers had been dominated by the idea that the main way a woman could act in the world was through a man. But Betty knew that she could just act for herself.

Unlike her mother, Betty wasn't strident about feminist issues, she was a balanced and stable person who was very well disposed towards men. Yet it was evident that she was so complete in her own right, enjoying her love of music, theatre, her engagement with the broader community in sport as President of the Sydney University Sports Association and the Women's Cricket Club, and in international affairs.

'Many of us who were privileged to be at college with her have turned into strong women when we may have tried not to be,' said Marie Bashir, 'when we would have perhaps, consciously or unconsciously wanted to follow the compliant model that better fitted that Australian male-oriented society. I can't think of one of my contemporaries who somehow have not received that, what is it … an anointment of going forth to do the best you can and don't cease.'[45]

But it seems Betty did have failings. In difficult circumstances she tended to put too much responsibility on the senior students. Such a situation arose when it became evident that one of them was a kleptomaniac, taking other people's clothing and watches. The senior students were expected to go through everyone's rooms, a demeaning task, to determine what was happening. It was only after some time that Betty finally acted.

The other failing was that, while not being neglectful, because of her Christian Scientist perspectives Betty rarely responded rapidly if somebody was sick, believing that they would soon mend of their own accord. The senior medical students who tended to minor complaints sometimes had to stress to Betty that a particular person was really sick.[46]

However, the greatest problem during Betty's stay at Women's College was her interaction with the Women's College council. Efforts were made on both sides. The council installed a kitchenette in the principal's quarters after Betty returned from England. This allowed her new privacy. Her salary was raised to £1000 in 1952. But while Betty's relationship with the girls couldn't have been better, there must have been considerable tensions between her and the council. And when Betty asked if she could have leave of absence to return to England for a rest in 1954–55 she said that she may not return. If the council did not like the uncertainty she said she would be happy to resign.[47] Some of the students were aware that the leave was because Betty was finding her role stressful and that all was not well.[48] In response the council agreed that she could take leave for up to a year and still receive nine months' salary.

The gulf between the principal and the council could have been due to the perception that while Betty had built up a fine spirit in the college, she wasn't maintaining the bricks and mortar as she should. In her early days, material changes to the college were minimal. It was soon after the war, there was little money available, and her priority was on consolidating education. Even so, in 1952 the Mary Fairfax Memorial Library consisting of four rooms was opened in the long vacation, new stairs were installed, and new bathrooms and carpets.

While Betty was overseas the acting principal, Miss Marsie Godfrey, seems to have been influential in undermining Betty's standing with the council and the students by drawing attention to the lack of systems in place for repairs, maintenance and housekeeping. At the end of 1954 the council minutes record that Miss Godfrey, while acting principal, attended to kitchen equipment, uniform laundering, gardening, eliminating damp from the laundry and cooks' quarters and other duties.[49] She suggested that the council consider re-establishing the house committee to deal with household duties, and that the finance committee set aside a sum for maintenance each year.[50]

In contrast, Betty, who had grown up in the Depression, was not overly interested in changes to buildings and structures. She didn't want curtains in her room and it seems there were lots of maintenance needs that she never noticed. Looking back on her eightieth birthday, Betty said that when she recently saw Women's College, which was spruced up and modernised: 'I began to realise what an incredible effect the Second World War had on one's attitudes to things like that. After quite a long spell of not doing anything, only absolutely necessary repairs, you didn't get anything new, you didn't embark on new bathrooms or new this or new that or anything. Arriving here at the end of the war in the WRNS and going to Women's College [it was instilled in me] not to spend any money on bringing things up to date. We had a bath at Women's College that used to rock on three legs and I thought that's all right you can have a bath in it, what are they fussing about? I was so imbued with the idea this didn't matter, the important thing was to educate people.'[51]

Betty looked instead to the life force of the college and creating a positive environment. This she achieved, many students testifying to the joy of being in college during her leadership. If there was disparity between Betty and the council, the students were on the principal's side. When she went on sabbatical Marie Bashir, senior student and a friend, offered to keep an eye on Betty's house in Galston. Although they didn't have cars of their own to make the hour long trip they co-opted male friends, whom they later married, to drive them there to look around and make sure everything was secure. Betty was very moved by their interest and concern. 'So I suppose there was this sort of reciprocity about sensitivity,' explained Marie. 'She inspired good feelings and good behaviour in you.'[52]

It is not surprising, then, that Betty's return from leave in July 1955 was embraced by the students. They felt she brought back a spirit and stimulus to college, and that through her personal interest in them she was a comforting presence. The students celebrated her return by ceremoniously piping her in with a bosun's whistle to the gaily decorated dining hall for a welcome-home dinner.[53] After dinner Betty spoke of conditions in Britain. This was not accidental. It seems that her trip was to determine whether she should return to live permanently in England. She weighed the benefits of each culture.

Betty saw the English, with their long and successful history, as more tolerant and understanding than Australians, who were still immature and consequently intolerant of views other than their own. They were too sure they were right and tended to be aggressive and one-sided. This immaturity showed in an inferiority complex which made Australians far too worried about what other people thought of them.

One of the unexpected results of England's maturity was its adaptability and readiness to innovate and experiment, particularly in the fields of industrial relations and the social services. Australians, however, tended to be unjustifiably self-satisfied about their schools and universities. Yet Betty concluded that the basic belief in equality in Australia was not only pleasant but healthy. It led to a friendliness and openness between people which was a great improvement on the 'we and they' attitude. Equality being a concept that had been fed to her since a child, Betty plumped for Australia.[54]

Returning to the council of Women's College was a different matter. The former acting principal, Julie Fitzhardinge, was still its secretary and Betty felt that the Fitzhardinge family was unduly influential on its development. What irked Betty most was her perception that, although she was the principal, the council backed Julie more for fear of hurting Julie's feelings.[55] This was not an unusual scenario for Betty. It is apparent throughout her life that because people saw her as a strong and self-sufficient woman they assumed she could take criticism and harder decisions more than those whom they believed need protecting. Betty's vulnerability lived at a subliminal level.

Decades later Dr Meg Mulvey said that if the council had known of Betty's feelings they would have been discussed. 'I think we made a mistake there. But I think that also, out of loyalty to Julie, we couldn't do much about it.' As for asking Julie to resign, 'I think it would have been impossible,' said Dr Mulvey's sister Helen Buchanan, 'it was her life.'[56] In fact Julie Fitzhardinge resigned at the beginning of 1957, after Betty announced her intention to resign. Not that the Fitzhardinge factor would have been Betty's sole source of dissatisfaction. Her inability to house her mother at the college could well have been projected back onto the council. However, there seems to have been a need on the council's part to contain Betty, to be officious, such as the time they objected to Alec Archdale's luggage being placed in the front hall.

Meg Mulvey says she has never been able to work out the misunderstandings because the council was anxious to help Betty run the college. 'I think Betty had the personality that she rather resented anybody in charge of her … and consequently her relationships with council were not as happy as they might have been. For instance Barbara Munro [appointed in 1949] was her great friend but she never spoke to Barbara once about any matter of the council. Barbara was on the council and it would have made it much easier. Well Barbara had said to her, "Betty what is wrong, what can we do to make you feel better?" and so forth. But Betty would never speak to her at all. And yet they saw one another socially, they went out a lot together.'[57]

In 1956 the college had a financial loss. It was Betty's second last year, but the council didn't blame her for it. The college had tried to keep the student fees as low as possible, and it was a miscalculation. Even when she resigned, Meg Mulvey said there was never a feeling of council wanting Betty to go. But members of council didn't quite know what was going on in her mind.

The mood seems to have been rather fraught. Peg Telfer, who was chairman of the council, decided she had to resign because she couldn't get on with Betty. Then Fanny Cohen, who was headmistress at Fort Street High and a member of the university senate, took the chair. She used to see things in black and white, and became so worked up that she had to take phenobarbitol before each meeting. Mulvey then became chairman and felt helplessness and an unnecessary strain in the awareness of Betty's antagonism without knowing what was at the root of it.[58]

In later life Betty, in discussing the council, acknowledged that she didn't get on well with the people she should have got on with, that she was a bit dictatorial and wanted to do things her way. 'I thought if I was head of the place, I jolly well should run it and I resented interference of council because I think I was used to places, schools and colleges, where the head really ran it and the council said yes or no as the case may be. It was partly inexperience on my side and partly inexperience on theirs.'[59]

In November 1956, despite not having a job lined up, Betty informed the council of her intention to resign at the end of the following year.[60] Years later she cited Julie Fitzhardinge, with whom she had diametrically different views on practically everything, as the main cause, 'I said I'd had enough and either she went or I did, and it was I who went'.[61] The council accepted her resignation with deep regret, noting that she had fulfilled all the expectations and more of the selection committee. The students' response was more emotional. 'It was with great sorrow that we learned of Miss Archdale's intended retirement,' wrote Janet McCredie, senior student. 'It is felt that College will be losing its most vital part. The influence on each student individually, and on the College as a whole is too profound ever to be evaluated. Those of us who have been in College in her time will always be sincerely grateful for having known and loved this truly outstanding woman.'[62]

The press was quick to comment on her retirement, one paper saying that Miss Archdale had one of the keenest academic minds in Australia. The reason for such public attention is that during her time at Women's College Betty had entered the public arena—through her public speaking and also through a popular radio program on ABC Radio, *Any*

Questions. It consisted of a chairman and a panel of intellectuals who were asked questions by the community at large. The panel members responded either entertainingly or sincerely, however they were moved. They were paid £3 per show and had a free dinner provided, very reluctantly, by the ABC.

Although there were four or five women invited to participate, they rarely appeared together, the mix was usually three men and a woman. The men included Felix Arnott and other academics such as Professors Alex Stout and Peter Elkin, Edgar Holt and Zelman Cowen. The balance suited Betty perfectly, as she often found herself talking more easily with men, both on committees and socially. All the participants enjoyed the experience and the mood of the program was always relaxed, the chairman Frank Legge handling the panellists very well. He made them feel that what they said mattered, and that he liked having them there, which was crucial when none of them had had any previous radio or (later) television experience.

The program was sheer pleasure to Betty. She enjoyed the stimulus of being put on the spot, she liked the attention and, despite being inherently shy, she enjoyed saying what she thought, including expressing views on the status of women which weren't necessarily popular at the time. In the late 1950s there was change afoot, it was a time of hope rather than achievement. On one show, when asked her definition of what it meant to be educated, Betty replied, 'When you know you're not and that you never will be'.

The public response to the program surprised Betty. A number of people wrote, but more spoke to her the next time they met. Her laughter became instantly identifiable. Colin Munro remembers going with his parents to the theatre in Sydney to see Victor Borge, the comedian and pianist. 'Within ten minutes of him being on stage, suddenly this joyous roar rang through the theatre and I said to Dad, "My God, Betty's here".'[63]

Betty was also involved in other cerebral pursuits and had a strong rapport with many of the intellectual people round Sydney.   Because of her war service and her involvement with the Australian Institute of International Affairs she was seen as a person with an understanding of world play. She had become especially interested in the settlement of Antarctica. It was the period when many countries were setting up stations there and Betty, who was concerned with the political possibilities, published a paper with the London Institute of World Affairs on 'Claims to the Antarctic'. It's an impressively researched case against government of the continent by the United Nations, arguing that a practical form of international cooperation between the countries working in the Antarctic was already in existence.[64]

Betty's forthright commonsense won her new speaking opportunities. In May 1956, on the centenary of responsible government organised by the NSW Call Committee, she urged each person to take responsibility not only in their political but also in their economic lives.

At a time when ABC radio programs featured programs on *Homemaking, Bless the Bride, Cookery Book*, other women's sessions and the never-ending serial *Blue Hills*, Betty delivered a lecture, 'Too Much Woman'. There was, she said, no such thing as a 'modern' woman. Women were much the same today as they had always been, and though they might think they were doing very nicely under so-called 'modern conditions', they were not. There was far too much emphasis on the word 'woman', and a tendency to forget that men and women were all human beings, with mere God-given sex variations.

Physical differences do not have any effect on mental capacity and people all start from scratch with equal brain power. Betty believed it was the social conditioning process to which women were subjected from the outset of their lives that put them where they eventually found themselves—despite their so-called emancipation—always in the place just slightly behind men. She said social pressures conditioned girls to behave in set ways and very few girls had the courage to stand up against them and do what they would like to do.

Betty held that there was too much rationalisation about women, with people frequently saying 'she has a very good position—for a woman'. Statisticians were too prone to claim that the fact that women were employed in large numbers doing monotonous routine jobs which require patience but not much brain proved that they were best suited to this type of work. In reality, most women took such jobs because they were readily available, or part-time, in order to help the family income.

She made the point that girls schools found it difficult to get the best maths teachers because of the assumption that girls 'have not heads for figures' and that teachers told girls not to worry about high school but to take the easier 'more suitable' courses in domestic science schools. Because of their alleged mental limitations, it was easy to discourage the mass of girls from taking higher education. But, she contended, since Australia was as much a part of the scientific age through which the world was passing as any other country, it needed every scientific brain which could be extracted from its small population—be they male or female. The discouragement of the training of girls was a waste of talent which Australia could not afford.[65]

This wake-up call for education of girls must have had some impact because two months later, when Abbotsleigh girls school at Wahroonga was in a crisis following the resignation of its headmistress after only two and a half years, attention was given to Betty as a possible replacement. Apart from problems of leadership, there was also concern about the school's financial position. The council needed a strong personality to set the school on its rightful path of inspired teaching for the daughters of the north shore middle classes.

It seems the council was divided over two applicants, so Betty was invited before a special council meeting in October 1957. Amongst those congregated was Betty's friend Margaret Peden, who had persuaded her to consider the position. There was also the unusual presence of Archbishop Howard Mowll. Betty had to wait in an office while the council conferred. Mowll, concerned with the state of affairs, refused to cast a determining vote. Instead he invited Betty Archdale to the position.[66]

'I didn't apply, they offered it to me ... I think I was very lucky. I had no Dip. Ed. and no teaching or school experience,' said Betty.[67] Nor was she, even more crucially, a member of the Church of England. So after the meeting, Mowll rang Felix Arnott at St Paul's College. Felix had been informally instructing Betty in theology for some months. Now, the archbishop asked Arnott if he'd confirm Betty Archdale as soon as possible. 'I've often had a good laugh about it,' said Betty, 'so I was confirmed rather quickly after that. I don't know whether it was tomorrow or the next day, but it was soon after, so that I was then properly eligible to be head of Abbotsleigh.'[68] The text was II Thessalonians 3:3: 'But the hand is faithful who shall stablish you and keep you from evil.'

When she came to Women's College eleven years earlier Betty had described herself as a Christian Scientist, but she had been so disillusioned by that faith's rejection of her mother's application to one of their hospices that she wanted no more part in it.

After Helen Archdale's death Betty said she went around feeling that she'd like to join something. Moore Theological College, on the Women's College boundaries, trained the vast majority of Anglican priests for the Sydney diocese. But its inflexible attitude to the place of women not only in the church but in society at large was poles apart from Betty's thinking. It was Felix Arnott, a biblical and classical scholar, who drew her to the Anglican Church. Betty was impressed by his very real faith and saw him as a good Christian and an intelligent one. He didn't expect her to accept doctrines uncritically, he didn't take the Bible too literally, he was honest.

Betty had more or less accepted the position of principal of Mary White College at the University of New England when the Abbotsleigh job came along. But she knew there was a strong element in Armidale that preferred someone else. 'I can remember thinking I don't want to go somewhere where I'm not really wanted,' said Betty. 'Whereas I felt Abbotsleigh did want me, because that goes back to the cricket and the Pedens—I thought, well, there are all my friends. I think I made the right decision.'[69]

13

ALEC AND GALSTON

Betty's caring qualities were not only expressed in concern for her girls, but also for her brother Alec.

After Helen Archdale's death, Betty recognised that Alec was very badly shaken, so she suggested that he come to Australia for a holiday. Betty never thought of Alec settling down, imagining that he would regard Australia as a primitive country with little culture. However, and much to Betty's surprise, Alec was so impressed he stayed and found work as an actor.[1] 'I suppose he was glad to have somewhere to live—I think he was probably broke—I never inquired too much into his financial side,' said Betty.[2]

Alec came to Australia in late 1951, at a time when Betty was yearning for a home. It seemed she was always living in a place that belonged to someone else, and she had a great urge to build a nest of her own. She may also have wanted to establish herself and Alec as a family. Their mother had died and a few years later, their elder brother Nick.

After being headmaster at Ashbury College in Ottawa, Nick Archdale went to Mackay College, a run-down expatriate college in Valparaiso, Chile. From there he rang his wife Sheila and said there was no need for her to come down and bring the whole family, because he was only going to be there for six months. He was also in the midst of an affair. Sheila responded by telling him she was taking the children back to England. Nick continued to care deeply about Sheila despite their separation, said their son Audley, 'but some people say that he never grew up, that he was still and always remained a boy, which is sad and I think his father [Theodore, who also flirted with women] was similar'.[3]

Eventually Nick returned to Canada, where he introduced basic educational facilities in remote areas. 'People absolutely adored him,' said Audley. 'I think they liked his energy. He was brilliant when he started to put on plays. He could enthuse and stimulate people to do anything he wanted them to do.'[4] But in December 1955 he had a heart attack when laughing at a play rehearsal at a school in Chilliwack, British Columbia. Betty always envied the manner of his dying. What a wonderful way to go, she would say—to die laughing.

The two remaining siblings, Alec and Betty, reinvented the Archdale family. While they both worked in Sydney they were restless at the weekends. Sometimes they joined the Peden family at their old beach house at Collaroy, but they felt it would be nice to have a bolthole of their own. Their ideas were vague, but sometime in the early 1950s they settled on a five-acre block at Galston, about 22 miles north of Sydney. The land was on the southern slope of a hill and ran from just below the road on the crest down to another road some 300 yards below. It was bushland, not cleared, but had been logged fifteen years earlier. Water, power and telephone services were available, so they had access to some comforts.

For financial reasons they decided to build some sort of a house by their own efforts, having fun in the process. Chance played a part as an architect friend was engaged at that time in building a large pisé house in Queensland. It sounded interesting and when Betty and Alec read a book on the subject it seemed to them that here was a method they could use themselves without any great technical knowledge or craftsmanship. So they settled for pisé.[5] Hornsby Council was horrified at the thought but Barbara Munro, who designed the house, patted the inspector's arm and said, 'Let's look on it as a grand and glorious experiment.' The inspector proved difficult once again when Alec went to have the plans approved. 'How are you going to lift that beam?' he asked. 'With a bowline on a bight,' said Alec. 'Oh, navy are you?' said the inspector, himself an old salt, and the plans were passed immediately.[6]

The house design was very simple, a rectangular shape with two monk-like cells for bedrooms at one end, a living room with a fireplace, and at the other end a breakfast bar and kitchen, off which was built a bathroom cum laundry.

Betty and Alec immediately erected a garage of partly prefabricated timber on a concrete foundation, but it took four years before they finished the house and moved in. Often the two of them were so tired from their various involvements that they'd go to the site, pick up some utensils, and just sit down and look at them. The main difficulty they experienced was in digging for the foundations.

After the concrete footings were poured Betty went away for a year and a theatrical tour on Alec's part extended the delay to nearly two years before they began seriously to consider getting on with the building. Friends became involved, some of them even slept overnight in the garage. Helpers included Nancy Lord and her Englishwoman friend Cecil Western at the end of their year-long tour of Australia in 1956.[7] With Betty they had gone down to the harbour to meet a ship bearing Lady Margaret Rhondda on her maiden voyage to Australia, only to find that she had fallen and broken her hip on the South African leg of the journey. Much to Betty's sadness, Margaret died in England eighteen months later, in 1958. The focus of her life, *Time and Tide*, suffered a dwindling death.

After some time, Alec and Betty poured a concrete base for the floor of the house, then mixed the earth for the walls, which took three levels of rammed earth to complete. As the walls were 12 inches thick, they kept the house warm in winter and cool in summer. The roof beams were sapling gums from the cleared site and the window and door frames came from a demolished house. Betty went to a wreckers' yard at Newtown and found a bath—a great coup, she thought.

Inside, the walls were plastered with a combination of dust from the floor and cow dung, a mixture, Betty asserted, that was recommended by experts. 'Initially the place smelt terrible, but only for a day or two,' she recalled, 'the plaster never flaked, and in cupboards where it has been left unpainted the finish is an interesting neutral brown.'[8]

Throughout the extended building process, Alec and Betty amused themselves thinking of a name for the house. 'Various Australian aboriginal names were sounded out and discarded,' Alec wrote. 'We never even considered Mon Repos or the like and eventually settled for NORTHIS. It was a puzzle name and we never explained its derivation and none of our friends ever made a successful guess. Very simple really—as we toiled along … we realised the truth of the statement that Rome wasn't built in a day, nor this we said, NORTHIS. And very nice too.'[9]

Betty found that building a house oneself gives an enormous feeling of achievement and a sense of belonging within it. And it was at Northis that she felt truly at peace—at one with herself.

While Betty was building a reputation as an educationalist, Alec was polishing his image as an actor. When he first arrived in Sydney, J. C. Williamson's had a monopoly in the commercial theatre and work at the Independent was amateur and unpaid. Radio was the bread and butter of all Sydney actors. It was not well paid but there was a lot of it and it was done very quickly.

Alec was in a short tour of *Black Chiffon* under the direction of Doris Fitton of the Independent. Then John Sydney Kay started a theatre in Phillip Street in the manner of the European repertoire system. The Mercury Theatre also opened to a good press and was welcomed on the Sydney scene. Alec played in *Point of Departure* by Anouilh at the Mercury, and directed and played in Strindberg's *The Father*, with Ruth Cracknell as his daughter Laura. But money was almost negligible and although the cast was as professional as Sydney could supply and turned in some fine performances, eventually standards fell. The principals could not afford to turn down any paid employment and the venture closed.

While the early days of the Mercury Theatre established Alec on the Sydney scene, a decline began in 1956 with the arrival of television. Radio stations cut back on local productions and Alec decided to go to RADA in London as a tutor. Before he left he and Margot Lee played in the first live television play seen in Australia. It was *The Twelve Look* by J. M. Barrie. 'Those who saw it were full of praise,' wrote Alec.

Alec later wrote: 'Looking back at those few years in Australia I am compelled to say that whatever the state of the theatre and its standards, the fault, unconsciously I will maintain, could have been mine that my work ground slowly to a halt. I took a senior executive of the ABC to lunch one day and asked him directly why I was not getting any work. His first direct answer was that I sat about in studios always looking as if I knew I could do it better than those performing could. Then he followed that up by telling me that he had heard that I thought him and another man to be the worst directors I had ever encountered. This was completely untrue. That I have certain impatience with fools and incompetence is true but that I could make such gratuitously rude statements as claimed is not true.'[10]

The ABC executive was not the only person to find Alec difficult. Ruth Cracknell noted that while Alec was particularly kind to her, he was difficult with others. 'He seemed to be a disappointed man who didn't realise his full potential, he had a chip on his shoulder. He couldn't compromise, he couldn't bend too much if he thought he was right, and he wasn't always. He found it difficult to settle into an Australian environment. He felt he could teach us a great deal more than we knew.'[11]

In an interview with the *Sydney Morning Herald* in 1986, Leo McKern said Alec was one of the most monstrous people he ever worked with: 'He was a bastard on the stage. He had the Wolfit complex, but where Wolfit had the monstrous talent to match his monstrousness, Archdale certainly did not.'[12] Whatever McKern said about Alec, Lyn Marchant-Williams says it would not have been half as bad as the things Alec said about McKern. Alec was jealous of him for winning the role of Rumpole in the television series that gave Leo such prominence.

At the time Betty was distressed by McKern's comments. She wrote a letter (not for publication) to the editor of the *Herald*, saying that: 'To say I was hurt by Leo McKern's remarks about my brother is putting it mildly. If Alec had been alive, criticism, however crude, would be legitimate. But within a matter of weeks of his death, when I and others are still mourning, I can only describe it as heartless and cowardly. Luckily one son lives in England and the other in California so neither will see the article.'[13]

Betty had an easy understanding with Alec and it was a matter of course to her to be living with him in absolute loyalty, to be his certain base when all else was troubled. It seems she supported him financially, which Alec hated, but she was not critical of him. 'I wouldn't say Alec was bad because he wasn't,' she explained. 'He was good and I think he'd be always very fair. But I would say he had no money sense, it didn't mean a thing [to him], if he had money he spent it—the idea he might need a bit next year …' she laughed.[14]

In fact Betty was fascinated that Alec was not a scrap materialistic, and she pointed out how important he was to her in the building of Northis. For although Betty had bought the land at Galston (for £600) and provided funds for the building, it was Alec who knew how to erect the dwelling, who made detailed drawings, who directed the hammerings and pourings, and who knew what a bowline and bight were. Betty was his admiring handmaid in the project.

Apart from tutoring, when he was in England Alec tried to write plays. But no worthwhile acting roles opened up to him apart from a television series called *Deadline Midnight*. In the late 1950s after four years away he was asked to return to Australia by the Australian Elizabethan Trust to direct Gordon Chater in *Charley's Aunt* and then star in *The Miser* and another play. He found the theatre scene had changed, the Australian Elizabethan Theatre Trust being largely the cause of an alteration in the attitude of the public and consequently of the profession. He played Falstaff in *The Merry Wives of Windsor* in 1961. Once again in Sydney, he was greeted as an important actor. But on a return trip to England he had a heart attack.

Reflecting during his recovery, Alec recognised that the theatre was his love, his business and, despite the odd setback, it had given him a good life. So he decided it was now his turn to give something back besides one or two good performances. 'I awoke the next morning with Australia large on my mind—recognising that a day of progress in the theatre was about to dawn,' Alec later wrote. 'Surely I could help in some way however small.'[15]

Alec dreamt of establishing a repertory theatre in Sydney—a provincial suburban repertory akin to those which were the great training ground of English actors. He decided it should be sited on Sydney's north shore, which was a fashionable residential area for both academics and businessmen. 'I must admit it was also an area where my sister's name was in high repute,' Alec wrote: 'I had a good name as leading actor over most of Australia and I would have to concentrate on building that name more widely getting this new theatre off the ground. I knew this would be expensive as I would have to turn down the little jobs, the bread and butter of the Australian theatre scene, and wait for the leading parts. I could live cheaply enough in the house we had built.'[16]

Alec wrote immediately to his friends in the theatre inquiring about the possibility of parts on his return to Sydney in 1962. To his delight he was offered the role of Warwick in *Saint Joan* with Zoe Caldwell as Joan. Alec didn't tell Betty of his plans until he'd returned to Australia. She seemed shocked, but weathered it well, suggesting that they hold a party of friends to get their views.

There is no doubt that Alec was a first-rate actor, a perfectionist. He drew his strength from his belief in classic theatre. But his propensity to aggravate is reflected in comments he made about the *St Joan* production. 'I found Zoe with great talent but rebellious to what I represented. It took her ten weeks of playing before she would accept me. When she did ask for help I was only too glad she did, but I had to make the whole thing official through the executive director of the Trust.'[17]

In establishing a repertory theatre Alec relied heavily on his sister's name, and on friends and contacts, many of whom contributed £200. Without Betty's status the project might never have developed. 'During the early planning days I was unsure whether my sister Betty took the scheme very seriously,' wrote Alec. 'With some of her friends we used to have a lot of fun going through the names of people they knew, listing them in three categories—would be interested, could be interested, would not be interested.'[18]

On train trips to town Alec saw a large hall known as the Soldiers Memorial Hall at Killara. It stood only 100 yards from the railway on the far side of a small park. Eventually the Community Theatre Company limited was registered and incorporated in March 1965. Meanwhile, Alec played in productions at the Independent and on ABC TV, directed a play at Williamson's and acted in a new play by Patrick White, *Night on Bald Mountain*, at the Adelaide Festival of 1964. One effect of this work had been to earn the attention if not the respect of journalists connected with the theatre. So when he arranged a press party in April in 1965 to celebrate the launching of the Community Theatre, they turned up in good numbers and in a friendly spirit. Alec also appeared that night on the popular program on ABC TV, *People*, and received phone calls to the studio from complete strangers offering help.

The five people who had consented to act as founding directors included Betty, Justice John Kerr, Patrick White, Ruth Cracknell and a solicitor, David Griffin, who became Sydney's Lord Mayor. In six short months 500 people had paid five to ten dollars each towards an idea and about 250 had turned up at a meeting to say they wanted to go ahead.[19] The actors involved staged *Krapp's Last Tape* by Samuel Beckett and *A Phoenix Too Frequent* by Colin Free at a nearby hall in Lindfield to raise funds.

But there was some resistance to the use of the hall at Killara, where deep conservatism prevailed. At a Ku-ring-gai Council in committee meeting, the theatre's chief opponent observed how grossly unfair it was that a gallant organisation like the dancing class, which for over 30 years had helped form fine Australian citizens of the future, should be turned out of its home to make way for a vested interest such as this community theatre.[20] It was hardly a valid objection, but the battle with council endured for a year.

As the hall was converted into a theatre, Alec lived in the caretaker's flat at the back and remained there for three years. After a period of frenetic activity, wiring, painting, insulating, and establishing the 320 seats, the Community Theatre opened on 28 March 1968. 'The curtain was due to rise at eight-fifteen,' said Alec, and I was hanging the last of these curtains about seven o'clock—when Bill called me to stop working and get below and eat and dress. I obeyed my stage director'.'[21]

The theatre opened with a large overdraft but otherwise not too heavily in debt. It had a state grant of $8000 and membership was growing. About the middle of the year it was informed by the Australian Elizabethan Theatre Trust that they had been instructed by the newly formed Council for the Arts that all assistance must be channelled through that council.

In successive years the Council for the Arts allocated less and less to the Community Theatre. At the beginning of 1970, after a reasonably successful year, Alec was dismayed to find that he had received an even smaller grant and he asked for an interview with Dr Coombs, the chairman of the Council for the Arts. Alec was told that the council had decided that the standards of production and programming of plays were better at the Old Tote and the Independent theatres. 'I withdrew with the certain knowledge that as long as I was running the Community Theatre we would get the same killing treatment,' Alec convinced himself. 'As long as the standard I set endured we were dangerous to the establishment.'[22]

When the Community Theatre opened for its 1970 season, Alec was no longer its director. 'Really he was a very naughty man in many ways,' said Lyn Marchant-Williams, 'he was his own worst enemy … it was his tantrums and his arrogant attitude to the Arts Council that lost them all their funds. That's why they threw him out. And she [Betty] thought they were dreadful; she withdrew her life membership and Lord knows what.'[23]

In a letter of application to an English theatrical agent in 1977, Alec wrote, fuelled by self-pity: 'Came back here '62 to start a professional Rep. where there was none. It worked well but antagonised the establishment. After nine years of working on it and directing it I left end of '70. What I might well call my own Theatre—still in healthy existence—has never offered me any kind of work whatever.'[24] Ruth Cracknell said that Betty had all the strength that in some way, for all his talents, Alec lacked. 'The element of self-pity is not within her for a second—I don't think she comprehends it.'[25]

'Alec was good [as an actor], there is no doubt about that,' said Lyn Marchant-Williams, 'and certainly the vision he had of the theatre was excellent. But he was nothing like as good as Betty thought he was. Betty would not hear a word of criticism about him. And she put up with all his girlfriends and everything else.'[26]

Alec's sex life, Betty would laugh ruefully, was at the other end of the spectrum to hers. She had no lovers, Alec had many. There were a lot of girlfriends, including an Abbotsleigh girl who was about 30 years his junior. But there was one particularly awkward incident. At Galston, Alec began an affair with the daughter-in-law of one of their neighbours and closest friends. The woman left her husband and rented a flat in Kirribilli. Alec packed up his belongings and left to live with her, but he was back with Betty at Galston the next day, just sitting, disconsolate. The woman had put all his goods on the pavement. 'Poor Alec,' Betty said. 'I just tried to be sympathetic. What can you do?'[27] But despite their indisputable closeness, Betty said she thought it better not to ask Alec about the humiliating incident.

Betty was very conscious that neither of her brothers was good to his wife. Despite her mother's example, both Nick and Alec placed men very definitely first. Yet despite this Betty enjoyed a strong relationship with Alec and they developed a life for themselves in relative isolation—initially in the village there was only a post office and one shop. They asked a neighbour, John Orr, to plant apple trees, pears, peaches, apricots and three varieties of plum trees. Alec built a shelter for his orchid collection. They installed a circular above-ground pool into which Betty, in her woollen costume with its cotton belt and buckle, climbed. And as an indicator that she was in residence, she hung her pedestrian underclothes on a string line wound round gum trees.

But most powerfully of all, they entertained interesting groups of people from the theatre and the arts and education—old friends, ex-students, cricketers, Wrens. It was at Northis, for instance, that Ruth Cracknell first met Patrick White, who lived down the road. Sir John and Peg Kerr would be there, Doris Fitton, Felix and Anne Arnott, actors Ron Hadrick, Ann Haddy and Peter Adams. Betty's way of entertaining was to push her books to the side of a table to make way for dishes of food. Then she'd go to the garage and bring in beautiful Wedgwood plates for her guests to eat from. She had quality possessions and knew how to use them, but that was all unimportant.

As an example of her unreal approach, Joyce Cole recalled: 'You know that little kitchen? It was nothing to her to bring you a one pint saucepan and I suppose half a packet of coffee and say, "Would you make the coffee for everyone?" Everyone being thirty or forty people. That was so typically Betty.'[28]

The mood was almost bohemian with informality of dress, Alec sometimes in a sarong. Both he and Betty had an enormous sense of fun, finding many things amusing and chortling over them. It was as if the guests were refreshed by the rustic spirit of the place, as if anything was possible. Everyone, so distantly placed from their defined worlds, relaxed and the exchange of ideas was strenuous and stimulating.

And it was that love of ideas and of exercising one's intelligence that Betty and Alec shared with relish. 'He had a much better brain than I had,' Betty claimed, 'he was very good that way—he was very well read.' They used to exchange books with friends, and built up their library which lined the walls at Northis and was recorded numerically in a long black book. Betty's taste in reading was non-fiction and religious books, and the lightest of fiction—just as in the theatre she was always delighted by farces. Alec's taste was much more literary.

'I liked having him around,' said Betty of Alec. 'He had lots of friends and he liked socialising. I was always quite happy and had plenty of friends, but at a different level from Alec.' Although Alec was friendly with Betty's personal friends, he found her professional friends pretty dull and he'd get bored with them, and show it.

Alec was also competitive, and was rather surprised by the attention and respect Betty received. In an article in the English *Sunday Times* in 1985 Pat Garrow said: 'Alex was very proud of his sporting skills. He played in goal in football, was a scratch golfer and a cricketer who could have been of county standard. I met him in retirement and one day in our club, the Savage, he was quite miffed when I discovered I was talking to the brother of Betty Archdale, the pioneer of women's cricket. Alex didn't rate her at all as a cricketer … Alex said "She used to play in the garden with my brother and me and she was no good." Did someone mention chauvinism?'[29]

Yet the siblings had an understanding which was convenient. Alec didn't question Betty too much about her emotions—he may not have even been interested—but this allowed her to have a certain space that was not understood by others who would have liked to have been closer to her. Nancy Lord noted that Betty was very aloof in her own way: 'She and Barbara [Munro] were bosom friends and Barbara was a very open sort of person and Betty's older brother [Nick] in Canada died and Barbara—I forget how she heard of it but it was some time after and she was really hurt that Betty hadn't told her because that's the sort of thing you tell your friends.'[30]

Although Alec had two sons overseas, and both he and Betty had nephews and nieces who could have added great richness to their lives, they seemed remarkably detached from them. It was as if they felt quite contented in their self-sufficient family of two. It was the shared joy with Alec of hosting and thinking and drinking before their innumerable open fires at Northis—this unspoken companionship—that was the emotional underbelly of Betty's life in the outside world.

14

ABBOTSLEIGH

Abbotsleigh has the reputation of being one of the most prominent private schools for girls in Australia. From its first headmistress, Miss Marian Clarke, who founded the school in North Sydney in 1885, the emphasis has been on academic achievement, high standards of cultural expression and sporting performance. After several moves it was established in Wahroonga which Betty was later to describe as—and she searched for the word—'a settled place—nothing exciting happens there'.[1] It was the first Australian girls school to have playing fields—no doubt contributing to the inclusion of former students Margaret and Barbara Peden in the first Australian women's cricket team in 1934.

In 1924 the school was sold to the church by its second headmistress, Miss Margaret Murray, becoming Abbotsleigh Church of England School for Girls. Echoing the ideals of conduct based on Christian teaching, the school's crest is a shield with two fish for Christianity, two fleurs-de-lys for purity, a lion for strength, and a motto which encourages drive: 'Tempus Celerius Radio Fugit' (Time flies faster than the weaver's shuttle). In the 1950s the school buildings bordering the Pacific Highway were mainly a mixture of old redbrick, heavily placed on a top corner of 21 acres of land which fell away to playing fields, courts, a pool and pockets of bush. A junior school was built in an avenue on the other side of the highway.

When Betty arrived in 1958 it was a prosperous school with a solid reputation. It housed boarders from country areas and catered for Sydney's north shore line. It was very appropriate for its environment which was growing in families of professional and business men who believed that church schools provided better character training than state schools, and who desired the best education available, one which would enable their daughters to participate in the highest strata of society.

The school population tended to be homogeneous, socially, economically and denominationally. In 1957 the council of Abbotsleigh allowed a girl whose parents were of 'mixed religions' to be accepted at the school, but members of the Jewish faith were to be refused admission.[2] Meredith Burgmann commented that she had left school before she met, to speak to, a Catholic or a Jew, let alone an Aborigine or a migrant.

The day girls were very much locally based and there was a great sense of people knowing each others' families. Even in the 1960s there were some people who felt it was social death not to live on the north shore line, and Meredith Burgmann recalls that, although she belonged to a respectable well-educated family, she just didn't feel fashionable enough. Many fine women emerged from the school who performed well in social and professional circles, coped well with adversity and had allegiance to each other.

Before Betty arrived, the main recent influence on the school had been the competent reign of Miss Gordon Everett for 24 years. She had an MA and a certain cachet for having studied French and linguistics at the Sorbonne. She was described as tall and spare, with golden hair, an athletic gait and a presence reinforced by her habit of carrying her deceased fiancé's army cane. She brought to the school administrative abilities, personal charm and a belief in the virtues of cultured womanhood. Miss Everett was regarded as a 'character' whose presence was felt throughout the school. And although she was not emotionally close, she saw that her 'gels' were encouraged to embrace their learning, their dress and behaviour with discipline.

Awarded an MBE for her services to education in 1960, well after her retirement, Miss Everett was an independent spirit dying, with style, on the Trans-Siberian Railway. Her successor, Miss E. Ruth Hirst, was a frightened person who resorted to strict discipline and her ineffectual two years at the school left it paralysed, gasping for direction.

When Betty arrived at Abbotsleigh it was as if the pupils were paddling in a distilled pond with hardly a ripple from the outside world. The students echoed their mothers particularly. Betty was conscious that the women 'up our end of the line' were still very conservative, more materialistic and less intellectual than the women she had previously mixed with. Some were clever and read a great deal, but a sense of being in touch? Almost blank, she surmised. Asked if Abbotsleigh, in its more parochial setting, was something of a backwater, Betty said, 'Abbotsleigh wasn't a backwater, but run by a church which hadn't got a clue. The girls themselves and staff were absolutely fine.'[4]

While she was thinking of applying for the job of headmistress of Abbotsleigh, Betty telephoned her long-term friend, the artist Janna Bruce, who was working there as an art teacher. She wondered what the job would be like, and did Janna think it would be worthwhile. 'I said well I don't think it is as it stands,' related Janna, 'but I think you could make it worthwhile if you try because they've had a very boring headmistress there before.'[5]

Betty came to the school with a salary package of £1850, plus an allowance of £150, accommodation and meals.[6] All her life she had vowed she would not teach because she belonged to the generation in which teaching was virtually the only thing a woman could do. 'So I landed up (it was all wrong really) being head of a school without ever having worked in schools. I was biased, but I thought it was a good thing. I felt I had much broader views, more experience of what went on in the great wide world, I wasn't so hidebound and rigid. On the other hand there was a heck of a lot I didn't know—basic stuff like syllabuses—oh no I knew nothing about that at all!'

Some months after she started Betty was making a tour of the school grounds with the newly installed Archbishop of Sydney, Dr Hugh Gough. 'And what educational training do you have for this position?' queried the archbishop. Betty threw her head back, roared with laughter and said, 'None!'[7] While she may not have had a Diploma of Education or experience of teaching in the classroom, Betty had brought with her qualifications in law and economics, leadership of groups of women in cricket, the WRNS and at a university college, a love of sport and an independence of thinking hewn by her upbringing amongst ardent feminists.

Betty also had within her another qualification which may not have been obvious to others. She had a nostalgic love of her old school in Scotland. When there was so much change in her childhood, St Leonard's had been a safe place. It was at school that she had received attention and shone for the first time in her life, away from her mother's strong presence and preoccupations. What is more, St Leonard's had challenged its students to believe they were quite as able as males in every respect. Betty wanted to give to the girls now in her keeping that same nourishment and belief in themselves. So from the beginning she was on the girls' side, as if she were identifying with their needs.

Her approach was even more potent because, fresh from a university environment, she was used to dealing with her students as adults. She had worked quite happily in that environment and apparently felt no urge to alter her way of relating. So the pupils at Abbotsleigh found themselves in the giddy position of having a headmistress who was very much at one with them, and treated them with the same respect as undergraduates. 'The Betty we saw was the Betty at the peak of her life—we really got the best she had to offer in so many ways—we were just lucky,' said Jane Plasto.[8]

Betty's manner was not the only apparent difference. There was also the matter of style. Miss Everett had a certain dash, Miss Hirst was safe … and Betty? Her friend Janna Bruce was perturbed about her clothing. She knew Betty would be involved in all sorts of public events and that the school council was interested in clothes. 'I can remember trying to persuade her to go to some sort of milliner because she used to wear a fisherman's cap with a big tassel here at the side of her face—a top that hung down with a big tassel—it looked ridiculous. And so I tried to persuade her to go to a milliner called Henriette Lamotte, but she wouldn't do it and I gave up at that stage and I was wise to give up because you can't do anything about it at all—quite impossible!'[9] Betty tended to wear skirts with twin-sets, and canoe-like shoes with thick heels. She considered her blue naval uniform still serviceable though it was shiny with age. In summer she tried to dress up with nylon frocks with full skirts.

Then there was her car. Canon Newth, chairman of the council at the time, said they were all concerned over 'her awful little bomb car'. The bomb was a dung coloured corrugated-metal shell over a deux chevaux Citroën. Betty had bought it in England because she and Alec needed a van to carry tools and materials while they were building their house at Galston. It was small and very cheap to run. Because it was registered as a van it had to have printed on its side, in big white letters, 'Archdale: Abbotsleigh'. When it sat outside the school on the Pacific Highway, no-one could fail to know that the headmistress was in. If one of the tyres was flat she would change it on the highway, rejecting the proffered help of the gardener. At the end of the day she would pull on her sheepskin coat, the one with a pucker where it had hung on the clothes peg, and lower her frame into the deux chevaux with an enviable artlessness. That is, until the council could stand it no more and gave her a large, pristine, white Holden station wagon.

'She was an amazing person. I shouldn't say she resurrected the place,' reflected Canon Newth, 'her personality showed itself. The school certainly came alive.'[10] Even so, Betty didn't come straight in and put everyone in their place. For the first year, when she attended council meetings she was very quiet, listening to all speakers.

Instead, she turned her attention to what was needed in the school to ensure it would be considered amongst the best. Initially, Betty was shattered at how few changes there had been in schooling since her adolescence. Teaching methods were the same, disciplinary methods were the same. The girls were far more worried about exams, but everything, especially social attitudes, was very conventional. 'It was extraordinary and I thought this is all wrong,' Betty told *The Bulletin*, 'everything else has changed.'[11]

Betty believed absolutely that, with education, women could do or be anything. So she was quick to underline that Abbotsleigh was a girls school not a ladies college. Looking at the clutch of private schools around her, she saw a discrepancy between the teaching of science to boys and to girls. Although boys were offered both physics and chemistry, very few girls were. She found it strange that education was still imbued with the idea that there were certain science subjects which were all right for a girl, such as botany and biology, but they didn't have to worry their heads about physics.

At Women's College Betty had noted how disadvantaged were the Abbotsleigh girls studying medicine, science and physiotherapy. While they had some knowledge of chemistry, they had no grounding in physics or higher maths and they had to be coached at college to make up for lost time.

In 1958 Miss Ellison had been teaching chemistry since 1942 and, as there was only one class, she taught biology as well. The school only had one and a half laboratories. Betty wanted to broaden the base of science so she responded positively in 1960 when Miss Ellison said she wished to attend a summer school on the teaching of physics staged by Professor Harry Messel. Physics classes commenced soon afterwards, but with a minimum of equipment and a great deal of improvisation. The first batch of girls to sit for the subject in the Leaving Certificate had completed five years of physics in two years. While none of them gained an A, they all passed.

Quite soon a new science block was built, and more science staff were engaged. Betty's enthusiasm for science skewed the ambitions of the girls. 'In our day, if you did biology or art you were considered stupid, the clever people did physics and maths,' said Meredith Burgmann. 'Archie was very into believing the girls should do science and maths—to the extent that for the Leaving Certificate I did maths 1 and maths 2, physics and chemistry—four of my six subjects which is just crazy.'[12] Meredith went on to study the humanities.

It also became apparent that the senior mathematics teacher, Miss Allen, was not qualified to teach honours in the subject. Miss Allan was a tiny but steely teacher who, as deputy headmistress, held enormous sway in the school. She had held Abbotsleigh's discipline intact during the latter years of Miss Everett's reign and Miss Hirst's tenure. For her to be found inadequate for the task of higher maths must have been galling.

Along with most of the older teachers, Miss Allen disapproved of

Betty's breezy manner, her untidy dress ('the teachers used to run smart dressing,' said one), and her lack of experience in schools. Miss Allen soon left the school and Betty tried to appoint suitably qualified teachers to take the girls to the highest levels of maths. But after her years in the university milieu she was surprised to find that at the school it took a while to find stability in good maths tuition.

Betty's emphasis was not lopsided and she was as much for the arts and languages as the sciences. But she was keen to make the acquisition of knowledge a taste instead of a task. Her idea of education was broad; rather than just sitting in a classroom learning facts, it involved experiencing all sorts of things. With Betty's encouragement students began to attend plays at the Elizabethan Theatre in Newtown and other theatres in the city. In her 1963 headmistress's report she noted that parties of girls had been taken to *The Cherry Orchard*, *Hamlet*, *The Visit*, *The Playboy of the Western World*, *The Cloud*, *Cyrano de Bergerac*, *Season at Sarsaparilla*, *The Fire Raisers*, *A Misdsummer Night's Dream*, *Richard III* and *Henry V*. In the same year the Young Elizabethans performed *The Tempest* and *A Midsummer Night's Dream* at the school, and a puppet show was organised by Alliance Française. That was apart from Shakespeare Day plays held on the lawn by the swimming pool, a school performance of *The Tempest*, first, second, third and fourth year plays, and excursions to see films including *Pride and Prejudice* and *The Longest Day*.

'We saw every theatre performance that was going, went to every concert put on for schools, jazz as well as classical music, which seemed very daring to us then,' said Wendy Blaxland. 'Wonderful as an education. After all, that's what I remember now, those hushed afternoons of magic in the darkened school hall, rather than the often excruciatingly tedious routine of lessons.'[13]

Betty realised that much that she had learnt at school was no longer accurate. So it was not the pursuit of storing information that she encouraged, rather the teaching of skills to embrace life in all its fullness so that the girls could be as flexible in their learning as the changing world demanded. It was a delicate balance because she was aware that there was also a rapid increase in the amount of factual knowledge children had to take in. It posed a problem as to how to divide school time.

The many extracurricular activities impinged on maths and science lessons. The girls loved it, but the staff sometimes got annoyed.

'In the morning she would say (to the staff) "At 11.00 we will have the Elizabethan Players in the hall"—not even a few hours notice for teachers—you might have had tests to give,' Elva Julien recounted. 'There would be an outcry, and Betty would say, "Well this is the important thing about education and years after the girls leave school they might not remember the lesson you were about to give, but they will remember this experience".'[14]

It was the wholeness of education that Betty aspired to for her girls. A few years after her arrival she said that science had come to be regarded as not a subject for the brilliant few, but as English has always been, for all. In 1964 she boasted that at Abbotsleigh, there was evolving a new type of pupil whose interests were varied enough to include drama and chemistry, poetry and physics, mathematics and music—all at the same high level.[15]

Since she wasn't bound by orthodoxy, Betty tried to broaden horizons, not that all her ideas could be implemented at once. For example, Betty was keen to introduce Chinese and Russian into the curriculum, but exotic languages were not introduced for some time. However, with Betty's reputation as a cricketer Abbotsleigh acquired a new intense interest in sport. All the while, change hung in the air, and not just for the sake of change but to keep the school in the forefront of education. Hence the new laboratories, the interest in the Wyndham Report, intelligence testing, vocational guidance and quicker reading. 'Nothing but the best is good enough for Abbotsleigh, the best in work, the best in sport and the best in our spiritual growth,' Betty enthused.[16]

Yet despite what people think, Betty wasn't progressive, she didn't rush to make radical changes to the curriculum. She was merely testing the waters and it was her attitude that was so different, her values that were so confronting.

'She didn't conform to any pattern,' said Christine Fox, head girl in Betty's second year at the school. 'So it was always a bundle of surprises. We'd go to assembly and suddenly things had changed, the routines were no longer there … And then she'd laugh when you weren't expecting it. You'd think, we're in trouble now, and she'd burst out laughing and suddenly the threat wasn't there any more, so you'd have to rethink where you stood. And that must have made us suddenly aware that teachers were not people that you just didn't talk to and I think she suddenly made the place human.'[17]

Betty emphasised that school was not a cocoon, it was a starting point, a place that you went away from. This was the girls' opportunity to learn and ask questions and not to take things for granted or to go along with something because everyone else did. It was always, why are you doing this? What do you think that's for?

In pursuit of these aims Betty made it quite clear that she wanted the girls to have a say in what they were doing. When Christine Fox's class held a sit-in demonstration (the first known rebellious act) because the school had decided to take the cobblestones away from the entrance, Betty asked the ring-leaders to tell her why they had done this. The girls said they felt that tradition was being broken and this was just one more example of modern ways coming into Abbotsleigh and ruining their lives. In response, Betty asked whether they had any compassion for the little old ladies with their stiletto heels who were busily breaking their ankles and their legs walking on the uneven cobbles. The girls had no recourse but to say yes, that was probably right and the cobblestones were pulled up. 'But she actually listened to us and she asked us to come and talk,' said Christine. 'That was amazing and it's something I'll never forget.'

The girls came to believe Betty was interested in them and in their development and they were very impressed that she took the time to come to the most junior in the senior school to welcome them and to ask them if they had any questions. Betty also suggested that the houses hold their own assemblies, run by the house captains instead of the teachers. The girls had never been asked to run anything before.

The school started to relax. What pervaded it was the very real sense of Betty's enjoyment of life, her emphasis on the positive, and her expectation that every girl and every teacher had something to contribute to the life of the school. When asked towards the end of her headship what she had accomplished at Abbotsleigh, Betty said, 'a certain cheerful atmosphere, a relationship between children and staff which is friendly, reasonably respectful, but friendly, and I think a general opening up of the [extracurricular] activities of the school.'[18]

Up until then the girls had experienced only limited models of women. Their mothers were war brides, upper middle-class wives, mostly in the home. Often intelligent women dissembled so that men felt they were in the ascendancy. Suddenly there was this woman with a large and open personality who not only totally eschewed fashion but the social scene as well—it was irrelevant to her. The girls liked her because, compared to their mothers, she was outrageous.

Occasionally Betty asked some girls to hop into the back of her station wagon and she'd take them to her mud house at Galston for a barbecue. She wore old clothes, jeans and sandshoes without laces, and although the girls were anticipating organised activity, nothing actually happened, she just enjoyed their company, treating them like adults who thought for themselves and took responsibility for their actions. Sometimes Alexander was there—the first vaguely arty person some of them had ever met. The girls were impressed with the warm relationship between brother and sister and with the fact that they had built the house themselves. They were struck that everything was so natural, there was nothing artificial and that Betty let them into her secrets there.

For girls who were used to well-harnessed mothers, Betty's freedom in being braless was fascinating. The cricketers used to encourage her to have a bat so they could see her heavy, hanging breasts shiver and shake as she ran.

From the beginning Betty was incredibly impressive, so massively there, quite plain, untidy hair, uncompromising in what she wore—an antidote to the nerve-rackingly well-bred girls at the school. She made the whole experience of school much more like real life. 'I instinctively felt, right from the beginning, when I was just a little girl, that this was someone who would definitely be on my side,' said Jenny Rowe. 'She was a straight woman. She wasn't going to go for any bullshit, whatever else happened. So it made me feel safe to know that she was there.'[19]

The girls were all impressed that Betty appeared on television and was heard on radio and said what seemed to them eminently sensible things. For many of them, she became the model of a woman they wanted to be like, free and independent, important in her world and visible in society.

Self-Discipline

At Abbotsleigh, Betty developed a policy of having the door open, of allowing the girls to come and talk to her. Annabelle Schmidt said that when she came to the junior school as a boarder at the age of eight she can remember Betty coming down to their residence, Poole House, and saying, 'I am Miss Archdale, your headmistress, and I want you to know that my door is open to you at any time.'[20] The next headmistress, said Annabelle, had a light put on the outside of her study door. If it shone red, she was unavailable, if it shone green, she still might not be available.

Betty felt the girls should be given more freedom and be allowed to make more decisions themselves. She was genuinely on their side and the girls appreciated her approachability and they her willingness to back them in idiosyncratic endeavours. Instead of asking 'Why?' to unusual requests, she said 'Why not?'

When Glynis Johns, now a doctor interested in homoeopathy and an MA in philosophy, was in fourth form she was besotted with films. She persuaded her mother to ask Betty if she could attend a week-long Greta Garbo festival which was being held at one of the arty cinemas in town in the early afternoons. There was no problem and Glynis remembers her years at Abbotsleigh as amongst the happiest of her life because she knew an enormous sense of freedom to explore her own ideas and to be what she wanted to be.[21]

Boarders weren't usually allowed to go on unaccompanied expeditions to Kings Cross. But when Susan Anthony, who was then fifteen, read about the Rev. Ted Noffs and his work amongst the down-and-outs at the Wayside Chapel, at the Cross, she begged Betty to let her visit him. Despite the fact that Noffs's venture attracted criticism that social work was not the role of the clergy, Betty gave the excursion the nod. Noffs showed the uniformed girls around the simple, cheerful building, introducing them to homeless people, drug addicts and others, trying to explain their lives and problems and giving them all a sense of shared human equality that Susan says she has carried with her ever since. 'In those days I had never met a man with a beard, a woman who had defied her family, or, most importantly, a man who treated me without condescension, as Ted did,' Susan wrote at the time of Ted Noffs' death in 1995.[21]

Because of Betty's response to them, the girls came to feel an increased confidence. She wasn't judgmental, and, although they admired her tremendously she wasn't a figurehead either—she didn't have that distance. It was as if she generously allowed her spirit to leave her body and placed it alongside the girls. 'It was like having an extra member of the family, whose love and interest you never doubted and whom you loved back with equal devotion,' said Wendy Blaxland.

Having herself been mischievous at school, Betty recognised that the recalcitrant were often the brighter girls who needed outlets for their restless energy. So she directed their attention to fruitful activities. If they wanted to put on a concert or a competition, she'd tell them to go ahead—they didn't have to justify it. She was thrilled if it kept them busy and prevented them from making the lives of other people miserable. Francis James spoke of this quality in Betty, 'this special, female creativity: the quite selfless gift of helping, nudging, stimulating people into creative channels, and doing it unobtrusively'.[23]

The school hosted the second five-day residential history conference for 200 students from NSW and interstate in the May holidays in 1966. Lecturers included Sir Howard Beale, former ambassador to the United States, and C. P. Fitzgerald, an authority on China, covering topics such as 'Women in the Ancient World'. Betty again said 'Why not?' when the Royal Australian Navy asked the school to send a choir to sing at a midnight service on Christmas Eve. Parents were less than pleased at the thought of the long drive late that night, so valiantly she returned the girls to their homes all over the north shore. She wouldn't have reached home until four o'clock on Christmas morning.[24]

The school became fun because there was so much going on. In response to Betty's faith in them, the girls had a strong sense of not wanting to disappoint her. And because they perceived that she was very much with them, Betty was able to bring about a different idea of discipline. At Women's College she found that the undisciplined undergraduates had come from strict homes and regimented schools. Betty had found in her own experience as a child at boarding school that punishment never altered her behaviour one jot, so at Abbotsleigh she always had doubts about punishment. She rarely saw any change in behaviour after girls were kept in detention and she also saw that some teachers gained satisfaction from exacting discipline, which was not the point of the exercise either. She sensed that because the young people were steadily being given greater privileges and allowed to participate more in the adult world, they would not respond to harsh discipline. So she relaxed the rules and tried to encourage the girls to think for themselves, to run their own lives.

Not only did the policy of self-discipline create a happier atmosphere, but better cooperation between pupils and staff made the running of the school easier. Betty was delighted to hear one of the staff comparing Abbotsleigh favourably with a nearby girls school which had 124 notices between the front gate and the school and one dog, tied up. Abbotsleigh, however, was untidy, unorganised, with no notices, a minimum of rules and a number of dogs, none of them tied up.

Yet the girls knew that, above all, honesty and integrity were Betty's absolutes. They were not to lie, cheat, or use force generally. They were to think of their neighbour. There was a strong feeling that if you were in the wrong, if you owned up and were straight with her, then you were okay. Betty would deal with the problem and that was the end of the story. Even so, she was regarded as being more lenient than some other heads of schools and the stories of her dealing with misbehaviour were legion.

Bill Farram, an accountant on the school council, said one of his children was a bit of a rebel and liked to bend the rules if she could. When she hit upon the idea of moving around on rollerskates during a Latin class Betty let out a merry chuckle and said, 'I think that's rather funny, but I won't think it funny if you do it again.'[25]

Betty's punishments were also unpredictable. One night, boarders from Vinden House shinnied down the verandah posts and ran across the top oval, down through the bushes to the swimming pool. They took their pyjamas off in the changing shed and went for a dip. As they laughed and splashed about they had not taken into account that Betty's residence, Read House, was the closest building. Betty came to the pool's side and asked them to get out of the pool, which they did, their hands fanning their nakedness. Her punishment was that they had to return to their boarding house, without their clothes, and get into bed on the second floor without disturbing the housemistress. Not another word was said.[26]

Some of the teachers weren't entirely happy with Betty's approach and thought she didn't back them up if they wanted a girl disciplined for being difficult. When Joyce Cole was about to reprimand one of the girls for rollerskating down a sharp incline towards the science block, Betty appeared and said to the girl, 'Good morning Madam President of the Roller-Skating Club'. She had given them that site to skate on, knowing it was problematic, in the hope that they would tire of it. By simply giving them a little rope, she maintained a close relationship with them.[27] 'Sometimes it felt like Arch and us against the reactionary forces of the staff,' remembered Wendy Blaxland. 'We knew how privileged we were to have a headmistress like this … I do remember the once or twice she told us off. It had a devastating effect, probably because it was so rare, and because we knew she was always inclined to take our side rather than the reverse.'

Penny Figgis said Betty's approach to her unruliness made a big impact on her. Several times her behaviour was bad enough for her to be sent to the headmistress, although sometimes for stupid reasons such as dyeing her hair purple. There was humour in Betty's reproach, but what really moved Penny was opening her reference when she left school. Although she had often been in trouble, had been preoccupied with boys, had been unhappy in her final years and was not a successful student, Betty wrote warmly of her, saying this is a person of considerable ability who will hit her stride. Indeed, since leaving school Penny has been vice-president of the Australian Conservation Foundation, on the boards of the Environment Protection Authority, the Australian Tourist Commission, Landcare Australia and Uluru National Park and was recently made an AM.[28]

Betty rarely suspended a girl for bad behaviour and only asked one girl, a boarder who wandered abroad at night with a boy, to leave the school. Years later she congratulated herself on having so few casualties. On the whole she thought the girls were terrific—that most of them did something for a lark, but they weren't really wicked. Because she didn't make large of small misdemeanours she encouraged the girls to laugh away pettiness. And in listening to them, she validated them, so that by the time they left school they believed they were strong, independent individuals with an ability to contribute to the community at large.

Current Affairs

It was when Betty suggested that she run classes on current affairs, initially for those in their final year, that the girls recognised the extent of her impact on them. The sessions were partly a means for Betty to communicate with her charges and, through discussion, find out what was happening in the school. But mostly they became a lever, lifting the girls' attitudes from the parochial to a concerned alertness about the world.

Betty would come into the classroom, always a charismatic presence, with a *Time* magazine under her arm. She would sit on a desk, with a leg dangling, and ask the girls, who were also sitting on their desks, what they wanted to talk about—what issues, what countries, what concepts. Then the discussion would begin.

Her audience didn't know that Betty's governess had been Emily Pankhurst's daughter, that she had attended the League of Nations with her mother in the 1930s, opening the way for the establishment of equal rights for women. They didn't know of her involvement with the Institute of International Affairs. She never mentioned or boasted of her past because she was not practised in speaking about herself—she didn't expect people to be terribly interested in what she'd done.

For the girls, it was in these sessions that the whole world opened up. And while some were simply stimulated by an awareness of a vaster picture, for others the current affairs lessons sowed the seeds for future activist adventures. Penny Figgis, who says her family didn't discuss such matters, remembers thinking this was the first time she had heard anybody talk about drugs or sex or abortion or politics or race. Although she couldn't always remember the content, here was an adult saying these things were really important. For Penny it was the start of her political awareness.

One of Betty's emphases was that, for people to live with each other, they should never be absolutely certain that the other fellow is wrong. Quarrels and violent demonstrations need two sides, both of which are probably partly right and partly wrong. She used to quote from the play, *The Captive*: 'Whoever says he is 100 per cent right is a fanatic, a thug and the worst kind of rascal.' Certainty lay behind the Inquisition, behind Hitler, behind every major catastrophe in the world's history. So Betty was keen to encourage uncertainty and doubt—which had given rise to most of the major discoveries of civilisation—and respect for other people's integrity.[29]

In about 1965 she asked a group of Africans to come to the school to tell of their struggles with apartheid. A group of 30 people came and after speaking in the assembly hall they went outside and gathered under a big tree and sang 'We shall Overcome'. 'I found what they were saying just so affecting,' recalled Penny Figgis. 'And then they sang, and I can hardly say it now without immediately beginning to weep … And then I went back to the classroom and there were these girls from Brewarrina or Walgett, country girls, saying, "bloody blacks, bloody boongs". And I can remember it like a slap in the face with a wet fish. I didn't know people thought like that, I'd never confronted it before.'

If Betty had heard these comments she would have been inflamed and responded sharply, as she did on another occasion. Rarely did she humiliate girls in front of others, but in this instance she did. An Abbotsleigh girl refused to show her pass to an Aboriginal ticket collector at Killara railway station and when he called out to her she ran away. The next day in assembly Betty said, 'Would all the girls who live in Killara please stand up?' and after they rose, with her passion to the fore, she strenuously rebuked them. Jill Auld said, 'It was only one girl and every girl that lived in Killara, and there were quite a few of us in those days, copped it. Awful! She didn't know [which girl it was] or if she did know she didn't want to single her out in front of the whole school. It was the first and only time in my life I felt ashamed of living in Killara.'[30]

Betty wanted the girls to understand that there were other ways of living, so she encouraged them to leave their sheltered lives and take American Field Scholarships and live overseas. Christine Fox, who was head girl in Betty's second year at the school, was the first to go. It altered the direction of her life and she later became involved in the anti-Vietnam War movement, producing a news-sheet in San Francisco and working with people who were being hounded by the authorities. She has continued to be involved in cross-cultural anti-racism, working with the Australian Peace Education and Research Association, Freedom From Hunger, Community Aid Abroad and consulting in teacher education in Third World countries. 'I don't know I would feel so passionately about anything if it wasn't for Betty Archdale,' she says. 'I'd give my life for that woman. I really think she is a very, very special person.'[31]

Betty seemed to feel a lingering responsibility for her more radical students once they left the school, as if she felt she had made them become the people they were. Meredith Burgmann became involved in the anti-Vietnam protest movement and was arrested, always for non-violent demonstrations, at least twenty times between 1968 and 1980. In the late 1960s Betty wrote and asked her to come and talk to the students about Vietnam, which Meredith thought was quite extraordinary. In 1971 Betty sat around on court benches for two days waiting to give a character reference when Meredith was given a two-month gaol sentence for running onto the Cricket Ground during the South African rugby union tour.

From the sidelines, Betty would have approved of Meredith's work—her doctoral thesis on the Builders Labourers' Federation and the Green Bans, her role as President of the NSW Upper House, and as a vocal member of the National Pay Equity Coalition, to press for equal pay for women. However, Meredith and other more activist former pupils felt increasingly alienated from Abbotsleigh, which they saw as representing the complacent middle classes. 'Even though Abbotsleigh was very liberal in its philosophy I still believe that those sorts of wealthy private schools are about the ruling class replicating itself,' Meredith said in 1994. However: 'I always found that if I shamefacedly admitted to having been at Abbotsleigh—this is amongst my new radical friends— they'd say "Oh, that's all right". They sort of excused me because that was Betty Archdale—it was obvious they had a respect for Betty Archdale.'[32]

It was no accident, for instance, that when Caroline de Costa (Downes), a former pupil, was in Damascus in 1965 that she saw a *Time* magazine billboard with the ample-breasted Megan Stoyles (one of Archie's girls) with no bra, wearing a T-shirt emblazoned with 'Make Love Not War!'[33]

Feminism

Speaking of Betty and the Melbourne educationalist Myra Roper, Francis James wrote in 1968: 'Both know, know quite well that women are superior in all important ways to males; but while both are content to know it—never dream of saying so. Though both are suffragists, accordingly, they use the weapon of under-statement in their fight.'[34]

Betty came to realise in Australia that the word feminist inferred that women thought themselves better or above men. She was brought up to use the term feminist merely to mean that women should have an equal go. But she found Australian men to be slightly old-fashioned, with a calm assumption that the woman was number two and could never do anything as well as a man. She felt that girls had been conditioned (even if unconsciously) to please their fathers and brothers, that they were reluctant to outshine them, and that this attitude was reflected in girls' education.

Betty came to Abbotsleigh at the end of the heyday of marriage. Throughout society in the early 1960s was the expectation that girls would, at some stage after leaving school, marry. There was no doubt, Betty observed, that the mothers' greatest desire was that their girls should make a good marriage. That that would be their fulfilment. Another factor that Betty had to cope with was that some of the girls had a strong feeling of anti-intellectualism and that the clever girls were sometimes made to feel that they were the ones who were different.

As both Betty and her mother had lost their fathers early in the piece, they had grown up in an absence of male influence. Betty was never given the impression that because she was a girl or a woman she had to kowtow to anyone. However, while the girls hadn't heard of feminism in the early days, Betty was feminism in action—a strong woman who made her own way and whose self-esteem didn't appear to be unduly influenced by what other people thought. It was empowering for young girls in her charge to see this profoundly honest, unflustered woman running very capably, and so professionally, a group of girls and the staff, who included men, and laughing uproariously.

Often if a girl has an overbearing mother, the daughter doesn't survive it very well. But Betty was the successful daughter of a strong mother, and her experience of charting a life of accomplishment, perhaps despite her mother's dominant presence, seems to have given her insight into helping the girls find their own way. Certainly, she challenged the girls to embrace a vision of what was possible beyond their perceived limitations by aiming for more demanding careers—in law, engineering, medicine or science.

At the same time, some parents attempted to trim their girls' ambitions, believing that they need not look further than teacher or secretarial training. Betty was frustrated by the conservatism of such an environment. 'Occasionally you get a child who rebels against the family, not very often,' she said. 'It's not really till they get out into the world with such rapid changes going on that I think they're going to wonder whether this is right or that's right.'

Regardless of home influences, Betty warned the girls not to succumb to generalising about the sexes. All of us are different, she emphasised. 'You should do what you want to do—women should not be pushed around. If they want to be married and have children and stay at home they should. If they want a career, or want to combine them both, they should. Part of what we suffer from is being generalised— women should do this or that—let women choose for themselves and organise their own lives. I am keen that we should be considered as people rather than as women.'[35] Whatever direction the girls chose, Betty would always wave them off with a laugh and 'Have fun!'—that was her expectation for them.

The girls sensed that Betty's viewpoint was important and they learnt from it. Caroline de Costa, who came to Abbotsleigh in 1963 for her final year only, said: 'Somehow, without being aware of it, the girls at the school were all doing the Leaving Certificate with the idea that they would do as well as possible and utilise it in some way for themselves, rather than as some marriageable commodity or the means of filling in time until they did get married. And I do think that with some of us [Betty] threw in that it wasn't necessary to be married in order to live a complete life. I'm not sure how she did it, but I certainly came out at the end with that impression which I didn't have when I started that year.'[36] The idea of Betty's that most impressed Caroline de Costa was that you could take hold of your life and do what you wanted to with it. She took heed and on leaving school studied medicine in Ireland, became a specialist in obstetrics and gynaecology, produced seven children and gives freely of her time to the Aboriginal Women's Health Centre.

Yet in 1985, fifteen years after leaving Abbotsleigh, when she was receiving an honorary doctorate from the University of Sydney on the centenary of the first women graduates, Betty commented that the expectations for women moved with an aching slowness. At the time of the ceremony, although only 44 percent of university students were men, there were only 6 female professors but 125 male professors, and 63 female senior lecturers compared with 370 males. That the ratio didn't trickle up from student to powerbroker, Betty attributed to social pressure from the cradle.

She had found at school that when a girl said she couldn't do maths those in authority tended to say, 'There, there, go down to the next division and do easier maths'. But if a boy couldn't do maths, somebody kicked him good and hard and said get on with it, work a bit harder and you can jolly well do it. Betty urged the installation of programs to change such attitudes and to encourage the girls to embrace the scientific or technological side of life. She could see that new technology was going to make it easier for more women to participate in the workforce, including through part-time jobs.[37]

At the same time, Betty's concerns were not exclusively academic. As a headmistress she was always conscious of those girls who were not academically minded. She would never hear them downgraded and was delighted when their forms won drama competitions or when they excelled in sport. One senior teacher said that she saw more of Betty's warmth with these girls than in any other relationship. One girl with a prominent role in the school seemed to be faring badly in the run-up to the Leaving Certificate. When she passed Betty sent her a telegram which simply said, 'Whacko! Archdale.'

Regardless of their skills, the girls' sense of their uniqueness was enhanced by Betty's ability to break through the conservative mannerisms of many of their backgrounds, in which they were geared to being good, aiming to please and to avoid trouble. She showed the girls that it was all right to be a bit unusual, to let go of expected behaviours, that one can survive not being approved of by absolutely everyone.

Sport

The girls were conscious of Betty's standing as an international cricketer, and her performances at cricket matches between teachers and girls underlined her reputation. Mary Smith, a maths teacher, said early in her career at the school she made the mistake of offering to be Betty's runner in a girls versus teachers cricket match. 'Good God no!' Betty responded. The teachers had to declare after Betty, who didn't run a single run, had hit the ball all over the place.[38]

When Betty arrived at Abbotsleigh, cricket was not a sporting priority. Suddenly there was a notice asking anyone interested in playing to go down to the oval. The girls felt close to Betty when she'd suddenly turn up, give them a few pointers and disappear again on her way to her house below the main oval. They were proud of having the first cricket bowling machine in a school on the north shore and Abbotsleigh's brother school, Barker, was annoyed, feeling its manly pre-eminence in sport challenged.

Betty tried to make sport more dynamic and accessible to all girls, without being compulsory. She asked Miss Palmer, who was at the school when she arrived, to leave because she felt she was too tough on the girls and then she employed teachers Rowena Butcher and Kit Raymond, who represented NSW in both cricket and hockey. While the school developed a good reputation not only in cricket but in tennis, hockey, swimming, athletics and basketball, Betty never hid the fact that she didn't like basketball and felt the girls should have been playing hockey. The basketballers used to shriek at her, 'Please stay and watch' but she'd just keep walking and laugh.

The Staff

Having come from a university, and without an intimate knowledge of curricula and school structures, Betty was initially at a disadvantage with her staff.

On the whole, the school society was cooperative and understanding, but when Betty started allowing the girls more freedom it aggravated those teachers who had been on the staff for a long while and had fixed ideas about what the girls should do. To them it seemed as though Betty had a casual attitude, but it was her pattern of headship to deal with situations logically and be completely unshackled by the past.[39]

Apart from disapproval of her ways, some of the staff felt that Miss Hirst had got a raw deal. And because Betty encouraged the teachers who weren't very good to leave, there was a marked exit, particularly of some of the older teachers, in her first years at the school. At the end of her second year *The Weaver* commented that the school was sorry to lose so many resident mistresses for the boarders, then announced the arrival of eight new ones. For the less staid teachers, however, the response was one of excitement—that here was someone fresh and with a marked status. Because Betty had been principal of Women's College the staff recognised that this gave her a background of association with older teenagers, even if she didn't have teaching qualifications.

Betty didn't go around setting guidelines. Her attitude was more that she had staff in whom she had confidence, and if they made a decision in a critical situation she would support them provided they told her at once what had happened. The teachers found that when an answer to a question was requested, she gave it firmly one way or the other—there was no dithering about. If she needed to consider matters further then she would reliably let them know. The staff were given a very free hand, including days off if they could get their work done in a set time. The teachers, in return, set out to please her.

Because she was not yet familiar with the school mores, Betty was particularly dependent on her deputy headmistress, Dorothy Hughesdon, an outstanding history teacher. She was intelligent, had integrity and was a cheerful, undemanding guide to Betty when she was new to the job and feeling her way. Dorothy and Betty had an unspoken friendship, but two and a half years later Dorothy contracted cancer and deteriorated rapidly. Betty was distressed when she died and ordered the girls to line the Pacific Highway as her coffin passed.

Delegation then became a necessity rather than a choice. For quality control of staff, Betty had to depend on the senior mistress or the head of each department. At the same time, in her search for first-class teachers Betty sought those with strong academic qualifications. She was aware that far too many second-raters were only teaching because they couldn't think of anything else to do and was staggered by the number of teachers who obviously loathed children.[40] Betty said it didn't matter tuppence whether her staff had teaching qualifications, she reckoned they could learn those in the classroom anyway. If you could teach, you could teach. A good teacher, according to Betty, must have an absolute love and knowledge of their subject and a genuine interest in the children. Betty came to recognise the benefits of having married women as teachers. Having raised children of their own, they understood children more intuitively. By the end of her time, 90 percent of the staff were married.

But attracting good teachers to the school, despite its high academic reputation, was inhibited by the fact that the pay was considerably behind that of the state education system. The school quickly took corrective action, salaries were increased and the fees took a meteoric rise. Betty was known to be impossible about salaries, according to Elva Julien, a former teacher[41]—she would pull them out of a hat but when she was able to appoint the staff she wanted Abbotsleigh took flight, soaring in its reputation.[42] However, the battle to keep abreast of the state salaries was ever-present. For example, in 1966 when the school was above its overdraft because of huge development costs, the chairman recommended that, considering the advantages of employment in an independent school compared with departmental schools, 90 percent of departmental rates would be considered satisfactory. On 14 December 1966 the council received a letter from the senior staff expressing disappointment at salary increases. But there was no fear of any resignation and Betty believed most of the staff who signed the letter were satisfied with their salaries and conditions.[43] Nonetheless, when some members of the staff who sought awards organised a book to be placed on the staff-room table and invited everyone to fill in their salary, Betty was so furious she didn't go to the staff Christmas party.

The council introduced a superannuation scheme in 1963 and equalised female with male rates of pay. And in August 1967 a scale of salaries was published for the first time, showing regular increments for each additional year of service. Conditions of service at the school became at least commensurate with those in the State system.

In comparison with employment by the state, while there were disadvantages of slower promotion if teachers wanted to stay in the same school, Betty was able to offer better teaching conditions, stability, a lighter teaching load, smaller classes and undoubtedly more freedom. If teachers had any bright ideas and wanted to experiment, she was only too pleased to hear them. But she required her teachers to take part in extracurricular activities such as drama, music and sport, which she saw as every bit as important as the time spent in the classroom. For this reason, she was under no illusions about the duties of teaching. When addressing girls considering teaching as a career she described the days surrounding her talk:

> We break up tomorrow; Thursday last week there was a Junior School concert, Friday and Saturday Fifth Year Plays, all Saturday junior sports, Sunday rehearsal for a concert, Monday a joint concert and Tuesday a joint concert with PLC. There is an excursion to Central Australia tomorrow morning … You will find in the independent school considerably more stress placed on this sort of activity, excursions here, there and everywhere.
>
> But please don't teach if you don't want to. Teaching is exhausting, frustrating, maddening, and infuriating. You are a cot case by the end of term. On the other hand it is rewarding, satisfying, and if this is why you want to do it, do it. But if you are not prepared to half kill yourself, don't think of teaching.[44]

Not surprisingly, Betty's approach in selection of teachers was idiosyncratic. 'She had a great nerve in choosing staff,' said Elva Julien. 'She loved people who were different and had a certain spark. We were lucky to have people who were eccentric on the staff.'

As she mistrusted references, Betty would simply chat to applicants. Judy Copeland, a geography teacher, was one. At her interview they spoke, as was Betty's wont, about world issues. Betty must have decided that Judy was of her ilk so she offered her a position. 'Now let me see,' she said, standing up and squinting at a vast timetable pinned behind her desk, 'oh yes, we've got a vacancy for a Latin teacher for first-year classes.' Judy, nonplussed, accepted. But when she started work she found to her great relief that she was to teach geography after all.[45] On radio Betty admitted her worst experience was when she selected a teacher and discovered later he was wanted for robbery and violence in some foreign land. The odd thing was he was a very good teacher, and she was rather sorry when the police caught up with him.[46]

Betty was not as assiduous as her predecessor in overseeing the staff, and she had some poor runs. In her first years there was a considerable turnover of staff, with some classes having three maths teachers in a year. If a teacher caused complaints shortly after the appointment, Betty tended to blame herself for misjudging the person and worried how she could deal with the problem. Towards the latter part of her time a man was appointed as head of the science department on Professor Messel's recommendation. He was inadequate for the task and there was quite a lot of unhappiness. But in those days before the fuller impact of the teachers' union, Betty was able to ask errant teachers not to return the next term. Sometimes she had to fill in the gaps until a new appointment was made.

The staffrooms were 'appalling' according to the teachers, small desks close together. 'Betty wouldn't have known about the staffrooms,' said Elva Julien. But once in situ, the teachers tended to stay, not because of salary but because they were allowed to put their ideas into practice. Betty attracted interesting people with diverse backgrounds, and on the whole she found the staff magnificent and their results very good. Joyce Cole feels that Betty was more prepared than subsequent heads with whom she worked to be friendly with staff. But it was a two-way stretch—they had to reach out and meet her halfway and if they didn't they couldn't expect particular rapport.

In reality, the girls had much freer access to Betty than the staff did. She would never shut her door against girls as a general rule, but she often refused to see members of staff—because she didn't want to see them or wanted to do something else.

'I think Betty could have made life easier for herself if she had been more consultative with the staff ,' said Elva Julien. 'She was more dismissive of them in a way. They didn't have the same importance as the girls. She was an emphatic kind of person—you felt she had a great personal strength, a strength that didn't depend on what anyone else thought of her… She could be abrupt and cruel if she thought things weren't happening as she wanted—she didn't worry. She was a larger than life person and most people remember that and appreciate it. She didn't go around patting people on the back. I suppose if you're a strong person yourself, you don't realise others could do with a little encouragement.'

As a result Betty didn't have staff loyalty from everybody and sometimes as many as half of them were against her, according to teacher Lyn Marchant-Williams. 'She scared them off, because she has always been insecure, and she was on ground there that she wasn't sure of. And they [the staff] knew so much more about what they were doing than she did. And I think this was half the reason she went for the girls who took her without criticism—and adored her.'[47]

Betty knew that her approach was causing trouble with the council and some of the staff … that they thought she was too friendly and not strict enough. But she reasoned that she listened to what the girls had to say and determined if they had a case. She didn't necessarily think that the staff were always right. According to teacher Val Street, there was some jealousy felt by teachers later on because Betty was so popular with her students.[48] And when, occasionally, Betty included staff in social gatherings at her house at Galston there was envy amongst those who were not included. Their lack of total loyalty allowed a teacher like the head of English, Mrs O'Dell, to join forces with Adam Lang, the school's chairman, to not wholly support Betty. Although she would not sacrifice principle, Betty was always upset at the thought of tackling somebody, and this situation was no exception. 'I know the effort that she had before she sacked Freddie [Mrs O'Dell],' said Lyn Marchant-Williams. 'It really was dreadful for her to have to do that. And it was the right thing to do. And strangely enough it didn't spoil their relationship. She still saw Freddie and Freddie used to phone her and send her Christmas cards. So it didn't ruin their relationship, which says an awful lot for the way she did it.'[49]

15

AGAINST THE WIND

Part of the reason for Betty's breadth of educational vision was that she had an energetic life outside Abbotsleigh.

In the year after she joined the school she was elected to the Senate of the University of Sydney. And there she stayed for 25 years, her longest serving position. The Senate consisted of an impressive group of academics, along with representatives of the community and of the student body. Here Betty was constantly exposed to the highest educational standards of tertiary students and to their social mores. Anxious to prepare her girls for the best that life could offer, the insights gained here helped her drive for better academic achievement at the school. Despite the fact that Betty said she wasn't assertive, she must have been known and trusted by the student body because in 1964, for the first time ever, a woman, Betty, topped the voting in a Sydney University Senate election.[1]

At the same time Betty became president of the NSW Branch of the Australian Institute of International Affairs, a position she held for two years. She was also a founder member of the Australian Branch of the International Law Association (ILA), which was a significant initiative in partnership with Carl Koenig. A Middle European refugee and a lawyer, Koenig had known the prestigious ILA in Europe. Their endeavour proved successful and a later president, Sir Laurence Street, became world president.[2] During her time as headmistress the Prime Minister, John Gorton, invited Betty to be a member of the Australian Council for the Arts (1969–70).[3]

In educational circles, Betty was president of the NSW Headmistresses Association in 1961 and was invited to be on the council of Tara, a Church of England girls school, by her school friend Elizabeth Hake. When attending meetings, Betty would drive the chairman, her friend Felix Arnott, who refused to take up driving.

The Abbotsleigh building program echoed the need to accommodate the Wyndham scheme, which was implemented in 1962, adding a year to secondary education. The new scheme consisted of a four-year course taken by all students, followed by an optional two-year course. Betty's initiatives in science teaching had placed the school in a good position for the compulsory integration of the sciences. Miss Ellison reflected that when she came to teach science at Abbotsleigh in 1958 it had one laboratory. When she retired in 1968 there were seven laboratories, demonstration rooms and a staff of eleven, teaching the full six-year science course covering physics, chemistry, biology and geology.[4]

In 1962 the staff said they wanted to form an Abbotsleigh Science Association among parents, staff and the girls. Betty asked fathers who were engaged in scientific fields to help. This they did with an open night organised by the Pacific Astronomical Society. As the association grew it staged a Radio Club evening and another for science counselling. It organised a one-day seminar on the place of biology with Sir Macfarlane Burnett as guest speaker, and another time Professor Sharman spoke on the biology of kangaroos. There were addresses by representatives of the UN and Freedom From Hunger on world food problems. In 1967 the school held a Festival of Science called A Woman in Sheep's Clothing. Scientists preached at a chapel service on the fact that there need be no conflict between science and religion.

So positive was the Science Association's influence that an Arts Association was formed along similar lines. Together the two associations staged a Festival of Light, looking at the scientific manifestations of light and its use in creative expression including photography and ballet. Musical groups also expanded, mushrooming into numbers of choirs, orchestras and smaller percussion bands under the jurisdiction of a full-time director of music, the composer Miss Tyer.

For Abbotsleigh the Wyndham scheme meant expanding enrolments and establishing four streams for the first four years to School Certificate and three each in fifth and sixth year—a total of 22 new classes. Betty was asked to aim for an enrolment of 120 for each of the four classes and decided to hold an examination for all girls on the secondary school waiting list, allocating open scholarships for full fees, so that she could ensure good entrants.

Because of the increase in the school population Betty introduced four houses—Paterson, Kendall, Gordon and Lawson—and a wide range of clubs were formed including the Code (cooperation, organisation, duty and endeavour)Club. Betty had already introduced the American Field Scholarship to the school with girls travelling to the United States and young Americans returning in exchange. She also encouraged the girls to form a school council, and she was impressed with their ideas to improve the running of the school. Within every initiative was a sense of Betty's liberal approach. She welcomed the presence of more modern books on the syllabus. *Sons and Lovers*? Oh most certainly, yes. She made sure that the girls knew that she regarded drama and debating as being as valid a contribution as sport.

Overall, she had a wonderful enthusiasm for the girls. Peter Duly recalls that during a fathers versus daughters cricket match Betty umpired the game and if one of the men made the slightest error, not enough to get out, she'd call 'You're out!' The girls found this enthusiasm for them, and the lack of inhibition in her imagination and in her actions, very infectious. Combined with all the building, the mood of the school changed—it had more confidence in itself, more pride.[5] 'The only thing that went down— it's what you'd expect—the girls' appearance became frightful,' said Janna Bruce, the art teacher. 'She did nothing about it and there was a lot of grumbling amongst the parents too … I don't suppose Betty thought it mattered at all, but I think the mothers thought it mattered.'[6]

Of course this was a reflection of Betty's non-materialistic value system, which was implicit in all she did and the girls were also taught not to judge others by their appearance. Val Street, who organised the outdoor education program for the Duke of Edinburgh Award, said that Betty was the only person amongst the heads of school to allow her to take girls to the Ultimo Teenage Centre to play basketball. Although the boys played without their dentures (having lost teeth from poor diet) and may have leered gummily at the girls during the game, the Abbotsleigh girls didn't have any problem in adjusting to the boys. It was the boys who had problems adjusting to the girls—mainly because the girls were much stronger than the undernourished boys.[7]

Betty's value system emphasised frugality, thrift and individual responsibility. She felt very strongly that to get ahead you had to work hard. You must not look for outside help or wallow in self pity. And she believed the individual to be more important than the institution. In the wider world she was concerned that big government might encroach on the right of each person to exercise her responsibility.[8]

But although Betty's whole life was distinguished by independence of thought and action, and in action she was lively, she was not radical. She approached complex contemporary issues from a basic morality that she'd worked out a long time ago. She had in her own mind a clear understanding of what was right and what was wrong. Because of her war experience, she felt strongly about Anzac Day, and while other schools had the day off, Abbotsleigh had a short compulsory ceremony.

The girls also sensed that Betty possessed a vast range of knowledge, to which she was always adding. Jane Plasto said that for all Betty's sense of fun and sport and Christianity, it was Betty's attitude to learning that had had the longest lasting impression on her.[9]

Betty continued to inspire both staff and girls to increase their knowledge, to develop their own point of view and express it. She tried to get the girls to have more contact with the outside world by asking an intriguing array of people to come and speak—the Begum Salima Ahmid from Pakistan, English cricketer and cleric the Rev. David Sheppard, Dar Pailes, Mr Atiase from Ghana; Felix Arnott talked on his recent trip to Greece, and later about his trip to Italy and Italian art.

With all the activities in the school Betty said the only people who got a bit worried were the teaching staff. But Betty believed that if the girls were stimulated generally and had a lively interest in everything that was going on they would get through their exams even if they missed a few classes.

In her memoirs Betty said a headmistress must always keep a sense of humour and a sense of humility and maintain complete honesty. Her earnest intent for the girls' advancement through education was always balanced by her humour, which the girls relished. A journalist said, 'Her practical sanity holds a thousand children to reality',[10] and certainly she never really took herself too seriously. Somehow one of the school dogs often seemed to precede her onto the stage at assembly. 'We never saw her as less than admirable, lovable, an ideal of strong womanhood,' said Wendy Blaxland. 'She affected a whole generation of us that way. We never ceased rejoicing in our good luck in having such an absolutely outstanding headmistress.' And such was the affection in which she was held that when Betty went overseas in 1968 a dozen of her former students went to meet her when she came back.[11]

Yet there were boundaries to Betty's affection for her charges. She had an intrinsic reserve and while she treated the girls with a humorous tolerance, she wasn't physically expressive—the girls never dreamt of her putting her arm around them. But in times of crisis, Betty's depth of compassion was unquestionable.

When Kim McConchie, a boarder, was asked to go to the headmistress's study she worried that she was going to be kicked out of science again. Instead, Betty said she had very sad news for her, Kim's mother had died unexpectedly. She then asked Kim who she would like to have with her as she prepared to leave the school. 'She came and helped me pack and she was with me the whole afternoon,' said Kim. 'I had another friend there with me as well and she took me to the airport— the whole bang lot and it's something that's really stuck in my mind. She was just fantastic.'[12]

Parents

Australians, unlike the English or the Chinese, tend to see things as black or white, right or wrong, according to Francis James. They over-simplify most things in terms of hard and clear categories. People are treated as conformists (most of us) or rebels (a minority) and you cannot be both. However, 'Betty Archdale is not simply an establishment figure; neither is she simply a rebel,' said Francis. 'She is both.'[13]

Betty recognised that one of the weaknesses within Australian society, especially the middle classes, was the pressure to conform. So at Abbotsleigh she tried very hard to counter that pressure. In doing so she had not only to convince the girls, but more particularly their parents. Because of her changes, and press coverage of Betty's ideas, there grew in some parts of the public imagination a picture of Abbotsleigh as being on a par with St Trinian's—a total free-for-all, with people running riot. A lack of knowledge of what was actually going on, coupled with anxiety, fed critical rumblings amongst reactionaries.

Some parents were anti-Betty. Believing the school should turn out young ladies who looked neat and behaved nicely, they were horrified when it became obvious that nothing seemed to be further from Betty's values. And so there was a polarisation of parents. Of course those who wanted their daughters to develop intellectually, to think for themselves and develop self-discipline thought she was wonderful. And at a time of changing expectations for girls in society, Betty's wide-ranging approach supported knowledge for knowledge's sake.

To her dismay, Betty found an irritating minority of parents were breathing down her neck all the time, querying why their daughter wasn't included in the top class, the top sports team, the top anything. They were active in their rankling, approaching school council members who sometimes took their side. One day Nancy Hyde, whose daughters had already left the school, rang Abbotsleigh on the first day of term and asked if she could speak to Miss Archdale. The voice on the other end of the line said, 'Miss Archdale isn't available'. 'Betty, you can't kid me, that's you,' laughed Nancy. Betty laughed in return and said she was about to exclaim, 'You're the ninetieth person who's rung today who insists their child should be in the top English class and there are only thirty children who can be in the top English class. And I'm not speaking to any more parents today!'[14]

In her memoirs Betty recorded that one mother who complained that her daughter had been passed over for an athletic distinction was rash enough to say, 'Only the daughters of the wealthy get anywhere at Abbotsleigh'. Betty said she just stood up and said, 'Get out'.[15]

There was a funny snobbishness at Abbotsleigh, Betty discovered. She wasn't certain whether it was worse 'up the line' than anywhere else, but she found that the parents liked to say, 'My girl is doing the Higher School Certificate and she's taking Latin and physics and going to have a shot to get into medicine'. Whether said daughter was able to or not didn't seem to matter. Such adults were usually embarrassed by a child's failure to do well and Betty believed their children were left with an 'appalling' sense of social stigma.

Answers to such a problem, Betty thought, lay in less importance being attached to the exam system, a reassessment of subjects for their vocational relevance, more scope for students to relate their work to natural interests and, surprisingly, a gradual lowering of the school leaving age. She firmly believed there were many non-academic children between the ages of fifteen and seventeen who would be much happier out of school, employed and training simultaneously. But the parents didn't like the idea by a long chalk and Betty felt the pressure showed up in the girls' results and in their behaviour in class. If she tried to put them in a class where they'd be happier, then the parents kicked up a fuss. A powerful family said it would take their daughters away from the school if they didn't have a particular teacher for biology. And Betty tried to make adjustments because she could see that they had a certain right on their side, that they wanted a more modern approach to the subject.

Over time Betty came to the conclusion that the strongest educational influence on a child came from the parents. While schools instilled many facts, none of this knowledge was as important as a sense of values, and it was the parents who gave children that sense of right and wrong … and a scale of what matters and what doesn't. If there was a divergence of values between school and home, the home won every time.[16] It frustrated Betty that parents who worried if a child did not come top were instilling the wrong set of values. What mattered was that the child was doing her best. The same principles and problems applied to sport, where children learn that life is often unfair and decisions are often wrong. It always intrigued Betty that while one couldn't hit a typewriter in an office without doing a course, there was no training for parenthood which was so important.

At the other end of the scale, Betty found some parents underestimated their children, and some simply wanted their daughters to get married when they left school and not use their intellectual ability. Her antidote to the home imposing intellectual limitations on the girls was to involve the parents in running the science and arts associations, inviting distinguished minds to the school and seducing the girls into unthought-of pathways.

There were of course many parents who did support Betty, and for them she was utterly grateful. She related particularly well to John Kerr, before he was knighted, when he was president of the Parents and Friends Association. When it came to conversing with parents whose child had a real problem, Betty was focused and humane. She could communicate on all levels and when she was with the parents she realised it was the child that they had in common and her ego did not get in the way.

Often she would laugh off situations. Jill Auld (Cowper) said:

Our form mistress in second year, Miss Forster, we sorted her out very quickly to the extent that she must have thought that we came from the most terrible homes possible. So she took upon herself to visit them, our homes, without any appointments or anything. And on this particular day the first port of call was Penny Garrett's house in Killara. Now Mr Garrett was home because he was having his dentures fixed—he had no teeth in his head. Tony, the son, was at home with a cold and he was sitting on the front verandah cleaning his rifle and up goes Miss Forster …

Just along the road of course were the Cowpers, and I was at home with a cold too but my mother had just gone to the shops and I heard this knock on the front door, and I can still remember it—it went knock knock knock… knock knock… knock. I peeped through the hole and saw who it was. Panic-stricken I pulled the blinds down all round the house and meantime there was the knocking on the door. Eventually I hid under my parents' bed—so full of guilt … not going to let her in. Anyway Mum came home and I told her and she was furious. She rang up Dad at the office, which was really an occasion because women weren't allowed to ring men at the office—never interrupt men unless a terrible emergency. So he got straight on the phone to Betty Archdale and she laughed and said, 'Oh Mr Cowper I didn't know this was going on … well Mr Cowper I'll do a deal with you. I'll speak to Miss Forster if you speak to Jill and all her little friends … she reeled their names off … they're a bad little bunch and I'll see it never happens again' … that was the way she handled it.[17]

Schools were very odd communities, Betty mused—you've got the children, you've got the staff and you've got the parents. With this mix there was one thing that Betty was sure of, and that was that as headmistress she should be in control, that if you are head, you are head. And yet Christine Fox said Betty must have had a rotten time with parents because years later, when Christine invited Betty to address the International Training Institute, Betty said, 'Chris, you probably won't like what I'm going to say today, because you've got different memories of me … I'm all against parents having any influence in the school.'[18]

Shortcomings

Inevitably, with her strong persona, Betty alienated not only some parents but also some of the girls.

Michelle Judzewitsch (Cotton) came to the school to board and felt there was a sense of inequality in the treatment of the girls. She found it offensive and reacted against the school's mores by deliberately failing exams, irritating Betty. After she and another girl were awarded Commonwealth Secondary Scholarships based on creativity and general knowledge, she said Betty avoided them because she was angry that the academically successful girls she had favoured missed out. The relationship between Betty and Michelle deteriorated to the extent that she eventually left the school, completing her Higher School Certificate at Bathurst High School. Michelle now lectures in veterinary science, and when living in Arabia compiled a significant collection of rare plants. She is keen that Abbotsleigh receives no credit for her success, although she suspects that her growing feminism may have been seeded by unconsciously absorbing Betty's belief system.[19]

Betty knew that Abbotsleigh didn't really cater well for the non-academic children. Although there were plenty of subjects like art, drama and music to choose from, with the exam system in place, if the child didn't measure up it wasn't easy. There was also the prevailing social pressure in which some sort of tertiary training was seen as crucial and the competition to be accepted for courses became steeper. Because young people needed academic qualifications so much, they tended to worship them.

Even so, Betty thought the school denigrated the non-academics.

She felt she had failed them and that somehow the school should have given them more kudos. But she also knew that taking these girls out of classes and devising alternate courses could harm the school's reputation for its academic record, which was the last thing Betty wanted to do. But she recognised that schools like Abbotsleigh hadn't yet realised the ideal system of giving each pupil what she needed as an individual.

It was the boarders that Betty fretted about most. She was strongly for young people getting away from home, becoming more autonomous and living with and tolerating other children. But she was aware that at Abbotsleigh the boarders, who were mainly from country areas, were often relegated to the lowest academic streams and, because it was an academic school, were not valued as much as they deserved. Betty used to wonder why the third stream in each year was 'chock-full of boarders'. Was it some physical difference, was it simply that living in the country meant their interests were in being outdoors, was it because people with a less academic type of brain tended to go to the country, or was it simply lack of stimulation?

Whatever the reason, a lot of the boarders during Betty's time at the school did not stay on to matriculation. It wasn't expected of them either by their parents or the school—there were more important things to get on with. Betty also noticed there was quite a separation between the boarders, who felt they belonged to the school, and the day girls who came and went. Yet she found the country children to be the most helpful, responsible and considerate—and thoroughly practical.

Whether it was because she fought for the underdog or because she had been a boarder herself from the age of seven years, Betty had a special feeling for these girls and she became their champion. An 11-year-old girl who had arrived at Abbotsleigh to board a year before Betty arrived had found the school intimidating and its disciplinarian approach terrifying. But with Betty on the scene there was a freeing-up and the fear had gone. Instead of having an authoritarian person at the helm, the boarders remembered most Betty's huge sense of humour, her throwing back her head to laugh in their midst. In turn Betty found great pleasure in watching the boarders grow up. Before television was introduced at the school she would read to them after dinner on Sunday nights. Those in first year high school went to bed early and sometimes Betty would come up and tuck them in.

Outside school time Betty tried to keep the boarders busy, to distract those longing for home. She halved the rule book and gave responsibility back to the girls for their own lives. Now they could go shopping in the city and attend football matches. It was a happier and more human place. The limited number of boarders who shared her Read House accommodation would have supper with her after church on Sunday nights. And occasionally she would take a small group of them to a concert.

A major concern was in finding suitable women to be housemistresses. When she was at school in Scotland the housemistresses were all 'ladies' and the head teachers in the school. They were a great influence on the girls in every way, academically and in sport, and the girls could talk to them about anything. But while board and lodging meant a lot to these women in 1920s Scotland, in 1950s Australia Betty found that teachers didn't need to live in to make ends meet and an appointment as housemistress was no longer a plum job. At Abbotsleigh, housemistresses were more the superior domestic type—nice women but more interested in keeping the house clean and seeing the girls got in at night.

While Betty was able to employ some good staff for the boarders, some others were unsatisfactory. Because the school was an achievement oriented society the housemistresses tended to have little status. Betty knew that there would be problems with the boarders if they didn't respect the woman in charge and this did happen, with girls stacking suitcases against the door of an unpopular housemistress and powdering and short-sheeting her bed while she was out at a concert.

In School House, a boarding house for the secondary girls, Kerry Taylor remembered the housemistress with a bulldog face who would come in at night and explode, 'You girls are revolting' and turn the light out angrily. And it was the same performance every night, the same spiel. 'I mean it was just impossible to be revolting every night,' said Kerrie. 'We were just normal kids—it was just part of walking into the room— it had nothing to do with what we were doing.'[20]

There must have been a lot of things about the school that Betty found frustrating, because she would never say to the girls, 'You've all been revolting'. At the same time she recognised that resident mistresses' living conditions were far from good. They often had to share bathrooms with the girls and Betty suggested that if a self-contained flat was made available, more senior academic staff would be prepared to live at the school.

Religion

'Religion?' Betty said in response to a journalist's question in 1965, 'Well this particular diocese of Sydney is pretty rigid, wouldn't you say? And rather anti-intellectual, I'd add. Marvellous, the diocese, for social services, I don't believe there's any to compare with it. But the theology from the pulpit? That's pretty medieval. The whole Sydney diocese seems to me to be run by rather dreary conservatives.'[21]

Betty believed that the young needed a belief in something outside themselves—something that was bigger and better. The trouble with a lot of Christians, she observed, was that their idea of Christianity was miles away from Christ's, and she thought it important to give her students a strong idea of God and Christ and His teachings. Her maxims were: 'You shall love the Lord your God with all your heart, with all your soul, WITH ALL YOUR MIND [her emphasis], and with all your strength' and 'You shall love your neighbour as yourself'.[22]

'She had a strong faith, a very firm faith,' said Freda Whitlam who was headmistress of PLC Croydon at the time. 'Four or five of us at headmistresses conferences would go to church, Kath McCredie from SCEGGS Wollongong, Miss Chisholm from SCEGGS Darlinghurst–there were a few of us it really mattered to. She was really up to date with movements in the church. She and I would go to listen if a prominent church person was out [in Australia]—that was where we met most. Always she took that side of things seriously without grandstanding.'[23]

For Betty, the best description of God was the one that defines God as meaning.[24] Yet while she was deeply religious she wasn't tied to dogma and her key word in relation to religion was tolerance. Girls with a variety of belief bases were accepted into the school. Betty's theological tolerance had an enormous impact on Susan Bures, whose Jewishness was accommodated. Susan's later interest in and appointment to the Ethnic Affairs Commission is something she attributes to Betty.[25]

Betty read widely on theology to help define her faith and when taking assembly said she just tried to be honest and say what she had found. As she read the prayers or talked, what was obvious to the girls was her inherent belief. They all knew it was genuine, there was no question about it and it was respected. Betty also encouraged other staff, who were not necessarily Christian, to take assembly and portray their faith through their own eyes.

However, she was powerless in deciding who should teach the girls religious studies. Because the school was Church of England, its chaplain was the local rector of St Paul's Church, Wahroonga, the Rev. Donald Begbie. Betty was dismayed that he was so dogmatic in his approach to religion and that he saw everything as black and white. It would be an understatement to say that he did not connect with those of his charges who did not espouse the same Low Church evangelical idea of Christianity. He certainly had great difficulty in controlling the unruly divinity classes and he used to express his frustration by throwing chalk at the girls and making rather desperate threats. Despite this, Betty liked Donald Begbie but thought he had joined the church because of his family's history of involvement. Instead she saw him as an artist with all the artistic senses. He painted a rather severe portrait of Betty as headmistress.

The Billy Graham Crusade came to Sydney in May 1959, and a new wave of conversions were ready for expression. But at Abbotsleigh, despite being a church school, Betty had little doubt that divinity was the worst taught subject. If any other subject was taught as badly, neither the parents nor the school would put up with it and the school would be out of business very quickly. Betty blamed the lack of trained divinity teachers. She had good Christian women who were sweet and kind, and the children trampled on them. She had one deaconess who, despite a degree and a Diploma of Social Studies, didn't know the meaning of Christian love. The children disliked her as much as she disliked them and she taught them to draw the little devils whom they were apparently to meet in the Hell for which they were so clearly destined.[26]

Another deaconess was liked by the girls, but she soon came to understand that her broader views counted against her advancement in the Sydney diocese and moved interstate. Betty, who was sorry to see her go, believed the number of people put off Christianity in Sydney must be colossal.

Basically, the divinity classes were the responsibility of the struggling local reverend. The girls usually reacted with disdain, and there was an insurrection at the end of 1963. A large number of the girls who were about to sit for their Leaving Certificate formed a circle between the administration building and the main senior classrooms. Because of building in progress the area was covered with rubble and looked desolate. Chanting and circling, the girls tore out pages from their divinity books and threw them onto a makeshift fire in the centre. Although Betty didn't witness the event she was greatly distressed by it, recognising that it could only have happened if the subject was not well taught. She told the ringleaders that although she did not disagree with their views on the teaching of divinity, they shouldn't express them in this way. Not because of the nature of the school, but because the minister was personally upset.

This might seem a mild rebuke, but the incident resonated in Betty and the following year she told the school leavers she didn't want any ructions. When the girls all brought teddy bears to their final assembly (which seemed a harmless farewell gesture), Betty, tense in anticipation, overreacted and, leaning over the lectern, told them they couldn't sit for the Leaving Certificate. In a towering rage she left the school. When a posse of girls went to her study to apologise and stood stricken before her, Betty threw her hands in the air and exclaimed, 'Oh Phoofff!' She saw them for what they were—completely chastised and appalled by what had happened—and she forgave everyone on the spot. She later told the head girl, Meredith Burgmann, that she didn't mind what the girls did as long as it wasn't in a religious ceremony. Over 30 years later the girls involved recalled vividly how badly they felt letting Betty down. 'I recognised then a deep religious feeling,' said Meredith Burgmann. 'It wasn't about the dignity of the school because I don't think that was terribly important to Betty, it was the religious aspect. She made a point of making that clear to me.'[27]

The incident forced Betty into working out ways to reform

religious instruction. She noticed that divinity was the only subject in which, for examinations, the children dished up answers they did not necessarily believe, largely because their results in divinity were included in the averages on which honour prizes were awarded. Betty believed that the girls were essentially religious and wanted to believe, but that the divinity teachers should guide children to Christianity, not bulldoze them. She decided that children must be taught the basic historic facts of Christianity in first and second years. And because of their curiosity they should be taught about other religions for comparison. In the higher years she suggested using a problem-solving approach based on issues and relationships that were relevant to the girls' lives. In the final years the girls should be encouraged to read a wide range of contemporary theological writers like Barth, Bultmann, Bonhoeffer and Tillich.[28]

Christine Fox said there had never been any religious discussion before Betty, because religion was so much part of the school that you never asked questions. 'And I remember sitting around with Miss Archdale myself and having this amazing conversation, and I was still very afraid of authority, but there I was debating whether or not there was a God. I don't remember whose side I was on—but it was so important to me—it was really a turning point in my life.'[29]

The real spiritual renaissance in the school occurred when a chapel was built in the school grounds, and the school 'got away from the Church'. It was opened by the Most Rev. H. R. Gough, Archbishop of Sydney and Primate of Australia, on 24 April 1965. Earlier, in December 1964, a service was held in the unfinished chapel for the girls who were leaving. Girls, staff and workmen stood among the scaffolding for a short but moving service.

A pattern of compulsory services evolved. But it was the voluntary services, run by the girls, in which Betty took greatest delight. She thought they were priceless and held more spiritual significance than the official services as everyone was there of their own free will, speaking and playing good music. To the voluntary services came a variety of speakers whom Betty admired from Aboriginal welfare, the Quakers, the Rev. Ted Noffs from the Wayside Chapel, Rabbi Brasch, Norman Webb, Bishop Hulme-Moir and a number of missionaries. The speakers demonstrated how different belief systems can work in fellowship together.

Betty often wondered how much the religious teaching in church schools had an effect on the girls after they left. But what is apparent is that at Abbotsleigh in the late 1950s and '60s, the girls were much more affected by Betty's attitude than by what they learnt in divinity classes. Because they admired Betty they felt it was valid to have a good faith.

Glynis Johns said that at the end of her fourth year she became very religious. Having always been rebellious (she was expelled from her primary state school), often in reaction to judgmental teachers, she suddenly wanted to be good. She said that this surge of faith was because, although she had been constantly in trouble, Betty had never made her feel she was a bad person. In an indirect way she was now saying to Betty, you've done a good job because you've treated me so well. Glynis has no particular memory of her christening, which was conducted in the chapel, except that it was extraordinarily moving. She cried throughout the service and when the water was put on her forehead she didn't know if it was water or tears that streamed down her face. It was a complete change in her heart.[30]

The Council

When Betty arrived there were 21 members on the council under the chair of Canon Newth. Four members were elected by the Abbotsleigh Old Girls' Union, and because it was a Church of England school two members were appointed by the archbishop and the rest were appointed by synod, including four clergy. The prevalence of church appointees posed problems and when a statement was made by the church, 'We need Christians on the council as well as Old Girls', the representatives of the Old Girls present were mightily annoyed.[31] The men and women were chosen for their churchmanship rather than their interest in or knowledge of education. When Jill Auld's father was on the council in the late 1940s he was told that if he wanted to remain on the council he had to join the Anglican Church League. Saying that no-one should tell him how to run his religion, he resigned.

Two years after Betty came to the school Canon Newth decided to resign from the chair because he felt it was ethically wrong to be headmaster of a small school, St Andrew's Cathedral School, and the governing principal of a major school such as Abbotsleigh. At the time Canon Newth had an up-and-coming secretary on the Abbotsleigh council who was 'dying to be chairman'. An ex-Shore boy with first-class honours in law, Adam Lang was keen to take over and become involved with the school.[32] A stockily built man with a round, florid face, glasses, and receding pale hair, he had joined the council the same year as Betty commenced her headship.

Meanwhile, the synod had a tendency to place clergymen's wives and other known churchgoers on the council. Yet the school had to harness tens of millions of dollars a year. As the church representatives rarely had exposure to that level of business, they could not make a contribution. One woman didn't make a remark in three years. Betty said the church on the council was 'pretty useless' except when they wanted to get their way—and then they stacked the meeting. Hours could be spent discussing the length of pupils' hair or skirts. On matters relating to buildings and gardens, the council members contributed well. But when Betty tried to advocate or discuss a real educational problem she found she was up against a brick wall.[33] Not only was she deeply frustrated by the church members' resistance to advances, she found some of the representatives of the Old Girls' Union also wanted things at the school to remain as they had been. As a result, Betty had to work with a group who did not really understand what she was trying to do.

Her power in the council arena was further undermined by the fact that she was not officially a member of the council but 'in attendance'. She could not vote, or propose or second motions, and was asked to leave when some matters were discussed. Betty felt she should have been a full member of the council and that she should be joined by two staff members.[34] 'Would any other business of comparable size to Abbotsleigh be run by part-time voluntary amateurs?' she asked, but 'I don't think I was easy on the whole', she admitted, 'I think I got my own way on things—as to what subjects we should do.'[35]

The main cause for friction however, was not the structure of the council so much as the relationship between the chairman, Adam Lang, and Betty. Lang was very focused on erecting a new order in the school. In doing so he locked horns with Betty, who believed that she should

38. Betty *(far left)* in line to shake hands with HRH King George V in 1940. (H.E. Archdale papers)

39. Second Officer Betty Archdale *(far right)* with Wrens about to leave for Singapore in February 1941. (H.E. Archdale papers)

40. Three of Betty's companions in the Persian Gulf—Flight Commander Hill (*centre*) and Lieutenants Inverauty and Richardson. (Photograph by Betty Archdale)

41. Miss Elizabeth ('Dusty') Miller, veteran Wren, at her home in Wickham, England, 1991. (Photograph by Deirdre Macpherson)

42. Betty on site as builder of the rammed-earth house, Northis, at Galston (H.E. Archdale papers)

43. The Women's College Sports Day, 1947. Left to right: Miss P. Nicol, Betty, and Helen Archdale (*beyond the enamel jug*). (Courtesy of the Women's College, University of Sydney)

44. Archbishop Hugh Gough on a visit to Abbotsleigh in 1962.

45. Alec Archdale imitating his sister as headmistress. (H.E. Archdale papers)

46. Television panellists discussing the controversial revue, *The Mavis Bramston Show*. *From left:* Mr Peter Westerway, ATN's director of public affairs; Miss Betty Archdale, headmistress of Abbotsleigh Church of England School for Girls; The Rev. Alan Walker, superintendent of the Central Methodist Mission; Mr Edward St John, QC; Father C.B. Keogh, Roman Catholic chaplain at Long Bay Penitentiary; and Mr F. Daly, Labor MP, who raised questions about the show in the House of Representatives a week earlier. (Courtesy of Fairfax Publications)

47. Betty, at the height of her public life, 1986. (Courtesy of Newspix)

48. The headmistress of Abbotsleigh, with her prefects, 1961. (Courtesy of Kristin Kerr)

49. Leaving the school on 7 May 1970. (Courtesy of Newspix)

50. Surrounded by Abbotsleigh girls on the day of her retirement, 7 May 1970. (Courtesy of Newspix)

51. Betty and Felix Arnott arriving at Albury en route to a seminar on human relations, 28 April 1978. (Courtesy of *The Border Mail*)

52. In retirement at Galston, 1972. (Courtesy of Newspix)

53. With Alec at the Barry Stern Galleries in Sydney, 1981. (Courtesy of Newspix)

54. At home, under the spotlight, Betty with her biographer in 1991.
(Photograph by Sally McInerney)

55. Betty after receiving an
Honorary Doctorate of
Letters from Macquarie
University in May 1995.
(Courtesy of Macquarie
University)

run the school. It was a muscular tussle, as they were both strong personalities.

Adam Lang became known as the 'building chairman' because he initiated the construction of the senior school library wing, classroom block, hall and chapel, science wing, extensions to the junior school and the acquisition of two large neighbouring houses which were converted to boarding houses. He saw to it that the lower oval was filled with thousands of tons of soil to extend it as a hockey field.

There is no doubt that his initiatives were important in raising the physical aspect of the school to contemporary standards. There is also no doubt that he was very proud of his achievements. In an article he wrote for the 1968 edition of the school magazine, *The Weaver*, he lists all these developments and more, expressing satisfaction that each of the buildings was opened by Archbishop Gough or his successor, Archbishop Loane.

There is no such recording of Betty's contributions to the school which, being transcendental, were much harder to define. Furthermore, it was not in Betty's nature to self-advertise. While she was grateful that the school's physical development catered for her ideas of more advanced scientific practices, and there was no doubt she delighted in the chapel, her emphasis at the school was different to that of her chairman. The essence of Betty's approach lay in how the girls felt, in widening their educational horizons, and evolving the school's general attitude.

And while Betty acknowledged that Lang was very efficient, she also found him at all times at the school, checking each development. Abbotsleigh seemed to have become his baby and she resented his forthright uninvited presence. After all, Abbotsleigh was the headmistress's responsibility and they quarrelled. 'We sort of didn't like each other because he tried to push me around,' Betty explained. 'Lang was the only one who'd make life difficult.'

Betty's strength and the fact that she loved difference would have challenged her chairman. And while Adam Lang said at the end of each year that he would like to thank Miss Archdale for her energy, enthusiasm and devotion, the tension in their relationship was evident to all. Yet Abbotsleigh was central to both of them, and with Betty encouraging the emancipation of thinking, and Adam Lang building up the school in a more literal sense, together they propelled it forward.

However, it was Betty, not the buildings, that the girls identified with. Jill Auld said: 'I felt terribly proud to have been there … I'd say, "We've got Miss Archdale". It never occurred to us that there could be a better school anywhere.'[36]

16

CONTROVERSIES

As headmistress of Abbotsleigh Betty seemed to unfold and shine in a way she hadn't cared to before. Those who had known her at Women's College to be relatively reserved in expressing her views were astonished by her metamorphosis, for she had developed a liking for giving her opinion and a wonderful articulateness.[1] Her new confidence was noticed by journalists, who saw her as a marvellous source of original, commonsensical, warm and funny comments on a wide variety of debates bubbling up in the public arena.

Charles Higham wrote in *The Bulletin* in 1965: 'Cricket performances, women's rights, husbands and wives in Australia, community theatre, the church's teachings, school uniforms, the Pill … you name it and as likely as not Betty Archdale will be quoted on it. Every time anybody wants to get public interest whipped up in a subject, sure enough she's on the spot, her name in heavy type, talking about it together with people like Sir William Yeo, the Reverend Ted Noffs, Andrea or Archbishop Gough.'[2] But it was a surprise to Higham, when he met her in person, to find Betty shy, kind, rather withdrawn and soberly dressed. She appeared to be genuinely embarrassed by her role as spokeswoman on every known subject from Anzac Day to the Zeitgeist.

Betty said the press quoted her anyway, even if she had not spoken to them, so it was far better to talk to journalists when they wanted her to. She never minded publicity for 'my girls' at the school either, as examples of the good side of youth. Often Abbotsleigh girls were asked for interviews or to join panels—all because they were at Betty Archdale's school. Looking through her press clippings, the content of what Betty did say isn't startling or extremely new. It was her persona, conveying ideas in a forthright and fresh way with conviction, that made her prominent. Kath McCredie, who followed Betty as headmistress of Abbotsleigh, said Betty made great statements because she really loved to rouse people from apathy. She used to throw down the gauntlet hoping somebody would take it up. 'I always remember that [above a story on marriage]"Why ask me? I'm a virgin" … and of course that was for the tabloids,' said Kath.[3]

Interestingly, Betty had few difficulties with journalists. She found them fair, maybe because they recognised that she was a giver. Ellis Blain of ABC Radio said, 'The moment you speak to her she's got a wonderful warm response'.[4] As a consequence, Betty not only made an enormous impact on the education of women and girls, but her influence extended far beyond this. She contributed to the life of Sydney, and even Australia, by what she was—a warm and outgoing person, a lover of life, a highly intelligent and independent woman and a keeper of the broad perspective; someone who had seen many changes, but had somehow often managed to be ahead of those changes.

So established did Betty become in the public mind that an article in *The Australian* in 1969 included her as one of the country's intelligentsia, and one of 100 opinion leaders they polled about issues ranging from abortion to republicanism ideals. Amongst her beliefs were that abortion shouldn't be a crime, that Australia didn't need Charles III, that God was necessary to her personally, that individual freedom was slowly being eroded by the increasing standardisation of society, that Australia was becoming too dependent on the USA.[5]

Betty was surprised by the extent to which she enjoyed her public role. However, as she seldom gave a damn what other people thought of her stance it is no wonder that her truthfulness sometimes landed her in controversy. The 1950s concept of suburban perfectionism in middle-class family life—the perfect home, Sunday school for children, long and golden beach holidays, the idealisation of childhood—was under attack in the 1960s. The young sensed that their parents were vaguely unhappy, even angry, trapped in gender and class roles, and they rebelled against them. Parents in turn were often enraged by their children's open pursuit of pleasure, sometimes drug-induced, their challenging of the Vietnam War to the point of going to gaol to avoid their duty to fight, their relaxation of sexual mores, their lack of self-control.

Sex Education

The airing of sexuality became a particularly hot issue. Only six years before Betty came to Abbotsleigh, Professor Alex Stout, Professor of Moral and Political Philosophy at the University of Sydney, had said that Hollywood films were one of the most harmful influences on character the world had ever known![6] In 1961 the NSW government set up the Curlewis Youth Policy Advisory Committee, of which Betty was a member. To it a Dr Victor Kinsella, a Sydney surgeon and amateur philosopher, sent a pamphlet, *Empiricism and Freedom*, which claimed that the empiricist philosophy and psychology taught at both Sydney's universities were corrupting the morals of youth. The Australian academic James Franklin describes how Archbishop Gough, Anglican Archbishop of Sydney, took up the cry and preached on the issue on 6 July 1961, saying that some university lecturers in Sydney were 'teaching ideas which are breaking down the restraints of conscience, decrying the institution of marriage, urging our students to pre-marital sexual experience, advocating free-love and the right of self-expression'. The archbishop called for state action to stem the moral decline.[7] There was an outcry by academics, with Professor John Anderson describing the charges as farcical. Felix Arnott, Betty's friend, swung into defence of the university and said that his archbishop's remarks were grossly uninformed.[8]

With the lability of such opinion in the community, and with her independent thinking and outspokenness, it was only a matter of time before Betty was caught in the spotlight and criticised.

Betty could not fail to recognise, when headmistress, that there was enormous sexual upheaval in Australian society. Sexual freedom was the mantra of the times and the introduction of the Pill emancipated women from the fear of unwanted pregnancies. At the same time there were greater opportunities for women to advance in society with the expansion of higher education and relative affluence. How to prepare her girls for the new sexual age concerned Betty, who initiated innovative sex education classes at Abbotsleigh, but there was a furore when some parents contacted the media to complain.

A journalist with the *Mirror* recalled, a decade later, a phone call to him in December 1962: 'It's an absolute scandal,' the voice was saying. 'When a girl of sixteen is taught things like this, action should be taken against the school. You can imagine what her father said when she asked him what kind of contraceptive he used.' The voice belonged to a woman, in her forties, who lived at Wahroonga. She was one of four mothers who phoned the newspaper that day calling for an investigation into sex talks given to their daughters at Abbotsleigh. Of the other three mothers, two complained in general terms about the frankness of the information given to their daughters; the other said that her daughter had information which she had not learnt until she was 25.

And so the inquiry began. Betty readily agreed to a reporter questioning the people who had given the lectures—one was Betty and the others came from the Marriage Guidance Council.[9]

Betty had become aware from the current affairs classes she took of the girls' concern about how to manage their sexual behaviour. Sometimes when she asked what they wanted to talk about, one of them would say, 'Why not the Pill?' So she'd discuss the 'wretched thing'.[10] When attempts by the Mother and Daughter Movement to talk about sexual matters failed, Betty was drawn to the idea of discussion groups organised by the Marriage Guidance Council, with a dozen girls each to a trained counsellor. It was not compulsory and the parents were given the chance to inquire about it before giving permission. The girls took the discussion group seriously and their questions were mostly concerned with looking for a code of behaviour to do with kissing, petting and how far to go with a boy. 'They wanted to know how to say no nicely, and still keep a boy who is pressuring them,' said Betty. 'It's a terrible problem for a girl of sixteen or seventeen. If she's too negative, she won't be asked out again. On the other hand she must know when to stop.'

Betty described the mother who reported her to the press instead of seeing her as a very silly woman. Luckily the issue was defused before the paper went to print and a mild article appeared, but by the time the next term started in February 1963 the school council was so jittery about the whole idea that the school had to drop the sex education classes.[11] It was up to the parents, stressed Betty, to make clear to their children that they had standards of behaviour in which they believed. And that they should explain why they had them. Parents often opposed sex teaching in schools because of their own sense of guilt about keeping quiet on the subject.[12] In the absence of the discussion groups, it was in the current affairs classes that the girls continued to probe Betty for her attitude and for information on the compelling subject. It was in one of those classes that somebody asked her if she was a virgin and she said, 'Yes and proud of it!'[13]

'I suppose it was possible to think of her as being a virgin who was perfectly happy to be intact and not to have been interfered with by any other person,' said Jennifer Rowe, 'because she was so self-contained—she didn't seem to need it. If you think anything, you would think of her as an asexual being—I mean she was womanly too you know—she's not mannish.'[14]

In 1959, in her final year at school, Meg Matthews said that one of Betty's cautions was, 'Never go to bed with a man till you've got him up the aisle and married him' and then she added, 'because you'll be asked in the next twelve months'. This was news to Meg, who remembers not only being stunned that Betty would say that, but that she was also so up-front about it. There was nothing in her message about shrinking violets waiting to be asked, it was get him up the aisle. It was so feminist.[15]

However, Betty's role as instructor in matters of sexual morality was a delicate one. Because Abbotsleigh was a church school she had, to a certain extent, to stick to the church's stance, which she didn't necessarily agree with. In an article she wrote for *Women's World* in 1973, entitled 'Teenage Dating', she quoted Bishop John Robinson's book *Honest to God*:

For nothing can of itself always be labelled as 'wrong'. One cannot, for instance, start from the position that sex relations before marriage or divorce are wrong or sinful in themselves. They may be in 99 cases or even 100 cases out of 100, but they are not intrinsically so, for the only intrinsic evil is lack of love. To the young man asking in his relationship with a girl 'Why shouldn't I?' it is relatively easy to say 'Because it's wrong or because it's a sin'—and then to condemn him when he, or his whole generation takes no notice.

It makes a much greater demand to ask and to answer the question, 'Do you love her?' Or how much do you love her and then to help him to accept for himself the decision that, if he doesn't, or doesn't very much deeply, then his action is immoral. If he does then he will respect her far too much to use her or take liberties with her. Chastity is the expression of charity—of caring enough. And this is the criterion for every form of behaviour, inside marriage or out of it, in sexual ethics or in any other field. For nothing else makes a thing right or wrong.[16]

That sexual mores will keep on changing, Betty had no doubt, but while behaviour patterns would continue to evolve, she advised adhering to the standards you believed in. She made it clear that she thought that sleeping around was unhealthy both physically and mentally, and bad for society.

When in 1966 Betty's friend Dr Grace Cuthbert Browne spoke at the headmistresses conference, she gave figures of the increasing incidence of venereal disease in the fifteen to nineteen age group and the high number of out-of-wedlock pregnancies. In response, Betty devised a pilot scheme stressing the importance of a stable family life and its influence on the developing child, and that full satisfaction in marriage cannot come to those who do not know how to love or the meaning of loyalty.[17]

In Defence of *Oz*

If the attention Betty received from the press about her approach to sex education shocked the Anglican hierarchy, her refusal to outlaw an obscene publication infuriated them more.

It was in 1964 when children of comfortable homes became freewheeling, peroxide-haired surfies, riding the waves by day and partying animalistically at night to the tune of Little Pattie's 'He's My Blond Headed

Stompie Wompie Real Gone Surfer Boy'. Martin Sharp, who along with Richard Neville and Richard Walsh was editor of the satirical *Oz* magazine, reflected the scene by writing a first-person monologue, 'The Word Flashed Around the Arms' (the Newport Arms Hotel), in the voice of a gatecrasher. The story, which was to revolutionise the country's attitude to censorship, ran:

> The word flashed around the Arms that there was a GAS turn up at Whale Beach Road, so we piled into the Mini Coopers and thrashed over. And you know what? The old man of the bird who was having the party said we couldn't crash—so Dennis belted him and we all piled in and had a helluva lot of grog. There were a few KING birds there, but they were all holding hands with these fairies—so Dennis belted them and we all go onto the birds and Frank got one of them so pissed that she passed out and we all went through her like a packet of salts—KING! And so it continued until Sid, the funniest bloke I know, kicked in the TV set and chucked in it. God it was FUNNY.[18]

A Detective Sergeant Green read the article after he had received a letter of complaint from a reader and he launched a prosecution. After interviews with the Vice Squad, the Crown opened its case against *Oz* in July 1964.

In law, a publication was obscene if found to have a tendency to deprave, corrupt or injure the morals of people into whose hands it was likely to fall. A work of 'literary or artistic merit' was exempt, so the editors searched for support amongst literary and influential figures. In his memoirs, *Hippie Hippie Shake*, Richard Neville said:

> A visit to the university was less dispiriting; several former lecturers agreed to testify. But still—we needed a heavyweight from the world at large. At Abbotsleigh Ladies' College in Warrawee [sic], Mart and I presented ourselves to the silver-haired headmistress, Betty Archdale. A Master of Law, a member of the English Bar, she sat on the Council of the Girl Guides Association. I drew her attention to the 'The Word Flashed Around the Arms'. 'Utterly disgusting,' she said.
> 'You mean the whole magazine?' Might she too be an agent of the Crown?
> 'Oh no. I mean the behaviour it portrays.' Her senior girls had complained of such 'goings-on'. Sharp's satire was 'salutary' and she would be

delighted to testify. The bell clanged and we floated from her office. Nine hundred school girls swarmed into the playground, hurling their straw hats over our heads and swamping us in their high spirits.[19]

The three editors managed to gather seventeen experts for the defence and, true to her word, Betty Archdale told the magistrate that the morals of the girls in her care would not be injured by their exposure to Martin Sharp's humour. In the *Sydney Morning Herald* it was reported that the headmistress of Abbotsleigh 'said the article was not one she would recommend to her pupils because it described incidents which were crude and unpleasant. She said the article would not deprave or corrupt the reader … Miss Archdale told Mr G.A. Locke SM that she thought two expressions used in the magazine were offensive, but not obscene.'[20]

Francis James, who headed the Anglican Press which was charged with printing an obscene publication, was also in court. It was significant that this champion of free speech, with an inherent sense of drama, dressed in an ankle length greatcoat and polishing his large contact lenses with a silk scarf, described Betty's performance on the stand before the belligerent magistrate as superb. 'One of the highlights of the trials, to us alleged criminals, was her reaction to a suggestive question by the Prosecutor,' he said. 'She straightened her spectacles, seemed to grow six inches taller, and looked sternly down on the poor man. A pause. Then "I—beg—your—pardon" she said in tones which conjured up the spectacle of First Officer Archdale on parade. The Prosecutor gulped "No more questions, ma'am" and retreated. Betty gave the Bench a cursory nod and stalked out of the box.' Francis James added that Archbishop Gough was extremely angry when Betty gave evidence in the *Oz* matter, because he held the same views as the prosecution.[21]

In September the defendants were found guilty and received gaol sentences. There was both a public outcry and an appeal, at which Judge Aaron Levine announced in February 1965 that 'The Word Flashed Around the Arms' did not glorify gatecrashers. On the contrary, it created feelings of 'revulsion, abhorrence and censure'. Might it corrupt young girls? No, he had been reassured by Betty Archdale.[22]

Betty's role in the case may in part have been responsible for the announcement in October 1964 of a Commission of Inquiry to study the responsibilities of the Church of England in public and private education in the diocese of Sydney. It was to be a thirteen-man commission including the headmaster of Shore, Mr B. H. Travers.[22] The following year Archbishop Gough urged Christian teachers to support the election of people of religious faith to positions of influence in the Teachers Federation.

But despite the church's disapproval of her stance in the *Oz* case, Betty's public standing seems to have grown because in November of the same year she was invited onto a panel, which included clergy, to review the satirical television review, *The Mavis Bramston Show*, which some found to be blasphemous and smutty. Her response was that if television programs are going to be geared to the sort of home which is nice and well-behaved and quiet then it might be just as well to throw the whole television system over.

However, it must have taken great skill to shepherd her girls through highly charged times. In 1965 students began a series of protests against the US and Australian involvement in the war in Vietnam. And then on 13 June 1966 an article appeared in *Oz* magazine which was considered defamatory of Abbotsleigh girls. The chairman received a number of telephone calls from parents and a letter from the administrator of the diocese of Sydney drawing his attention to the article, but legal opinion advised that it would be difficult to sustain a charge against the publishers.[24]

When the fear of drug usage was mounting, Betty was brave enough to say that there was evidence that pure marijuana, on its own, did no harm at all—although there was also evidence that 90 percent of hardline drug addicts used marijuana as a starting point. She said that the drug problem was not as bad as newspapers painted it but it was bad enough for parents to be constantly on their guard. Youngsters went to parties where they were offered drugs, usually 'soft stuff', she said. Pressed by a questioner as to whether marihuana should be legalised she said she honestly did not know.[25]

By 1968, Abbotsleigh under Betty Archdale had grown in reputation enormously. It had a current waiting list extending to 1978 and parents had to register their babies at three months old to have a chance of acceptance. But internally, trouble was brewing.

When Peter Duly joined the council in 1967, and became honorary secretary, he immediately perceived the terrific problem that existed between Betty and Adam Lang, the chairman. It wasn't as if there were major problems within the school. In 1963 Betty received a letter from a university lecturer from Melbourne saying that his choice of Abbotsleigh as a school for his 4-week-old daughter was because he had been impressed by the Abbotsleigh girls when interviewing applicants for the science faculty.[26]

Writing about the visit by Abbotsleigh girls to the Wayside Chapel in 1964, the Rev. Ted Noffs said: 'Let me assure you that they impressed me at one and the same time with their sense of Discipline and Responsibility [sic], coupled with a lively interest in all that was happening around them. They were a fascinating group and they certainly speak well of the training they are receiving at Abbotsleigh. You have every reason to be very, very proud of them.'[27]

At that time Abbotsleigh was on top in all ways—academically, in sport and with this wonderful feeling that had been built into the girls. The problems between Betty and Adam Lang were purely to do with who should be at the top of the hierarchy of power. They were both trained in the law, both highly intelligent and strong personalities. Both were confident of their ability and in their own judgment. Both spoke their minds. Each was a catalyst to the other and their partnership was never dull. Adam Lang's wife, Joy, said: 'I think they were like oil and water. Peter Duly and Kath McCredie [later chairman and headmistress respectively] stroked each other's feathers. Ad [Adam] would never stroke feathers. They were both lawyers who perhaps wanted to be cock of the roost.'[28]

'I'm sorry that I quarrelled so much with Lang,' Betty later reflected. 'But really what got under my skin was he wasn't loyal. If parents, as they frequently did of course, went to him and complained, he didn't say go and see the head about it, he took their side always, and came to me to try and put it right. Well that doesn't work, and I got very annoyed and rather rude … so we were at arm's length.'

Peter Duly said that Bill Farram, who was the school's honorary treasurer for years, told him that it was embarrassing travelling into town on the train with Adam Lang because he wouldn't lower his voice, so the whole carriage heard what he was saying about Betty Archdale.[29] Betty hated such disloyalty, and although she was slow to anger she felt that if someone let her down she could never feel the same way about them again. She did bear grudges, and it took her a long time to forgive.

School council meetings became the arena for the expression of mutual hostilities. Adam Lang was renowned for organising every meeting beforehand so it progressed without hiccups. Such an approach only annoyed Betty, who believed it was healthier to discuss matters.

Lang's modus operandi was particularly evident in the selection process for Betty's successor. The third-last meeting was to reduce the applicants to three, then the next meeting was to reduce the three to two, and at the last meeting the council would reduce that two to one. But Archbishop Marcus Loane turned up at the penultimate meeting and in typical fashion said, 'Mr Lang, I found that I had a free evening and I thought that I would attend this meeting'. According to Peter Duly:

> Adam Lang was ropeable, he didn't want him there, he wanted him at the last meeting. But of course the archbishop was the president of the council and that took precedence over the chairman and he said, 'Mr Lang, I think that we could possibly save a meeting by reducing the three to one this evening'. And Adam Lang was furious—you could see him, he was sort of containing himself, absolutely seething, that here was this man who had the temerity to interfere with his program …
>
> Anyway, getting back to this situation—so she [Kath McCredie] was chosen. Then Adam Lang got up and said (in a raised voice), 'Mr Chairman I then propose three motions' … and he repeated, he sort of stuttered these three motions and they were long motions, and I thought completely unnecessary. And the first was that having made the selection we then had to put the motion to the council that we select one of those three. After that had happened Adam Lang said, 'We must be unanimous,' so the motion was then that we appoint Kath McCredie as headmistress—so that it was a unanimous vote.
>
> That was the first motion and he phrased it in all sorts of fandangled words and the other two motions were constitutional motions and I for-

get them. But the archbishop said, 'Yes, Mr Lang, we will take each motion separately. Now the first motion' and he repeated it word for word
(he hadn't been briefed on this), so we discussed that, then we voted on it.
And he said 'your second motion was' … and the same with the third
motion. And I thought, 'Wow'. And Adam Lang was completely speech-
less after all this, being so annoyed.[30]

According to Peter Duly this was an indication of what happened
in council meetings. Betty could only feel riled by Lang's dominance
and she reacted by being difficult, without appearing to be so. In the
meetings she would either say or do unusual things. It wasn't until her
book, *Indiscretions of a Headmistress*, was released that Duly discovered
that Betty and another member of council (Barbara Clarke) used to
have a contest to see who would use an obscure word first. Betty's only
independence from the chairman's scrutiny was the chapel fund—monies
earned by the chapel for services and weddings. She was emphatic that
no one interfere with it and she used the money to enhance the chapel
or other aspects of the school as she saw fit.

Although Betty liked to be in control, she did not see herself as a
powerful person, a person who could get others to do the things she
wanted them to do. To fight it out with Adam in the council meeting
was not her style. Usually, provided she didn't disagree intensely, she
liked to gain agreement with people, due partly to a desire to please—to
be considered pleasant and intelligent.

At one stage during Betty's headship, a group of the synod members
of the council came to Peter Duly and asked him if he would stand
against Adam Lang at the annual council election because they were so
unhappy about his dictatorial ways and his treating people with disdain.
Peter said he couldn't be party to it, for even though Adam Lang had
antagonised the headmistress and it was a difficult situation, he had served
the school well and given it a lot of his time, so he had to leave of his
own accord.

It soon became clear that not only did Adam and Betty frustrate
each other within the council meetings, they got very annoyed with
each other on occasions as well. Although new to his position of honorary
secretary, Peter Duly decided to call on Betty in her study to discuss the

problem. It was in the last nine months of her time as head and he was a little bit wary of her because he was young and inexperienced. But he could see a 'bust up' between Betty Archdale and Adam Lang looming and, as she didn't have too long to go, he asked if she could try not to have any 'big insurrections'. 'And she looked at me very benignly and I could see her, figuratively speaking, patting me on the head as she would a little boy, with whom she was reasonably happy, looking at me and saying, "I will behave". But I could see the expression on her face. There was devilment in the corners of her mouth, her lips were sort of grinning, there was a smile on her face saying, "Yes how delicious this moment is with this guy who's so nervous about saying this to me"—and then this wonderful "I will behave!" I could never forget that.'[31]

With Adam Lang unanimously re-elected as chairman by the council in February 1965, with a vote of thanks for the unstinting way he had given of his time and energies, Betty had to curtail her behaviour. At times, when she felt under siege, she would lock her study door and pull down the blinds and pretend she wasn't there. A dark and lonely sanctuary.

Betty lived in the grounds of the school in Read House, away from the main buildings, down below the top oval. She had a housekeeper, Miss Filose, who mothered her, devotedly mounting the stairs at six o'clock each morning with a cup of hot water and making Betty's meals at night. Betty had living rooms downstairs and two bedrooms upstairs. Partitioned off were two small dormitories for boarders in their final year. They never disturbed her and she felt quite private.[32]

While Betty had marvellous friends, she didn't make them easily, as she once said, due to a reserve, tied up with shyness … or self-centredness, she added ruefully. Being at the top of an organisation is a lonely role, and Betty, without a partner, was vulnerable in her isolation. She found the eleven years at Abbotsleigh, while enjoyable, were nevertheless exhausting. She was on the job seven days a week and had little freedom in the holidays. She'd escape to her house in Galston on Sundays for a few hours, mow the lawn and dig up flower beds to rid herself of anger.

In times of severe strain she reminded herself of a book which she said was particularly important in her life, *Living Time* by Morris Nichol. The book emphasises a universality of being that is not material. The real person is invisible and capable of living on a higher dimension that cannot be measured by linear time. It enhanced her spiritual understanding and provided a perspective that eschewed pettiness—that the world would not come to an end if an Abbotsleigh girl didn't wear a hat or if she ate a bun in public. 'What is this strange now and then which when perceived together cause the mind to tremble on the verge of new meaning,' read her brother Alec Archdale in a radio interview in which she discussed the book.[33]

The youthfulness of the girls to whom she was relating also marked her sense of aloneness. At Women's College the limited numbers enabled her to have much contact with students, and as they were undergraduates she could talk to them directly. At Abbotsleigh, with more than 600 girls in the senior school and the associated huge amount of routine work, it was impossible to have the same degree of interaction. While Betty probably had a greater influence on the girls of school age than those at Women's College, she was also aware that with a schoolgirl one had to be faintly on guard with progressive ideas—otherwise the mother might come in the next day and say 'what do you mean?'

When at Women's College, if she was worried about anything she could talk to Felix Arnott at St Paul's College or Bert Wyllie at Wesley, but at Abbotsleigh she had no peers in the immediate vicinity with whom she could discuss or share problems. A marked degree of intimate support fell away when her first deputy, Dorothy Hughesdon, died and Betty never had the same relationship with other deputies. The headmistress of PLC Pymble, Dorothy Knox, was domineering and had completely different views on how a school should be run. Neither did Betty have a rapport with the headmaster of Knox, Dr Ross McKenzie. She did get on quite well with the headmaster of Barker, Trevor McCaskill, but it wasn't of the same depth as her friendships with the university college men.

Resignation

Betty was often quoted as saying that a principal can best serve the interests of the college by accepting the job for not less than five years and not more than ten. After ten years at Abbotsleigh, in 1968, she was tired of the demands of the job and the ongoing battles. She was getting bad tempered and irritated and she knew it was time to move on and fight again.

Apart from her constant chafing with Adam Lang she was becoming more frustrated with some of the parents. Then there were the boarding houses. Somehow she hadn't hauled them into line by attracting good housekeepers. Some of the housemistresses shut themselves up in their rooms each weekend and smoked like chimneys and Betty had allowed this to happen. The fact that her successor quickly cleaned up the boarding establishments made hollow Betty's protestations that good people weren't available to run them.

Betty was further frustrated by the rigid and old-fashioned examination-ridden framework of the bureaucratic education system. She thought the Wyndham scheme would have been fine if it hadn't been increasingly constrained by the culture of exam results as the ultimate mark of success.[34]

Yet the school's academic standards remained intact. The staff was of a high standard and the students came from a population that was interested in education. People praised the school to the skies. Some described Abbotsleigh girls of the time as being too outspoken, too powerful, too pushy, arguing the toss about anything, not accepting the baseline of the new hierarchies they entered on leaving school. 'People were able to pick us out in the dining room because of our laughter,' admitted Merilyn Bryce, who went from Abbotsleigh to Women's College at the University of Sydney.[35]

When Betty expressed a desire to retire Adam Lang recommended that she travel overseas for three months, at the council's expense, to study modern trends in education. He was keen to have as Betty's successor Miss Kath McCredie, who was headmistress of SCEGGS Wollongong, but as she wasn't ready to make the move to Abbotsleigh Lang wanted Betty to remain in situ until the circumstances were ripe for the changeover.

After her trip to the USA, the UK and the Continent Betty was welcomed home in July 1968. The finances of the school were in better condition than they had been twelve months previously. She recommended raises for teacher salaries in 1969, up to 90 percent of the departmental rates, with an increase in fees. When the senior mistress, Mrs Tyson, left at the end of 1968 Betty recommended that there be two senior mistresses appointed. Eventually Betty wrote to the council on 3 December 1968 tendering her resignation. The council accepted her resignation, including in its statement that it 'is grateful for the friendly relationship between the Headmistress and the council which has existed throughout her term of office. It believes that Miss Archdale has been one of the great headmistresses of the school.'[36] The council also placed on record that:

> Her time at Abbotsleigh has been called a 'breath of fresh air' and that generations were established of people who will benefit from this time.
>
> The girls who have passed through this school over the past 12 years have been subjected to a most unusual form of discipline. There has been guidance with a minimum of control and regimentation. This has produced a questioning frame of mind that allows girls to contemplate breaking down all existing concepts if they felt that a better way of living or of doing things could be achieved by doing so. That is, girls have emerged from the school who were capable of real individual thought. Yet at the same time, they have an appreciation of why it is necessary to conform to the important concepts of our society.[37]

Her Significance

There is no doubt that Betty was in the right place at the right time. Her vision for the education of girls uncannily anticipated the new role of women in a maturing Australian society. Being free of sex stereotyping and self-limiting behaviours, she was able to show her students how irrelevant were the restrictions imposed on married women before and after the war. Instead she represented a contemporary, career-focused role model for young women.

It was her student-centred orientation in the school that revealed an attitude well ahead of her time, wrote Dianne Henshaw. Instead of conforming to a male-dominated value system which was evident in school administrations during the 1960s, she believed that the academic needs of students had to be served by administration and not dominated by it.[38] She was forward thinking, and experimental in curriculum design, yet she was practical. She created a positive educational climate for girls and dismantled the hostility she had perceived between the staff and the students by attracting teachers who could relate better and who were able to excite the girls in their subjects.

While she described her style in dealing with staff as dictatorial, Betty's lack of teacher training also allowed her to be tolerant with staff and students because she was aware of their different backgrounds. She was successful in balancing an administrative leadership style and an inspirational, pastoral element. Her standards of behaviour were expected, and if students transgressed she expressed disappointment.

Betty was very mindful of the reasons why students were sent to independent schools and was advanced in recognising that the parents were, after all, the school customers. She was equally aware that parental interference in the running of the school restricted her autonomy, but she clearly believed that only one person can run a school, and that must be the head.

Most significantly, Betty showed the girls that there was greater honesty in nonconformity. In doing so she prepared them well in advance for the emergence of female power.

In 1970, the year Betty finally left the school, *The Female Eunuch* was published, with Germaine Greer exhorting women to reject every institution and assumption about their lives. The new picture she painted was the world of a woman who had decided to stop trying to please, to stop waiting to be loved, a woman who owed nothing to anyone but herself. 'Unlike the first wave of feminists who having gained the vote, were then at pains not to disrupt society or unseat the God, this was Greer's real aim—Revolution not mere rebellion,' wrote Susan Mitchell of the book and its impact. 'Like de Beauvoir she encouraged women to question their entry into the institution of marriage, and if trapped unhappily, to run away. She encouraged them to experiment sexually, to be economically independent and emotionally self-sufficient.'[39] Not that Germaine Greer saw women who set out on their own journeys as having an easier or even more pleasant time. 'Liberty is terrifying, but it is also exhilarating,' she said.

When Betty announced her retirement, the press leapt into print in response. Under the headline 'The Swinging Head Who Is Retiring to Have Fun', Janet Hawley wrote:

> Betty Archdale's glasses slid casually down her nose as she leaned forward, saucer-eyed and grinning and said, 'I'm leaving because I want to have fun. I'm going to retire and have a marvellous relaxing, swinging time … '
>
> The announcement of Miss Archdale's retirement comes as the proverbial bombshell to her 1100 pupils and their parents who regard her with immense friendship as a 'fabulous, with it, top-drawer' person.
>
> It will disappoint those many people who have booked their children into Abbotsleigh purely because Miss Archdale is its head.
>
> For they've seen this progressive, open minded woman, frequently criticised by other schools for her belief in free self-discipline for her pupils—turn the school into probably the most energetic in Sydney.
>
> At 61 Miss Archdale is a vital enthusiastic and gregarious person with none of the stiff reserve characteristic of headmistresses.
>
> She's forever throwing her head back, slapping her knees and roaring with uninhibited laughter whether she's at a school assembly or a well-wined dinner party.
>
> She'll vigorously uphold the right of her girls to wear their uniforms mini-length and be up with the fashion if that's what they want.
>
> This is characteristic of her whole attitude she says, 'I try to say yes to any girl's request whether it is starting up a new subject or discussing drugs, Vietnam, sex or anything else that is on their minds'.[40]

Quoting Betty's boast, 'I always tell my girls the truth', papers said that her many controversial statements, some of which surprised even her students, will live on after her. In the *Mirror*: 'Miss Archdale has altered the image of the private school from that of a stuffy education machine to a place where girls can voice the problems they face in adolescence; where groundwork is laid for social sophistication and where a girl can get what Miss Archdale calls "a wide education". The public has certainly not heard the last of her. She said she had "not entirely frivolous thoughts of writing a book".[41] That book, which would help her to get a lot off her chest, would be light-hearted and definitely libellous.

Betty suddenly became society's sage on education and it seems that whatever comment she made, however flippantly, found its way into print. However, her greatest and by no means flippant message was that it was not more money that was needed in schools so much as a great deal more thought.

She pointed out that adult authority increasingly was being challenged, first in the universities, now in the sixth forms, and that it would work its way lower down in the school as well. Pupil power stemmed from student discontent. With the additional year of schooling, teachers could no longer treat young adults of sixteen to eighteen years like children. She saw the students of this age group as being as mature as their mothers were at about age 22. They were drinking and their life outside school was dramatically different from that at school. If teachers were to retain some control they would have to share it with their pupils.[42] There was increasing pressure coming from students to express their view on the kind of education they wanted, and she added that girls were much franker at school now than in her day. They talked things over with their teachers more than she ever did, they had more poise and were not as socially gauche.

Betty argued for the diversification of schools. Society ought to fit the schools to the children and not, as now, the children to the schools. She saw the need to give bright children the type of education that will stretch them to the limit and prepare them for tertiary studies. Otherwise the schools could expect boredom, antagonism and anti-social behaviour. 'As long as all children have equal opportunities to attend schools, what is wrong with one type of school for the academic, another for the artistic or musical and a variety of others for the non-academic?' she asked.

For some 50 percent of children, education outside an academic school would be better. Why shouldn't education be carried on in farms, in factories, offices, shops and garages for those who dislike and are bored with the academic approach? Betty recommended first-rate school counselling and children being free to move back into school or from one type of school to another. Schools should be integrated with the community, with classes being open to any interested adults in the area. The mixing of youngsters with another age group would improve the discipline in schools.[43] She liked the idea of separate schools for pupils in their final two years, like the Canberra colleges. And also the establishment of learning centres where anyone, of any age or educational standard, could go and be taught anything they wanted to know.

Betty was convinced that there was too much teaching in the schools and not enough real learning. Students often learnt more on their own. She felt it was important that students be encouraged to seek out information for themselves to develop an inquiring mind. And while she would hate to see all schools become coeducational, Betty thought that if males and females were going to live together it's just as well if they were schooled together. But the social mores must equate girls and boys, women and men, and in the 1960s a teenage girl still seemed awfully concerned with pleasing boys. 'I have no doubt coeducation is right because children in this situation develop a healthy disrespect for the opposite sex,' she said.[44]

Regarding teachers, surely, Betty said, a test could be devised to eliminate those who were lazy or power seekers before they reached the profession, and allow only hard workers with patience, humour and a love of children to teach. On the whole, secondary teachers were extremely conservative and needed to be pushed along. It was up to the rest of society to do the pushing. Education follows society, it does not lead.[45]

Betty said she envisaged a time when a school would have two heads—one administrative and the other concerned with education—because it was increasingly important for the head of a school to be forward-thinking and innovative.

She also noted that the cause of most of the troubles in schools was the sheer quantity of knowledge that was increasing at a frightening rate. This, plus the competitive nature of society, put a strain on educational facilities. An answer could be for primary and secondary schools to concentrate on the techniques of learning—how to work out problems, how to manipulate figures, how to express themselves freely in written and spoken English and in other languages—and leave the mass of factual learning to the tertiary stage.

She encouraged parents to become literate in educational trends, to read the Williams Report, a national inquiry which examined secondary and tertiary education and its effects on employment and which recommended extensive revision. She believed new technology could enable children to do their work in half the time. This in turn could allow schools time to inspire students, to teach them that consensus is more important than confrontation, that competition isn't all that important, that the essential thing is to communicate with others and socialise well. She felt there was panic in the community about educating for jobs. But she saw it as more important to help people determine what to do in the seventeen hours a day they were not working. Many people hadn't the faintest idea what to do, they didn't read, or go to concerts, or plays, they weren't interested in exploring nature. People needed to be encouraged to use their leisure time effectively, to be self-sufficient.[46]

On the subject of the Higher School Certificate, Betty questioned its single mark's accuracy as a fair test of knowledge and ability. Ideally there would be two examinations. One would test what students had learnt in six years of secondary schooling. A certificate would show the subjects studied and the level achieved. The other examination would test the intellectual powers needed for admission to university faculties, CAEs (Colleges of Advanced Education) and technical colleges.

As for quotas, she thought it would be fairer to interview students who were three marks above or below the cut-off lines and consult their school records. In fact Betty felt so strongly about the issue of one mark only being considered for admission to universities that in April 1969, at the time of the restructuring of the HSC, she wrote to Professor Taylor, chairman of the Professorial Board of the University of Sydney: 'We have to advise students to take not necessarily the best subjects for them educationally and not the subjects which will prepare them best for the University course, but subjects at which they will amass the biggest total— thus gaining entrance to the University and Faculty of their choice and a Commonwealth Scholarship.'[47]

She was also concerned that students who were keen to do medicine and who had good academic ability, who related easily to others and who were humane, warm and stable, responsible and mature, were failing to gain sufficient marks to be included in university quotas. In a letter to *The Australian* in conjunction with other teachers and doctors, she wrote: 'The only way such pupils can gain sufficient marks is to do little else but academic study, especially in their final year. They are thus the poorer because they are deprived of worthwhile experiences in matters social, intellectual, cultural and physical. The school is the poorer because their experience and influence as leaders are not available.' She suggested that a number of marks be added to the HSC aggregate on the basis of information supplied by heads of school.'[48]

Betty also believed that it would be an advantage if there was a greater mobility of university students between universities. And she could see the beginning of a quaternary form of education, of continuing education through refresher courses, and adult education courses for the whole of life. Not only should those engaged in technical or professional work keep up to date, but the knowledge explosion was such that none of us could afford to stop learning.

The Succession

On 21 May 1969, at a special council meeting with the Archbishop of Sydney present, Miss Kathleen McCredie received an absolute majority over the other two candidates to follow Betty Archdale as headmistress of Abbotsleigh. She had been headmistress of SCEGGS Wollongong for fourteen years and was known as an able administrator with a distinguished sports record.

Tension soon surfaced when Betty, who had been prevailed upon to stay at the school a year longer than she wanted, realised that Kath McCredie would not be coming at the beginning of 1970. Kath was waiting for the completion of a building program at her school, after she which she wished to travel, including to Oberammergau, before commencing at Abbotsleigh. A tired and angry Betty wrote to the council in September 1969 expressing her displeasure with the situation.[49] She was understandably unhappy that the council asked her to meet Kath McCredie's needs rather than giving dignity to her own. Because of Betty's disquiet Kath's proposed date of arrival was brought forward to July 1970. As this was still not mid-term, Betty again wrote to the council expressing her disappointment.[50]

Kath McCredie said that she and Betty met at a heads dinner and

Betty made some caustic comment, something like 'I'll never talk to you again'. It was a childish sort of comment but it really hit home. 'I was quite hurt,' Kath said. 'However, we've been good friends since and I must say she never came near the school. Once she went, she went.'[51] While she saw her as a nice person, Betty wondered if Kath would be too conventional to perpetuate the changes she had introduced, and if the diocese, in pursuit of her successor, was more concerned with churchmanship than education.[52]

Eventually it was noted that Miss Archdale would officially retire on 7 May 1970. But the delay in her departure was at a great emotional and physical cost to her. There was an extraordinary amount of nervous energy involved in dealing with children and conciliating staff, while the constant fighting with the council and particular parents was exhausting. In the end Betty described herself as 'a cot case'.[53] Peter Duly recalls one particular morning: 'I was down there looking at the lower oval [with its drainage problems] and I was away in the middle of the oval and she came from Read House up the steps to go to her office and she only just about made it to the top of the steps. She was so tired … she looked so thoroughly worn out this particular morning.'

The consequences of Betty's tiredness meant that the school had slipped towards the end of her time. Peter Duly described an evening at the school which included both boys and girls and one of the mistresses came to Betty and said, 'I believe they are smoking pot' and Betty said, 'What do you expect?' and didn't do anything about it.[54]

The changeover of headmistresses was very unhappy. Betty wasn't in control, she was in a makeshift position—a stand-in—and she didn't see it as her role in life to be a stand-in.

Yet for Betty her time at Abbotsleigh was one of her richest experiences. Although she felt she had not adequately achieved her main aim to make Abbotsleigh an up-to-date school, in touch with the twentieth century and leading into the new millennium, she decided that she had succeeded enough to make it all worthwhile. When asked, after she had left the school, what she was most successful at doing, Betty replied that it was in making a group of people happy. 'I liked the girls, with few exceptions,' she said, 'and I think, with few exceptions, they liked me. I don't know why—but I sort of make a group get together.' She attributed this skill to her personality, to a certain lack of confidence that meant she didn't dominate. Mainly because she was never quite certain if she was right.[55]

Several years into her retirement the ABC interviewer Ellis Blain asked Betty what was her most valuable memory of Abbotsleigh. Her reply was unusually emotional. With great speed and warmth she said: 'Oh the children—a few individual children but I think more en masse—their general friendliness, their responsiveness, the way they smile and say thank you and hello and whacko! almost and this sort of general friendly attitude is terribly rewarding.'[56]

The more the ferment of controversy clothed Betty in her last days at Abbotsleigh, the fiercer was the girls' loyalty to her. 'Quite the nicest bouquet I ever received was when an eight-year-old told her mother,"She's not much to look at but she loves us".' The older girls loved her because she stirred up the dinner tables of the north shore line. 'I still reckon that the people that gave the bad name to Abbotsleigh were the mothers at the card tables,' said Jill Auld. 'My mother would play cards and I'd come home and she'd tell me all the things that were supposed to be happening at Abbotsleigh. It was nonsense, they were so jealous!'[57]

The girls were not the only ones who were upset. Some of the teachers were also hurt on Betty's behalf. For example, the College of Education gave fellowships to people who had contributed substantially to education. Despite other heads receiving fellowships, Betty, who had also served on the Senate of the University of Sydney for 25 years, was not included, despite nomination.[58] There was a feeling that some heads of schools thought she was a bit way out, they were scandalised by some of the newspaper comments, and while some respected her intellectual ability few respected her idea of discipline.

Freda Whitlam, who was headmistress of PLC Croydon during the period of Betty's headship at Abbotsleigh said she felt closer to Betty than to any other of the heads:

'She never grandstanded amongst headmistresses. She wasn't personally ambitious—she was there to serve the girls. She was thoroughly contemporary—she knew what was going on more than most heads did … I never thought of her as terribly academic but she was more than most heads were. It always struck me that she was doing her own thing—she was a liberated spirit.

' I doubt she was always appreciated by her council. If there were any difficulties with the council I suspect I would be on her side—I don't think she would lick boots. I thought she was terrific. I think the girls saw the best of her—perhaps the seniors most of all. Some maybe thought she may not have crossed all the t's and dotted all the i's like some heads are expected to. But she was a true person with a very deep spirituality which was so much part of her she didn't need to advertise it. I think she would have got on better at Abbotsleigh than at SCEGGS which was more connected to the diocese.'[59]

Betty's legacy remained in the school, with the staff always putting the girls first. 'What they give to the school is incredible,' said Elva Julien. Betty's name and approach continued to be linked with the school long after her departure. Kath McCredie found following Betty's headship one of the hardest things she had to do in her life. 'I mean still people say to me if they don't know anything about Abbotsleigh, "Oh that's where that well-known cricketer was head"—and I sigh. But … her vision. Yes, her vision was very extensive.'[60]

Goodbye Archie

On the eve of her retirement Betty said, 'It's the end of having a lot of keys on a key ring. Now I have only one, my front door key.' The lightness of tone camouflaged her real feelings. 'I was very upset the day I left,' she later admitted, 'I can remember that. Oh yes I missed it—I hurt.'

The last assembly was described by the *Mirror*:

Goodbye Archie 850 school girls yelled as they farewelled a living legend yesterday. Many had tears in their eyes. Betty had a rousing send off on her last morning at the school … From early morning they were slipping into her office in twos and threes to make their private farewells, then in mid morning the senior girls gathered in the gaily decorated school hall for the end of term prize-giving.

Miss Archdale made the presentation in the same matter of fact way she had done for 12 years as principal. She seemed not to notice the huge banner which faced her from the balcony. It said simply 'Goodbye Archie'.

After the prize presentation, the school senior prefect Elizabeth Quinnell moved on to the stage and handed over a gift with the words, 'thank you for everything. Thank you for everything. Thank you for allowing us to be individuals. We are sorry to lose you.'

There was a call for three cheers. And then all hell broke lose. Streamers were hurled from all parts of the hall towards the stage and the full blooded piercing screams of 850 girls rent the air.

An obviously touched Miss Archdale—after throwing a few streamers back playfully—fled from the hall.

But the cheering girls surged after her down the school avenue. They spilled onto the Pacific Highway oblivious to the passing traffic and cheered and cheered while Miss Archdale sought the refuge of her car. Her lips were trembling as she uttered an almost curt 'bye bye'. A moment later she was gone.

Back behind the mass of pushing cheering girls there were many who wept privately. The kind of girls who had first called on Miss Archdale, the shy and the timid and the introverted. They were the ones who felt her going the most. For Miss Archdale the most controversial, respected and outspoken educationalist in Australia always had time to sit down and listen to the girls with a problem. Senior prefect Elizabeth Quinell said, 'She has given an incalculable amount, not only in terms of time and ideas, but of herself.'[61]

17

FREEWHEELING

Jung believed that a person is happiest and most effective in life when his perceived social self is close to his subconscious, internal self … but that too many people act according to how they believe society sees them, rather than being in touch with their real feelings. He stressed how important it was for people to come back to living a very simple existence. In returning to Galston, Betty was happy to exist with little artifice. When she was at her busiest, she once said in an interview, the thing she valued most was time, time to live, time to do. Now she had it.

When Alec was alive they were self-sufficient in vegetables and fruit, picking oranges, apples and pears from the trees they had planted and making jam and plum sauce. Betty took great pleasure in walking down to the bush on her land, through lovely trees, checking the potato crop. Sometimes she could hear Alec shout out in the bush the lines of the latest script he was learning. Outside the house she would shower the stone terrace with crumbs and birds of all kinds would peck them up while Betty addressed them as 'dear'. And there was the daily ritual of gathering and cutting wood. Participating in the rhythms of nature and being in her own space were important to her.

She hungrily read a wide range of books. She was able to spend more time with the neighbours with whom she had a special bond—those who had helped with the construction of the house. When Helen and Alec first arrived the Bells lived opposite. Dennis Bell was a scientist who lectured at the University of New South Wales. He and Alec got on very well and would sit outside and talk. The Watsons and the Lowndes lived down the road.

The area was made remote by the gorge and it was mainly rural. The social tone was unpretentious and friendly. It was a small community in the 1960s and '70s, everybody knew everyone else and neighbours formed groups to assist each other. Betty became involved with the Galston Neighbourhood Centre, helping organise transport for the sick and elderly who had to visit doctors on the other side of the gorge. In her later years a neighbour, Margaret Brownscombe, invited Betty to participate in monthly readings of Shakespeare. When asked what her part was in the play of the moment, she said she thought she was 'noises off'.[1]

Initially Betty attended St Jude's in Dural, where she had a lot of friends. Three services a year were held in a lovely old stone church in Galston. When it needed a new roof Betty chaired the committee to raise money. But it was closed by the minister of St Jude's, who alienated Betty by saying she could have no say in the matter because she hadn't been to church for a while. Betty was welcomed at St Colomb's, the little weatherboard branch church at Arcadia, which had an active congregation, mainly women. After a series of poor sermons from rotating clergy Betty, aged 82, wrote to the vicar and suggested that in lieu of a sermon he hold a discussion—which he did, with an animated response. With the increase in tertiary education, Betty predicted people would find it more difficult just to sing a few hymns, mutter a few prayers and sit and listen and believe what they were told.

In this gentle world, Betty found that she was regarding herself as more Australian than British, and had come to like the 'funny' feeling of equality and the way everybody talked to each other. She liked the casual way of life, of being outdoors and the freedom of discussion.[2] She didn't know at what precise point she became an Australian, but in her retirement she found herself saying, 'we do so and so here and they do so and so in England'. Betty became an Australian citizen on 31 May 1974.

Controversy Revisited

Indiscretions of a Headmistress, Betty's promised irreverent *cri de coeur*, hit bookshops two years after her retirement from Abbotsleigh. Not only had she wanted to express the frustrations she had experienced as a head of a girls school, she also had the more serious intention of making suggestions about the structure of school councils, the type of people who should teach, how children should be dealt with and understood and the part old girls and parents should play in the school. She didn't want it to be a deep educational treatise, but funny and light-hearted.

In *Indiscretions* she referred to backstabbing, intrigue and 'gutless parents'. She also mentioned the time that she was 'dobbed in' to the press at the time of the sex talks. One chapter headed 'Parents, Possible and Impossible: Old Girls, Old and Young' was introduced with the Lewis Carroll quote, 'And thick and fast they come at last, And more, and more, and more'.

Treating the readers as if they were friends, Betty wrote candidly about her ideas on education and value systems without pomposity. The lingering impression was of her breadth of humanity. Disarmingly, she ended the book with a rough analysis of why she considered that she failed as a headmistress, citing poor communication skills in getting her view across to parents, staff and to the school council. She thought she had been lazy in taking the easy way out in the face of fights and disagreements, preferring a peaceful compromise. Her main regret was that she hadn't been more progressive, leading Abbotsleigh into the twenty-first century.

> My real field of success was with the girls. I liked them and treated them as friends, which they were. I trusted them and although a few let me down, most did not. I would rather be bounced by a few than not trust the majority …I think I was successful with the girls because I accepted them as they were and because I remembered my own schooldays. I did not expect them always to be good and do as they were told any more than I had done.[3]

With a photograph of Betty laughing uninhibitedly on the cover, the book attracted a wide readership and stayed on the bestseller list for at least four months. It even sold in England, the title intriguing readers. A traveller taking a copy of the book to her daughter in Portugal was held up at Rome airport, the security men being suspicious of the words 'indiscretions' and 'mistress'.

Betty received numerous letters, her chapter on what she believed unexpectedly drawing the most comment. Courageously, she stood outside the conventions of Christianity and explained why she accepted some and not other tenets of the faith. It was reproduced in the *Sunday Australian* in April 1972 under the heading 'What Easter Means to Me'. Again Betty received many letters from people who, with some relief, said she had enunciated their own spiritual understanding.[4]

Odd Jobs

Betty quickly became involved in an extraordinary variety of activities, the most humble being the processing of information at the Bureau of Census and Statistics at Central station. The most controversial were her television endorsements of Norman Ross discount products, for no pay, but with the assurance that a percentage of sales profits would go to the Aid to Humanity Foundation. Even so, the Council of the Australian Consumers' Association, of which Betty was a member, wrote asking her to resign because of her endorsement of products.

She wrote a weekly column on education for the *Mirror* newspaper, stating her opinions with a light pen. She was seen in Dymocks Booksellers television commercials reminding parents that textbooks were an important aspect of their children's education. She conducted weekly interviews with educationists on ABC Radio's *Morning Call*. For twelve years, as representative of the Association of Heads of Independent Girls Schools of NSW, Betty worked on the Veterans' Children Education Board, excusing herself at the age of 82. She was invited on the committee for the Hornsby TAFE for four years and was involved with the Girl Guides Association and the Outward Bound Trust. For little more than a year she was on Macquarie University Council before being asked to step down to allow a government appointee to take her place. Betty didn't approve of the government's interference and was indignant at being put aside.

Betty also worked for seven years in the establishment of a new, independent coeducational high school, Northholme, in Arcadia. She helped determine its educational policy and her presence on the board attracted students to the school.

She served as vice-president of the International Law Association and was a member of the Consumer Association. She was a member of the Privacy Committee when it was first established in 1975 because of concern about the availability and amount of electronically accrued information on individuals. Opposed to state-controlled information, Betty was always on guard for the underdog.

From 1973 to 1975 Betty was chairman of the NSW division of the Arts Council, where her concern was the funding of theatres including those which toured country towns. It was a position she landed, she said ingenuously, because of the association with Alec. She resigned after two and a half years, explaining that her main frustration was the pressure and competition from the Australia Council and its opposing philosophy about the quality of touring productions and funding of amateur activities. At the time Betty was also on the board of the Independent Theatre.

When her friend Francis James was imprisoned in China for three years for alleged espionage activities, Betty joined a group who energetically worked for his release. But after he was freed she was dismayed by his behaviour, feeling he was rude to those who had helped free him by querying what were they fussing about.

Betty's main activity was in taking classes for adult education at the WEA and speaking to VIEW clubs, The Queens Club and other community groups on current affairs and international and constitutional law. Even sixteen years after retirement she would go every Tuesday morning to the Baulkham Hills Council Leisure Learning Centre and talk about current affairs. And she helped initiate a Senior Citizens Current Affairs Group held at Abbotsleigh, where her reputation attracted the influential and famous to talk to up to 60 people.

Her longest serving role was as a fellow on the Senate of the University of Sydney—from 1959 to 1984. It was one of the best committees on which she had served. Betty, as head of a college and then of a large prestigious school, was renowned for being pro-student and never ceased to argue that the university's method of selection was unfair to country students and those from small schools generally. She was also opposed to the trend to amalgamate universities with colleges of advanced education, and she was puzzled by the fact that even in 1984, in spite of the abolition of tuition fees and greater student allowances, the university was still not getting students from 'good old working-class backgrounds'.[5]

The Senate gave Betty the chance to become an acquaintance of many influential people, and friends of some. Her feminism was most confronted by Sir Hermann Black when he was chancellor. Although she couldn't help liking him and found him to be honest, Betty saw his attitude to women as old-fashioned and deplorable. He was very nice to women, she said, especially if they were good looking, patting them as he came into meetings, but he didn't take them seriously as academics or as anything else.[6] Sir Hermann's attitudes were embarrassingly evident at a farewell dinner the university gave Betty. Ken Coles, a respected industrialist, was horrified when Sir Hermann, in toasting Betty, said she had strangely come to Australia as a cricketer! Whether he laughed or his tone was incredulous, he managed to indicate his disapproval. The speech went downhill from there, according to Ken Coles, and Betty sat with her head in her hands, but when it was finished she gathered herself and made a dignified response.

So embarrassed was he by the patronising speech that Ken Coles wrote Betty a note the next day:

> I feel I must write to you and disassociate myself from the Chancellor's speech last night. I am quite certain it was unconscious and unintentional on his part, but nevertheless I think it was the most demeaning and disastrous M.C.P. speech I have ever heard.
>
> When I saw you sitting there with your head in your hands I could only wonder what was going through your mind—perhaps it was some measure of despair that having taught so many girls and women to hold up their heads, you have failed to make any impression on Sir Hermann.
>
> If the speech he made were reported verbatim in the *University News* today, there would rightly be a thousand women clammering at his door to seek an apology at least or a resignation in retribution.

Only the tone of voice and twinkle of the eye saved the occasion, and I can only commend you for the way you responded.[7]

Ken Coles recalled receiving a touching letter in reply.

A Republic?

Since studying constitutional law at London University, Betty had remained deeply interested in the subject. The sacking of the Whitlam Government by Sir John Kerr prompted her to look at it again.

With talk of Australia becoming a republic Betty began to worry about changes to the Constitution. In a letter to Kerr after the dismissal she said that although it was not easy to conduct a theoretical defence of any hereditary office, she would place Canada, Australia, New Zealand and the Scandinavian monarchies amongst the best governed and most truly democratic of countries. She believed that Australians weren't conscious enough that they were treading a dangerous path, and that the country could be at risk of a dictatorship.[8] She queried whether the Australian Constitution, which in her mind had been superb for the best part of 100 years, was going to cope with the speed and efficiency created by the technological revolution. As democracy was neither speedy nor efficient, Australian society needed to ginger it up.

She also questioned whether Australia still needed both state and federal governments and the resulting clumsiness in decision making of a large bureaucracy. The states were necessary and did a very good job when it used to take a week to get from one capital city to another, but she didn't see the state structure as so necessary now. Instead she considered a better central government and a stronger local government would be more effective.

Gradually she wrote down her ideas, contemplating a book. But it was too casually compiled and her publisher, Angus & Robertson, politely declined. 'We suspect it ("Do it Yourself Democracy") would not really satisfy those previously enchanted by "Indiscretions", nor does it have a sufficiently sharp edge to find its own audience,' wrote Richard Walsh.[9]

More Headlines

Betty's public speaking still attracted headlines. In April 1978 she and her friend Felix Arnott, now Archbishop of Brisbane, were asked to address a seminar in Wodonga on human relations. It followed the release of the report of the Royal Commission into Human Relationships. Felix was one of the three commissioners. The organisers had chosen to focus on the section of the report concerned with family development, the role of the Department of Social Welfare and allied services.

A Catholic priest at Wangaratta, Fr F. P. Hickey, said the seminar was an 'exercise in deception' and accused the archbishop of talking 'pious nonsense' about the report. He paid for a half-page advertisement in the *Border Mail* on the day of Felix and Betty's arrival. In it he listed recommendations of the report ('dangerous document') including the decriminalisation of incest, the decriminalisation of rape, wide dissemination of contraceptives to all age groups, and abortion on demand (a 14-year-old girl could have an abortion without her parents' consent).

'These are just some of the recommendations. When you see the line up of trendy liberals, pro-abortionists, women's electoral lobbyists and gay libbers who did the research you don't wonder,' wrote Fr Hickey.[10] He said the report was a savage attack on the family, the dignity of the person and on life itself—especially the life of the unborn child. He maintained that Felix Arnott and Betty Archdale were there to sell the document as a whole. The Wodonga and District branch of The Right to Life Association joined forces with Hickey and accused Arnott of having 'blood on his hands'. It also called on the Anglican Church to defrock and excommunicate him.

Felix was not new to contention. The Sydney diocese, which Betty said had treated him badly because of his views and tipped him off everything, had already considered him too liberal. While the report's recommendations may seem extreme to some, Felix had been greatly moved, during the commission's inquiries, through his exposure to people who had been hurt by life. He said that, tragically, much of the criticism of the report had come from families who were comfortable and simply did not realise the stresses and strains some families did face.

'I never realised quite how serious the battered wife and battered children syndrome was until, again and again, from all sorts of people who weren't alarmists, we heard the story,' he said. He was deeply disturbed after some teenagers he met at a women's refuge told him that they were afraid to tell their parents they were pregnant because they'd be thrashed and thrown out. 'What do you do in these sorts of circumstances?' Felix Arnott appealed. 'This is the dilemma. It's not an easy choice in most of these moral questions, between an absolute right and an absolute wrong. It would be jolly easy if it was. But in nearly every case it seems to me it's a choice between the less good and the greater good.'[11]

Betty and Felix were photographed leaving the plane at Albury side by side to enter the fray surrounding the seminar. By now friends for over 30 years, they walk together as if controversy surrounding their fresh and honest thinking is inevitable.

Alec

Betty and Alec built an outside room with the idea that there might come a time when they would have someone living there to look after them. In the end, when Alec eventually came to Northis to live there permanently he said could he go in there rather than in the spare room in the house. Very wise too, said Betty, because he kept different hours from her. It also allowed Alec the pursuit of relationships away from Betty, who admitted she never really understood what attracted him about his girlfriends. 'I think it fair to say they were never terribly intellectual and he was very quick off the mark. None of his girlfriends spoke the same language as I did. They were very much girlfriends of the boy.'[12]

The living arrangements worked well. They were independent and yet together. As Alec obtained less and less work, Betty's frugality served them both. But gradually Alec's health deteriorated. Just old age, thought Betty, who was ingenuous in matters of health. He seemed to be in hospital quite a bit, and while she never heard anything about cancer, he smoked like a chimney and from other people's remarks Betty gathered he drank quite a lot.[13] He was also becoming confused. Betty knew things were getting out of hand when about three in the morning he woke her up and asked if she would like to join him for a drink. She steered him back to bed.

Towards the end Alec was having fits and turns. He was hospitalised, and then had a massive heart attack. He died aged 80, on 13 May 1986. The death certificate notes 'organic brain syndrome'. Alec's last wishes were: 'I desire to be cremated and that my ashes should be scattered to the four winds. $100 to each niece and nephew. Everything left to Betty with the hope that she distributes some part of my residuary estates equally between my two sons' (Dominic, 50, and Anthony, 41). Dominic came for his father's last days. He was a quiet, intelligent man, a little ill at ease amongst the people who knew his father and his aunt better than he did.

As time sloped on, Betty began to feel increasingly lonely. She recognised how important it had been for her to have Alec's companionship. While she provided Alec with a stable foundation to his life, emotionally and financially, his intelligent, theatrical and creative presence, along with his handyman skills, balanced her more earnest preoccupations. In creating the house and, through his need for people, a sociable interaction with those around, Alec in turn cared for Betty. She believed that in a funny way he was quite proud of her. 'I think he thought I was a bit odd but he was very, he really was quite understanding—and I think he was prepared to stand by me—in any rows I had with anyone.' In 1988 Betty told the interviewer Caroline Jones, 'We were extraordinarily close, which is odd. We disagreed on everything. He, look, he was a male chauvinist of the worst kind.'[14]

Betty said she felt missing Alec was partly a selfish experience. She missed having him to talk to and say this happened, or that. She kept coming across things he had made at Galston and she thought she hadn't really thanked him enough for what he did. She also saw him as a much finer person than she was, who did what he thought was right, not worrying what others said, and took on projects such as establishing the Community Theatre without the intention of making money out of it.

Betty tried to shrug off her sense of loneliness. It was something she never thought she would experience. But for the first time in her life she started to regret that she hadn't married. Not only had Alec died, but so had most of her close friends, and Betty came to rely on her godson, Colin Munro. But she said that if she were unfortunate enough to live again that she would make a real effort to marry and have children and grandchildren.[15] 'I wasn't good at social relations,' Betty said, 'I was very lucky with friends. I think I was a bit self-centred all my life—I think if you are a woman making it on her own you do become self-centred.'[16]

She also felt she had missed something in not having a sexual life. She knew that she had been accused of being a lesbian. When Ron Chambers, headmaster of Northolme, the school she had helped establish, was asked to resign because of unprofessional behaviour, he wrote a nasty letter to Betty saying 'everyone knows you are a lesbian.' 'I am not homosexual at all,' she protested, but the allegation affected her deeply and she became noticeably depressed. She saw it as a tragedy of the present day that it is assumed that every unmarried man or woman is homosexual.[17]

After the release of *Indiscretions of a Headmistress* Betty received a letter in 1975 from an Englishman, Paul Berry, who was the literary executor for Vera Brittain and Winifred Holtby, the author of *South Riding* and other novels. He asked Betty for her impression of both Vera and Lady Rhondda adding, 'It's been fairly widely said that Lady Rhondda was a lesbian—don't get me wrong, some of my family and best friends are either homosexual or lesbian—but Vera, of course, was a totally feminine woman and completely a man's woman, although NEVER interested in sex I imagine'.[18] Once more Betty said that Margaret Rhondda was not a lesbian, and that she should know, having lived with her and her mother for some years.

But it seems that Betty was sometimes in the midst of homosexual women, without being one herself. Looking back on her life, she said: 'I don't know whether there is some physical thing in my make-up that although I like men, I get on very well with them, real love—which means you'll give anything, doesn't it? ... I haven't felt it with any of the men or women that I met.'[19]

Airport Protest
In 1974, the *Mirror* cried out, 'Archie Canes Gough' and 'Archie Slams Labor'. The hue and cry was over Betty's decision to embarrass the Labor Party by releasing a letter sent to her by Evan Williams, the press secretary

to the prime minister, Gough Whitlam, which asked her to be a signatory (along with other eminent Australians) of a letter supporting the return of a Labor government.

Betty thought the government must be joking asking for her support when it had recently tried to force an unwanted new international airport on Galston. Local reaction was intense and Betty's opposition was important. So she wrote back asking, 'Do you want me to be lynched in the village?' She went on to outline her disappointment with Labor in the undemocratic way it had comported itself on several questions such as the allocation of school aid, the substitution of 'Australia' for 'Commonwealth' as the country's title, and the discreditable Gair appointment. Betty then released both letters to the press. An editorial in the *Sydney Morning Herald* on 2 May stressed she was right to do so, 'for the implications of this incident are, like much comedy, not laughing matter.'[20]

As demonstrated by the airport kafuffle, Betty was a swinging voter, although her tendency was to vote Labor. But each election she had a good think, not being party tied for fear of compromising her beliefs. She was sympathetic to the Labor Party in 1972, opposed it in 1974, and voted for the Democrats in 1980, not only because she agreed with some of their platform but because she hoped they would gain the balance of power in the Senate and so annoy both the major parties.

As for Sir John Kerr's sacking of the Whitlam Government on 11 November 1975, Betty could never understand why the Labor Party kicked up such a fuss. In the circumstances she felt Kerr did the right thing and she wrote to him: 'I've often wondered why Whitlam did not resign with the reason that by delaying the granting of funds the opposition was thwarting the democratically elected government. He would have quite rightly got a lot of sympathy, and probably been re-elected. As it was he put himself in the wrong and made it worse by his later behaviour.'[21]

It was a strange quirk of fate that at one of Betty's parties, Barbara Munro walked up to Sir John Kerr and said, 'That was a pretty brave decision, John'. And he said, 'Oh don't be silly, Barbara, I had a precedent'. He was talking about her father Sir John Peden, who had advised the Governor of NSW, Sir Phillip Game, before he dismissed the NSW premier, Jack Lang.[22]

In 1976, on the eve of their travelling to the UK to celebrate the centenary of women's cricket, Betty and Barbara Munro were given a farewell party by their friends at Galston. Betty invited John Kerr, who was still governor-general. She said he wouldn't come because of security problems, but that she would like him to be asked just to show that she believed in him and supported him. However, the Kerrs did come to the party. Sir John had diverted his plane to Sydney so he could say goodbye to Betty because he admired her tremendously. When Ruth Cracknell and her husband Eric arrived late they couldn't join the party until one of the Kerrs' security men knocked at the door to validate their entry.

Betty's attitude to John Kerr was an example of her loyalty. Underneath her complicated crust was a sweetness, a naivety. She could not believe ill of anybody to whom she had once given her trust.

Letters to the Press

Despite her retirement, Betty never left public debate. Because she saw very clearly the rightness of things, she had a desire to shock, to say something outrageous to wake people up and prevent them from being self-satisfied. In pungent letters to the *Sydney Morning Herald* or *The Australian* she commented on puerile sports commentators, the male-dominated media and the lack of balance in coverage of women's sports, sermons of poor quality, the ordination of women, the constitutional monarchy, the individuality of aged people … Her letters were energetically written and filled with suggestions for alternative stances on issues. 'I am often wrong,' she said, 'but rarely negative.'

In a letter in 1986 she steamily suggested that television sports commentators be trained to understand that their audience can *see* the game. 'Sitting in the stand at the Sydney Cricket Ground, we would be horrified if all day a loudspeaker described what we could perfectly well see for ourselves … All we need to be told are those things we cannot see or know owing to not being there physically at the ground.'

Another of her letters was disparaging about Fred Nile's generalisations on gender expectancy in his submission to the national inquiry into teacher education. He had referred to the 'mother-care' female role or the 'father-protector provider' role. Betty wrote:

And how about the 'I've got to look after my parent' female role, or the 'I want to be a teacher/doctor scientist politician/artist/actor' female and male role. And whacko for the 'I want to be a Church of England priest' female role.

Please can't we let men and women play the role they want without interference from either Mr Nile or groups of self-opinionated teachers?

I'd settle for 'there is neither male nor female; for ye are all one in Christ Jesus' (Galations Ch. 3. v 28).[23]

In the days following Betty received a postcard from Felix Arnott which read: 'Have just read your letter in yesterday's paper which gave me great joy … say it over and over again; Australia needs it so much. Especially the Diocese of Sydney … Love Felix.'

Feminism

In 1975 Betty said women were still second-class citizens and that the media depicted them as 'mentally deficient twits interested only in their looks' and as self-centred and not interested in what is going on in the world. Against that, said Betty: 'Our image of ourselves is of hard working women, interested in many things, including helping other people. The double image—of what other people think of women, and what women think of themselves—could be applied to other groups such as students, migrants, Australians and city and country people … This gap reveals ignorance and can lead to a real division of opinion and hates.'[24] She said it was important to bridge that gap through more communication.

The element of choice for women's occupation was crucial to Betty, and she was stunned by objections to mothers going out to work and leaving their children in care. She thought the trend for women to work outside the home had strengthened the family rather than weakened it, and that the idea that a woman had to choose between marriage and a career was as dead as a dodo:

No-one ever seems to object to a married woman working inside the home. For all anyone cares she can work 24 hours out of 24, seven days a week, with no annual holiday and no pay, as long as this is done within the home.

She can also work without pay outside the home for any number of charities, ladies' auxiliaries, church groups and similar socially approved activities, and earn nothing but praise. It is only when she works outside the home that people start talking about delinquent children and neglected homes.

This is certainly a man's world still and anything considered even potentially dangerous to the economic interests of men soon gets rationalised into being morally and socially wrong.[25]

Betty had seen the status of women change as the economic system changed and she predicted that the technological revolution would be good for women, reducing hours of labour and making it easier to find part-time work. But there was still a lot of secondary discrimination, largely in expectation and attitudes. At the same time she felt strongly that women should take responsibility for themselves and she resented paying heavy taxes to give pensions to women silly enough to become pregnant without the means to support their child.[26]

She endorsed the Women's Electoral Lobby (WEL) for getting down to specific jobs such as campaigning against textbooks that show inappropriate images of females. But she had reservations about quota-based affirmative action schemes, believing that the best person for the job should always be appointed. She was also careful to point out that men should not be regarded as scapegoats for women's dissatisfaction. Women unquestionably played a significant part in the behaviour of men, which meant they must accept their share of the responsibility too. In their misguided efforts to rule the world, men had certainly made a mess of it, but Betty was sure that, while women are endowed with just as much brain, character and capacity of every kind as men, they were just as likely to be stupid and greedy and bad-tempered and selfish: 'So I really doubt that we would be likely to make a better job of the world … even though I'm equally sure we couldn't do much worse.'

Public Tributes

Some great contributors to life go unnoticed, but not Betty. She had the thrill of being acknowledged in many different ways—from being a clue in a cryptic crossword to receiving Honorary Doctorates of Letters from both the University of Sydney and Macquarie University and being voted one of Australia's hundred 'Living Legends'. And an article in the *Sydney Morning Herald* on the likelihood of a woman becoming prime minister noted of Betty that 'she has brains, she could certainly talk and would never be nervous on the platform. If she felt something should be said, she'd say it. No doubt about that.'

In 1990 the Ku-ring-gai Municipal Council decided to recognise the significant contribution Betty and Alec had made to the welfare of the community by naming a park in Wahroonga after them. A plaque naming Archdale Park in Neringah Road was unveiled by Betty in the company of friends and Abbotsleigh girls who sang in a small ceremony.

But whatever praise Betty received, her sense of self never became exaggerated. When a group of famous people was asked for their favourite recipes Betty responded with: 'Junket—made with milk and rennet or tablets. It must be served with oatmeal, as well as cream and sugar. It is the medium or coarse oatmeal sprinkled on top that makes the junket delicious. I prefer brown sugar but that is a matter of taste. You can make it in two minutes—can't go wrong!'

When she was 88 Betty was asked to give the Occasional Address at Macquarie University where she was to receive an Honorary Doctorate of Letters. There had been some consternation at the thought that she might not be up to the task, and when she stood central stage to receive her doctorate, without the required velvet hat, her academic gown was pulled back from her shoulders by the hood she was wearing and white skin declared her vulnerability. But when she came to speak, she said, 'I had to take my bonnet off—it had come down round my neck. I must have over-exaggerated the size of my head!' The audience laughed and the tension of the moment fell away.[27]

One of the most unexpected and exciting honours Betty received was the last. In 1999 she was unanimously elected by the committee of the Marylebone Cricket Club at Lord's Ground in England to become an Honorary Life Member —amongst the first ten women allowed into the inner sanctum. When informed, Betty exclaimed, 'I haven't! I think that's superb. I am thrilled. It's the best thing that could have happened to me at this age.' 'I'm glad they've done it,' she later reflected. 'It doesn't hurt anyone, but it pleases a lot.'[28]

Friendship

Even though she might have been regarded as a source of wisdom by the community, Betty was always grateful for small expressions of friendship or kindness, quickly thanking people as if any service to her was unexpected or even undeserved.

Elizabeth Hake, who had known Betty since they were at school together in Scotland, said in the 1990s that Betty was one of the most unchanged people she had ever known. What stood out at school was very much what defined Betty over 70 years later—her intellectual ability, her absolute intolerance of anything dishonest. She was down to earth, practical, and what she said went.[29]

Even so, Betty found it hard to make friends, so when former students, cricketers, Wrens and teachers maintained a relationship she was pleased and quickly and dutifully responded to cards and letters. While they might have wanted more from the relationship, some people, after making a great effort, came to realise that the friendship was superficial to the extent that Betty wasn't fully engaged with them. Janna Bruce, who had know Betty since the 1930s in London, said 60 years later, 'I've known her for so many years yet I don't feel I know her at all—can you understand that?'[30]

Subscriptions to plays and concerts gave Betty a base for socialising. But in later years she was almost passive, expecting people, particularly the Marchant-Williams family, to organise birthday parties for her. Nor did the usual reciprocity in a friendship come so easily. Nonetheless, a loyal coterie of people kept her social life on a low simmer.

In September 1980, Felix Arnott and his wife Anne moved to Venice where Felix took up the chaplaincy as the Vicar General to the Anglican Church. It was a suitable appointment because for years he had been the Australian member of the International Anglican–Roman Catholic Commission working on the theological basis for church reunification. In a letter to Betty he wrote, 'Hope I shall see you either in Venice or later in Australia'. But Betty never saw him again. Just before their departure from Australia it was found that Felix had a malignant tumour. While at the time he said the prognosis was good, he died not long after, and Betty lost an unconditionally loyal friend.

Elderly neighbours moved away to warmer climates or to be near their children. Galston changed character, with the newly affluent moving in and building garish mansions. As the attrition rate of friends grew with the years Betty methodically crossed out names in her address book with a blunt pencil.

With increasing age, Betty tried to find more definition in her spiritual beliefs. She read *On Purpose* by Charles Birch and *The Mind of God* by the physicist Paul Davies, she attended lectures on the Dead Sea Scrolls by Barbara Thiering, and she commended them for the courage to try and think for themselves. The many factual and detailed beliefs of the various churches were not so important to her. For example, she didn't believe it mattered whether Christ was born of a virgin. Other religious leaders were also said to be born of virgins—to indicate something very special about the birth. What mattered was the fact that Christ lived and by his life and teachings gave future generations living proof of the existence of some force behind the universe.

Again, Betty didn't believe that Christ's body rose physically from his grave to disappear in the sky. What made her heart beat faster and with joy was that the men and women who lived and worked with Christ were convinced that they saw, talked and ate with him after his death. 'The belief changed them from downcast, defeated and completely disillusioned men and women into fervent believing Christians. They faced derision, persecution and death. They started a church which has spread into every country of the world and is the faith of some millions of people 2000 years later. This is not the kind of thing men and women do on hearsay or gossip but only on very strong and convincing evidence.'[31]

To Betty, the resurrection was proof of a purpose in the universe and that death is not the end. She was not afraid of death, but was uncertain of the kind of existence after life. She believed in some kind of mental recognition of those one has loved. And frequently she said she would be most upset if she didn't 'see' her mother and Alec again. As more and more people she loved died she had an increasing certainty in some form of continuing relationship. She liked the idea of Heaven as a union with the force behind this world and Hell as separation from it. In so far as we try on earth to live up to the teachings of Christ, who represented the purpose of the world, we are in that state which is called heaven.

Nightly, Betty prayed on her knees, with joined hands, not for specific things like money and success, but for 'character things that I want—integrity and honesty'. Then she prayed for guidance, after which she got into bed with a sigh and hoped for the best.[32] She was never certain that her prayers were answered, specifically, but in a general sense she thought they had been, believing that she had felt she was 'pushed' in a particular way by something outside herself. Mainly, however, she thought prayer had a positive effect on oneself. While she liked familiar prayers, she believed that real prayers were those that came from the heart. In her nineties she admitted that her constant prayer was that she might die, but it didn't seem to be happening.

She said that throughout history man has known so little about the world and himself that he attributed such events as spring, the winds, floods, earthquakes and even illness to God. Now our knowledge both of the world and ourselves has progressed to the stage where we know the answers to so much, and can control and alter so much, that we can no longer blame God or hide behind God. We have got to live like mature men and women, responsible to ourselves. Our increased knowledge involves an increased knowledge of God. Men and women are standing on their own feet and taking responsibility for their own acts. 'I think at least we are getting a glimmer of the real God,' she said, 'not a father figure admonishing us from above, but a purpose in this world.'

Betty thought if Christ returned today, He would consider that fundamentalists were old-fashioned, especially in their attitude to women, because they were relying too much on words spoken thousands of years ago in a different setting. In almost every profession women were zooming up, but on Sunday in church 'you go back 100 years', Betty wrote to the *Sydney Morning Herald*.[33] In another letter she wrote, 'Surely all Christians and other churches deserve to have the best men and women teaching and guiding their members'.[34]

She was astonished when, in response to a letter to the *Herald* about the ordination of women, she received a lengthy letter from the

Vicar-General of the Anglican Catholic Church of Australia who said Communion described the unique fellowship of the Church on earth with the Church Triumphant. Its effective sign was the Eucharist, in which the Church (the Bride of Christ—a feminine body) and her divine Groom become one, in Holy Communion. It is the bridegroom who presides as the 'alter Christus'. It is necessary that he be male. As the church is a feminine body—the Bride of Christ— for a woman to stand at the altar as the 'icon' of the bridegroom is to portray the relationship between Christ and his Bride as a lesbian one.

In Betty's response she said she found it hard to agree that the church is a feminine body, and she thought he was a bit hard saying that the pressure for ordination of women came from the 'soft, corrupt and decadent Churches of the rich, industrialised West': 'I would say the increasing standard of education, the opening of all professions and trades to both men and women, the strain of modern living leading to a greater need for religion, has led women in particular to view their exclusion from the ministry to be an anomaly and misinterpretation of Christ's teaching.'[35]

Ultimately, Betty decided, the purpose and meaning of the world must win. Its very existence implies it cannot fail.

Pure Luck

The interviewer Barbara Sinclair said to Betty in 1975 that some people would think she'd achieved a great deal. A reasonable amount, Betty said, but not all that much. If you're in the right place at the right time and the right job comes along you'll have reasonable success anyway. She put it down to chance and said her family motto was 'Data Fata Sequutus' (fate having being given, it so follows). And she had just followed the fates. She had been amazed at how one job turned up after another.[36]

When reviewing her life Betty would say in her Harrods hunting voice, almost with a rhythm of a song: It's all because of cricket. If I hadn't come out to Australia with that cricket team, when the war started I wouldn't have been sent out overseas with the WRNS. If I hadn't been with the WRNS I wouldn't have ended up here at the end of the war when the Women's College wanted a principal. If I hadn't been at

Women's College I wouldn't have got the job at Abbotsleigh even though I'd never taught.

'I've had a lot of fun since I've been retired, doing all sorts of things. Someone rings you and says how about doing so and so and so I give it a go and if it's no good I don't do it again.'[37] Always the recitation ended with, 'But you know, all my life I think I've been quite fantastically lucky!'

18

GOODBYE GALSTON

The fourth day of Spring arrived in 1991 and was greeted with dread in Betty's solitary soul. It was the day she was to leave her Galston home and enter a retirement village, Lourdes, at Killara. Various friends had put their names down for the same village and it was conveniently placed in the middle of the north shore.

Betty had been getting tired. Instead of chopping firewood all morning, after half an hour she had had enough. She used to pick up tools without even thinking about it. Now she thought, God this is a weight! She supposed her whole muscular system decided to retreat, and although she wore a Vitacall alarm around her neck she was fearful of falling on her land and not being found. After a recent fall outside the kitchen she went to the chemist for iodine, only to be told to go to the doctor who then needed to insert six stitches—the wound was so deep.

In fact Betty had rather hoped she'd drop dead before she had to move. But the property was sold and now she had to go. On the morning, Muff Munro, Colin's wife, was there, and so were two removalists— Graeme and Junior. A rattled Betty had a variety of battered cases which she was filling with random objects. She was wearing an off-white shirt, green woollen pants and nylon sneakers. Her bed was dismantled—a red divan with a red mattress and a rubber mattress on top of that.

Graeme started packing glasses. 'No, leave them!' said Betty sharply. The men were agile in jumping out of her way and jollying her in a forced manner.

Noel West, the new owner, arrived. Outside, his new black four-wheel drive gleamed at the base of a turpentine. Betty was pleased that he would retain Northis as his office although he planned to build a big home further down the block. Naively, she gave him books on building your own home.[1]

Betty fretted that the fly screen wasn't fitted to the outside of a window. 'All the bugs will come in,' she said.

As the newly formed cardboard boxes were filled with her meagre possessions, the house looked reduced, denuded of spirit. There was a .22 rifle behind her bedroom door. Everywhere dust and cobwebs. 'Should I take this mirror?' she asked. It was circular with an imitation brass surround and speckled glass. She rubbed it with her forearm and stuck it in a case along with a few vases.

It was a balmy spring day outside. The bush orchid was crowded with tight yellow blooms—fronds fanned generously over a large area. Clumps of freesias scented the air.

'Once I go in the car will I have to come back?' she asked querulously. 'No,' we replied.

The men finished packing. 'Would you like a drink?' she asked them—her last act as hostess at Northis. 'Wouldn't say no,' was the reply.

Betty had a tantalus ready for moving—an ornately carved wooden carrier for three square decanters. Its handle was locked into position (to inhibit servants of yesteryear from secretly imbibing) and Betty was perturbed that she didn't know how to open it. But Graeme found the right keys and the handle fell to one side. The tantalus was engraved with:

Presented to
Capt. T. Archdale R. F.A., D.S.O.
On the occasion of his marriage
by the officers of the Lancashire Field Artillery
October 9, 1901

Accepting that there were to be no more rituals, Betty allowed the glasses to be packed. She left behind the big grey armchair that was given to her by former students of Women's College because it was too big for the single room to which she was moving. But she took the large wooden chest given to her, she said, by some man who had been in love with her, despite it having been 'a darned nuisance to haul around'.

Betty put boxes of drink into the boot of her dented, mustard-coloured Mitsubishi and laughed at the idea of being caught with them. Then she turned to her helpers. Often her embraces were perfunctory, but this time there were no barriers.

Muff, down to earth and caring, said that Betty tried to take too little. She was storing Betty's things at her house and would return them as required.

At Northis a hundred empty coathangers were taken down and thrown in a heap with tattered curtains. The ship doorknocker swayed back and forth. But as if refusing to let go of the past, the smell of decades of open fires clung tenaciously to the house.

19

TOWARDS THE END

In her room at the retirement village Betty sat and invited death. The novelist Morris West had written to her: 'I try to spread the good word that death is not a fearful matter, but the end of one chapter of human existence. All we have are intimations of immortality, but we've been fortunate enough to experience life as a gift of love—so we can surrender it also with love.'[1]

But in the slow surrendering of life, Betty was lonely. She occupied herself by completing crossword puzzles neatly clipped for her from the *Sydney Morning Herald* by the Catholic priest in residence. There had been a lot of people in her life but she was curious as to where they were now. Part of her feeling of isolation was because she believed that she was different from the other residents—many of whom had been housewives and had not worked in the outside world. We speak a different language, said Betty, after finding her table companions were uninterested in discussing news items she had gathered from the daily papers.

Some years earlier Betty had said: 'I'm good at talking to friends, people I really know, that's easy, but not when it's with someone I half know, not with strangers. I think I'm lazy. You know, I think it's my fault, I think I'm not interested enough in them really.'[2] Betty's difficulty with small talk seems to be because she was always engaged in thinking with a world view.

One day I took her to the funeral of a former teacher. To our dismay, there were very few people in attendance. Betty turned round and said 'Where's Abbotsleigh?' Afterwards I assured her it would be quite different for the funeral of a headmistress. But we both felt low, so on the way home I suggested we visit a relative of mine. We were offered tea in cups that were usually kept locked in a glass cabinet. As Betty rattled her cup in its translucent saucer, I remarked on their use. My relative smiled, leant forward and said, 'And Miss Archdale, are you interested in china?' For the first time that day Betty became alert. 'Well I've been to Hong Kong,' she said excitedly, 'but never made it to China. I would have liked to!'

In her later years she was asked where she now most found meaning in life—contentment, satisfaction, beauty? Betty replied, 'In improving things, in making life better ... in doing something worthwhile'. But she added that she had had a good life and that she was ready to go, that at her age there was not a great deal she could do—she was not going to turn the world upside down or reform anything. She added, 'There comes a time when you're out of date.' Asked if there was any pain in that, Betty said, 'No. On the whole there's a bit of a sense of relief. I haven't got to worry about that anymore.'[3] Quietly she suspected that she hadn't fought enough for causes, unlike her mother, of whom she said, 'She was a magnificent woman, a magnificent fighter'.

There is no doubt that the suffragettes were the real pioneers of the women's movement. But it was also difficult for the second generation feminists who had the job of developing and consolidating the work that the earlier generation had initiated. The suffragettes won the vote and made their mark, but whether they could have gone on and built up an organisation and worked with men is debatable. Their successors who have done that are, in a way, just as important.

Betty was significant in that she made good use of the opportunities that first generation gave. She did this not only through her exceptional work in women's education and women's sport, but also by making a niche for herself in the wider community, at the same time enjoying an easier relationship with men than her mother had.

Helen Archdale set the moral tone and Betty took on the mantle of liberal thinking and of not believing one had to conform to things if they weren't right. But Betty didn't have to have that extra fight to keep spearheading things. Her breadth of contribution to the arts, privacy, human relations, education and sport, and to piercing complacency in society, has drawn many descriptions including 'great'. A psychologist recently listed seven traits common to great people, including survival skills and willingness to take risks. Betty's persona incorporated all the traits, but they do not include her most important gift to those around her—and that was that she gave more than she received.

Yet despite accolades, Betty sensed a quality in life that eluded her. She once said that she felt Alec was a much finer person than she was because he could get closer to people. She saw her difficulty in doing so as a flaw. If she had been a better person, she used to say to herself, she would have been able to have had more personal relationships.

Throughout the writing of her biography, I have been aware of Betty talking about her life in the treble clef, punctuated with, 'Oh look, I've been terribly lucky!' followed by a quick sigh of a laugh. At the same time I've been aware of a subliminal vibration, as of a bow being slowly drawn across the bass strings of a cello, a sense of longing for a closeness that she didn't know how to attain.

For all her education, Betty hadn't been schooled in the language of love. In her last days, I went to see her. She was sleeping fitfully. I waited until she stirred, then said, 'So then, how is my darling woman?' Summoning strength and with her eyes closed, she said, 'Enough of that!' She died a week or so later, on Tuesday 11 January 2000.

EPILOGUE

Betty Archdale's love was for people as a whole, expressed in giving time and encouragement, wise counsel and leadership. And she had a unique kind of intimacy with people, one that was able to sway their orientation to life. Her intimacy lay in the fact that the goodness of her nature and her purity of purpose were apparent to all because she hadn't learnt the usual social camouflaging behaviours. Even if she didn't know individuals, everyone knew her and what she stood for. In this way she touched a large number of people.

Towards the end of a 30-year reunion of schoolgirls Betty, then aged 82, asked to be taken home. As she moved to go, the room became urgent. For some time Betty couldn't leave because one woman after another came up to her, grabbed her hand and said over and over again, 'Archie, I just want you to know you changed my life!' … 'Archie, I just want you to know you changed my life!'

While the mystery of Betty Archdale's power remains, the gifts she gave to one generation of women have been passed on to their children and their children's children. For decades after her retirement people continued to send their daughters to Abbotsleigh in the hope that they may be affected by Betty Archdale's philosophical legacy. For even in her physical absence her influence hovers—her strength, her humanity, her honesty, the sense of endless possibilities for us all, and the presence of an undercurrent of humour which at any time may bubble through to the surface and make us laugh.

ACKNOWLEDGMENTS

The book was commissioned by the Abbotsleigh Old Girls Union. I thank them for allowing me the privilege of writing Betty Archdale's biography.

So many people gave of themselves in interviews. They were: Audley Montgomery Archdale; Audley Nicholas Archdale; Helen Elizabeth (Betty) Archdale; Mervyn Archdale, Betty's cousin; Diana Ashcroft; Jill Auld (née Cowper); Prue Barron (née Evans); Marie Bashir; Jo Bastian; Charles Birch; Janna Bruce; Merrilyn Bryce; Helen Buchanan; Mary Bullen; Meredith Burgmann; Verity Burgmann; Helen Campbell (née Kenyon); Felicity Charles; Joyce Cole; Ken Coles; Audrey Collins; Kath Commins; Ruth Cracknell; Daclan, employee, Archdale Castle, Department of Environment; Carolyn De Costa (née Downes); Anne Deveson; Norah Devonish-Meares; Mollie Dive; Peter Duly; Sheila Duncan-Smith; Barbara Edmonson; Dorothy Ellison; Aline Fenwick; Penny Figgis; Christine Fox (née Carter); Betty Hake; Jan Haskins; Janet Hay (née Cowper); Elizabeth Hassall (née Ferris); Molly Hide; Sue Holmes (née Cadell), Glynis Johns; Elva Julien; Michelle Judzewitsch (née Cotton); Doreen Langley; Joy Lang; Anne Le Couteur (née Bullen); John Lincoln; Nancy Lord; Myrtle Maclagan; Kim McConachie (née Brown); Jan McCredie; Kath McCredie; Dr Robin McMurdo; Prue McCullagh (Docker); Mary Maltby; Lyn Marchant-Williams; Meg Matthews (née Giblin); Margaret Maxwell; Penny Meagher; Elizabeth Miller; Deborah Moore (née Farram); Meg Mulvey; Colin Munro; Canon

Melville Newth; John Orr; Liz Palmer (née McGrath); Janie Plasto (née Parkinson); Phyll Puttick (née Holmes); Anne Robson (née MacWatt); Margaret Rodgers (née Hodgson); Jenny Rowe (née Oswin); Willy Shannon; Jenefer Shaver (née Hyde); Sue Smith (née Gorrick); Dr Tom Stapleton; Keith Steel; Val Street; Kerrie Taylor (née Bremner); Mavis Thorn (née Mackenzie); Dr John Watson; Wal Watson; Julia Welsh (née Ward); Freda Whitlam; Elizabeth Wilkinson and Julia Wokes (née Fisher). I am also indebted to Elizabeth Miller, a former Wren, who gave me a copy of her unpublished memoirs, with permission to draw on them.

Thank you as well to Dr Rosemary Annable, archivist at the Women's College, University of Sydney; Tim Robinson, University of Sydney archives; James Graham, Chairman of the Abbotsleigh Council, for allowing access to the Council Minutes; Avril Condren, archivist, Abbotsleigh; Ann Robson, archivist, St Leonard's School; Cheryl Szatow who gave me tapes of her interview with Betty Archdale in 1986; Julia Thorogood; Rosemary and Ian Spittle, Christine and Russell Stewart for rooms to write in; Val Sheppard and Sholto Macpherson for reading the manuscript when it was first finished; Ros Lloyd-Phillips and my father Ernest Hyde and Jocelyn Hackett for assistance; Peter Gluyas, whose computer skills rescued the book from oblivion more than once; Peter O'Hanlon and Peter McDougall of Seven Worldwide for scanning photographs; and Carl Harrison-Ford for wise editing, and for becoming a friend.

I am utterly grateful to my friends at large for continuing to believe in me despite my 'sheer cliffs of fall'. Special thanks to Marg Bisley, Carolyn Fletcher, Sue Holmes (née Cadell), Dimity Riley (née Wood), Penny Stratton and Ros Tindale (née Spencer); and to Sally McInerney, who quietly encouraged at every stage from the most primitive text to the book's final form.

NOTES

Chapter 1: In Love

1. Betty Archdale (BA), interview, 8.v.1990.
2. W.B. Yeats, 'The Lake Isle of Innisfree', *Selected Poetry*, ed. A. Norman Jeffares, Macmillan, 1962, p. 16.
3. Exhibition notes, Castle Archdale Museum Display.
4. Audley Nicholas Archdale, Liphook, interview, 4.xi.1991.
5. Theodore Montgomery Archdale, son of Nicholas Montgomery Archdale and Adelaide (Ada) Porter, was the youngest of their eight children. They were of the Riversdale line of Archdales ('the true line', according to Betty's cousin Mervyn Archdale of Omagh, interview, 7.xi.1991), living in Fermanagh.

Remnants of Castle Archdale where the cousins the 'Castle Archdales' lived can be seen on the shores of Lough Erne. During World War II the castle catered for up to 2000 crew and support staff of Sunderland and Catalina flying boats in the war against U-boats. (Castle Archdale exhibition.) But most of the estate was sold in 1954 to the Ministry of Agriculture (Forestry Division).

Denis Archdale, who inherited the remainder of the property, developed the site as a caravan park. It was opened to the public in 1966. But he overreached himself, dismantling the old manor to create the leisure centre for the caravan park. In 1974 he finally sold the remaining 200 acres to the Department of Environment. There exists now the Castle Archdale Museum Display, a marina, a youth hostel, and a caravan and campsite. So finished the great Archdale landlords of County Fermanagh in which they played a prominent part.

Riversdale, the large house at the core of the Riversdale Archdales, suffered a similar fate. In a letter to Betty Archdale from her first cousin, Sir Edward Archdale, Bt, of Comber, on 25.x.1991 is the following piece of history: 'Grandfather Edward Mervyn died in Nov 1943 at 90 but my father then I/C civil defence in Londonderry was not able to consider taking over Riversdale until after the war. My mother, and I am now sorry to say, myself, were against it and so he sold to the Dept. of Agriculture for very little and we moved to England, where he, and later my mother, died. Riversdale has since been pulled down, as also Castle Archdale.'

6. Theodore Montgomery Archdale (TMA), father of Betty Archdale, entries from diaries 1895 to 1917 (years 1904 to 1913 missing).
7. After Clondalkin was included in the Irish Free State on 6.xii.1921, the family moved to Northern Ireland, settling just over the border in Rostrevor, County Down.

8. TMA, diaries.
9. *The Landed Gentry of Ireland*, 1958, p. 28.
10. TMA, diary, 1900.
11. Ibid.
12. Audley Montgomery Archdale, Edinburgh, son of Osmund Audley Archdale and Vita Thorneycroft, interview, 12.xi.1991.
13. *The Scotsman*, 19.vii.1876.
14. Magnus Magnusson, *The Glorious Privilege: The History of the Scotsman*, Nelson, 1967.
15. Ibid.
16. Helen Carter was born in Forfarshire according to Scots Ancestry Research Society Report on the Maternal Ancestry of Helen Russel, 2.x.1991.
17. Helen Archdale (HA), 'An Interfering Female', unpublished ms, ch. 1.
18. Alexander Archdale (AA), 'Take One Actor', unpublished ms, ch. 1.
19. HA, 'An Interfering Female', ch. 1.
20. *Encyclopedia Britannica*, reprinted 1986.
21. TMA, photograph album.
22. TMA, diary, 1900.
23. HA, 'An Interfering Female'.
24. TMA, diary, 1901.
25. Ibid.
26. Ibid.
27. HA, 'An Interfering Female'.
28. TMA, diary, 1901.

Other Sources:
Henry Blackwood Archdale, *Memoirs of the Archdales, With the Descents of Some Allied Families*, The Impartial Reporter Office, 1925.
H.W. Coffey and M.J. Morgan, *Irish Families in Australia and New Zealand, 1788–1983*, revised vol. 1, *Abbott–Dynan*, self-published.
Mary Rogers, *Living by Lough Erne*, self-published, 1910.

Chapter 2: Falling in Reality
1. BA, interview, 7.viii.1990.
2. TMA, diary, 1901–2.
3. TMA, diary, 1903.
4. HA, 'An Interfering Female', unpublished ms.
5. Ibid.
6. Ibid.
7. Birth certificate.
8. HA, 'An Interfering Female'.
9. BA, interview.
10. Ibid.
11. AA, 'Take One Actor', unpublished ms.
12. Ibid.

Chapter 3: Deeds not Words
1. Midge Mackenzie, *Shoulder to Shoulder*, Alfred A. Knopf, 1976, pp. 6–61.

2. HA, 'An Interfering Female', unpublished ms, ch. II, p. 1.
3. Anne Archer, librarian, Bedales School, letter, 3.v.1994.
4. BA, interview, 31.x.1994.
5. HA, 'An Interfering Female', ch. XI, p. 5.
6. Ibid., ch. II, p. 8.
7. Ibid., ch. II, p.11.
8. Ibid., ch. III, p.1.
9 Ibid., ch. III, p. 3.
10. Ibid., ch. III, p. 5.

Chapter 4: Harrowing Holloway
1. HA, 'An Interfering Female', unpublished ms, ch. III, pp. 5–6.
2. AA 'Take One Actor', unpublished ms, ch. 1, p. 3.
3. Ibid., ch. III, pp. 9–10.
4. Ibid., ch. III, p. 11.
5. BA, interview, 8.v.1990.
6. BA, interview with Hazel De Berg for the National Library, 24.x.1972.
7. HA, 'An Interfering Female', ch. III, pp. 11–14.
8. Ibid., ch. IV, p. 1.
9. Midge Mackenzie, *Shoulder to Shoulder*, Alfred A. Knopf, 1976, p. 197.
10. HA, 'An Interfering Female', ch. IV, p. 2.
11. HA, 'An Interfering Female', ch.V, p.1.
12. BA, interview, 5.iii.1991.
13. BA, interview, 8.v.1990.
14. Verna Coleman, *Adela Pankhurst: The Wayward Suffragette, 1885–1961*, Melbourne University Press, 1996, p. 51.
15. Coleman, *Adela Pankhurst*, p.53.
16. HA, 'An Interfering Female', ch.V, p. 4.
17. Coleman, *Adela Pankhurst,* p. 53.
18. Adela P. Walsh (née Pankhurst), letter written 22.iv.1945, from Flat 11, 6 Duke Street, Kensington, NSW. Early in the letter she writes: 'I have never spoken to anyone of the painful business of my coming to Australia so nobody but you and I know the facts—and there are some you don't know—but I have no objection to your version being given forth, if it is of interest to anyone.'
There is a note on p. 51 in Coleman, *Adela Pankhurst*, which says: '(According to Vida Goldstein, Helen [Archdale], too, was eventually discarded by Emmeline and Christabel [Pankhurst]).'
19. Coleman, *Adela Pankhurst*, pp. 53–4.
20. HA, 'An Interfering Female', ch.V, pp. 4–7.

Chapter 5: War
1. HA, 'An Interfering Female', unpublished ms, ch.V, p. 7.
2. D. Wetherall and C. Carr-Gregg, *Camilla: C.H. Wedgwood, a Life, 1901–1955*, NSW University Press, 1990, p. 12.
3. AA, 'Take One Actor', unpublished ms, ch. I, p. 5.
4. BA, interview, 22.v.1990.
5. Anne Archer, librarian, Bedales School, letter, 3.v.1994.
6. BA, interview, 22.v.1990.

7. BA, interview, 8.v.1992.
8. Archer, letter, 3.v.1994
9. BA, interview in *The Greening Years*, presented by Jill Lennon, ABC Radio, 22.iv.1982.
10. HA, 'An Interfering Female', ch.V, p. 7.
11. Mary Phillips, *The Militant Suffrage Campaign in Perspective*, Edward O. Beck, 1957, p.14.
12. BA, interview, 25.vi.1991.
13. HA, 'An Interfering Female', ch.VI, p. 1.
14. Ibid., ch.VI, pp. 1–3.
15. Ibid., ch.VI, p. 3A.
16. Ibid., ch.VI, p. 5.
17. AA, 'Take One Actor', ch. I, p. 4.
18. HA, 'An Interfering Female', ch.VI, p. 6.
19. Ibid., ch,VI, p. 6A.
20. Audley Archdale, nephew of BA, interview, Liphook, 4.xi.1991.
21. *Irish Times*, 11.x.1918, p. 4.
22. Ibid.
23. Ibid., p. 2.
24. Christopher Plantin (translated by J.T.R. Gibbs), 'The Happiness of This World', sonnet, found in TMA's photo album.
25. BA, interview 15.v.1990.
26. HA, 'An Interfering Female', ch.VI, p. 7.
27. BA, interview, 8.v.1990.
28. BA, interview, 19.111.1991.
29. BA, interview, 22.v.1990.

Chapter 6: St Leonard's and Margaret Rhondda

1. BA, interview in *The Greening Years*, presented by Jill Lennon, ABC Radio, 22.iv.1982.
2. BA, interview, 22.v.1990.
3. BA, interview with Ellis Blain, ABC Radio, recorded 24.vi.1969.
4. HA, 'An Interfering Female', unpublished ms, ch.VIII, p. 8.
5. Viscountess Rhondda, *This Was My World*, Macmillan & Co., 1933, ch. XV, p. 234.
6. Diana Ashcroft, cousin and look-alike of the actress Dame Peggy Ashcroft, interview, London, 14.xi.1991.
7. BA, interview, 30.iv.1991.
8. J.S.A. Macaulay, ed., *St Leonard's School, 1877–1977*, St Leonard's School, St Andrews, 1977, p. 27.
9. Elizabeth Hake, interview, 14.vi.1991.
10. Anne Robson, interview, 11.xi.1991.
11. Diana Ashcroft, interview, 14.xi.1991.
12. HA, 'An Interfering Female', ch.VIII, p. 9.
13. BA, interview, 22.v.1990.
14. BA, interview, 25.vi.1991.
15. HA, 'An Interfering Female', ch.VIII, p. 8.
16. Ashcroft, interview, 14.xi.1991.
17. Hake, interview, 14.vi.1991.
18. Miss K.H. McCutcheon's reference for BA, 24.v.1935.
19. BA, interview with Cheryl Szatow, 1986.

20. Ibid.
21. Magnus Magnusson, ed., *Chambers Biographical Dictionary*, 5th edn, 1970.
22. Viscountess Rhondda, *This Was My World*, p. 97.
23. Magnusson, ed., *Chambers Biographical Dictionary*.
24. Ibid.
25. BA, interview, 14.iii.1994.
26. BA, interview, 19.iii.1991.
27. HA, 'An Interfering Female', ch.VII, p. 1.
28. BA, interview, 5.vi.1990.
29. Viscountess Rhondda, *This Was My World*, p. 298.
30. HA, 'An Interfering Female', ch.VII, p. 3.
31. Ibid., ch.VIII, p. 1.
32. Shirley M. Eoff, *Viscountess Rhondda: Equalitarian Feminist*, Ohio State University Press, 1991, p. 120.
33. HA, 'An Interfering Female', ch.VIII, p. 2.
34. Diana Reich, letter to BA, 17.ii.1982; Eoff, *Viscountess Rhondda*, p. 120.
35. Anthony Lejeune, *Time and Tide*, vol. 39, no. 30, 26.vii.1958, p. 903.
36. Ibid.
37. Eoff, *Viscountess Rhondda*, pp. 120–2.
38. Ibid.
39. T.S. Eliot, *Time and Tide*, vol. 39, no. 30, 26.vii.1958, p. 904.
40. Eoff, *Viscountess Rhondda*, p. 121.
41. Ibid., p.112.
42. BA, interview, 14.iii.1994.
43. BA, interview, 5.iii.1991.
44. BA, interview, 5.iii.1991.
45. Eoff, *Viscountess Rhondda*, p.109.
46. BA, interview, 8.v.1990.
47. Rebecca West, *Time and Tide*, vol. 39, no. 30, 26.vii.1958, p. 912.
48. Ashcroft, interview, 14.xi.1991.
49. BA, interview, 26.vi.1990.
50. BA, interview, 26.vi.1990.
51. BA, interview with Cheryl Szatow, 1986.
52. BA, interview, 19.iii.1991.
53. Macaulay, ed., *St Leonard's School*, p. 33.
54. BA, interview with Cheryl Szatow, 1986.

Chapter 7: McGill

1. AA, 'Take One Actor', unpublished ms, ch. I, p. 9.
2. Ibid.
3. BA, interview with Cheryl Szatow, 1986.
4. BA, letter to HA, 27.x.1928.
5. BA, letter to HA, 3.x.1927.
6. HA, 'An Interfering Female', unpublished ms, ch.VIII.
7. BA, interview with Hazel De Berg for the National Library, 24.x.1972.
8. BA, interview, 30.iv.1991.
9. HA, 'An Interfering Female', ch. XII.
10. Shirley M. Eoff, *Viscountess Rhondda: Equalitarian Feminist*, Ohio State University

Press, 1991, p. 112.
11. BA, interview, 19.iii.1991.
12. Margaret Haig,Viscountess Rhondda, *This Was My World*, Macmillan & Co., 1933, p. 302.
13. Eoff, *Viscountess Rhondda*, p.113.
14. Alan Judd, 'Henry James', in *Writers and Their Houses*, Hamish Hamilton, 1993, p. 221.
15. Eoff, *Viscountess Rhondda*, p. 114.
16. HA, 'An Interfering Female', ch. IX.
17. Ibid.
18. HA, letter (17.vii.1928) to *St Leonard's School Gazette*, November 1928, p. 214.
19. HA, 'An Interfering Female', ch. X.
20. *The Gazette*, Montreal, 27.v.1929.
21. BA, cable from Montreal, 21.v.1929.
22. BA, interview, 22.v.1990.
23. BA, interview with Cheryl Szatow, 1986.

Chapter 8: London Law
1. BA, interview with Hazel De Berg for the National Library, 24.x.1972.
2. BA, diary, 7.ii.1934.
3. BA, interview, 16.iv.1991.
4. BA, diary, 18.iv.1934.
5. BA, 'When Cricket Was Fun!', unpublished ms, ch. 1; BA, interview, 27.xi.1991: 'Since the war I went and had a look at the Pavilion, there were people living in it. It had been turned into a little house. The ground had gone of course.'
6. Felicity Charles, interview, 5.xi.1991. Felicity's father was Archdeacon of Canterbury for 15 years. They lived in a beautiful old house in the precincts of the cathedral. Betty and Barbara Peden went to her wedding.
7. Ibid.
8. Audrey Collins, interview, 1.xi.1991. A cricketer whose contribution to women's cricket was recognised in 1999 when she was, with Betty, amongst the first ten women to be made an Honorary Life Member of the Marylebone Cricket Club, Lord's.
9. BA, interview with Candace Sutton, *Daily Telegraph*, 5.i.1985, p. 20.
10. BA, *Time and Tide*, 10.vii.1937.
11. BA, letter to HA, August 1932.
12. BA, *Indiscretions of a Headmistress*, Angus & Robertson, 1972, p. 16.
13. BA, interview, 23.x.1990.
14. BA, interview, 30.iv.1991.
15. Sheila Duncan-Smith, telephone interview, 20.i.1994.
16. BA, interview, 8.v.1990.
17. BA, diary, 27.viii.1934.
18. BA, diary, 1934.
19. BA, 'When Cricket Was Fun!', ch. I.
20. V.M.M. Cox, letter to BA, 9.vi.1934.
21. *Herald* (Melbourne), 3.ix.1934.
22. BA, interview, 25.x.1991.
23. *Herald* (Melbourne), 11.vi.1934.
24. Newspaper clipping.

25. Letter of reference from H. Lauterpacht, Lecturer in International Law, London School of Economics and Political Science, 29.iv.1935.
26. BA, diary, 18.x.1934.
27. BA, 'When Cricket Was Fun!', ch. II, p. 4.
28. *The Star* (London), 19.x.1934.
29. BA, diary, 19.x.1934.
30. Ibid.

Chapter 9: Cricket
1. BA, 'When Cricket Was Fun!', unpublished ms, ch. III, p. 1; BA, diary, 6.xi.1934.
2. *Daily News*, 12.xi.1934.
3. BA, 'When Cricket Was Fun!', ch. III, p. 3.
4. BA, interview, 13.viii.1990.
5. BA, 'When Cricket Was Fun!, ch. III, p. 3.
6. Myrtle Maclagan, interview, 29.x.1991.
7. *West Australian*, 22.xi.1934.
8. Carlie Hansen, *Courier-Mail*, 21.xii.1934.
9. BA, 'When Cricket Was Fun!', ch. II, pp. 5–6.
10. Ibid., ch.VII, pp. 1–2.
11. *Women's Cricket*, magazine of the Women's Cricket Association (England), May 1935, vol. 6, no. 1, p. 6.
12. BA, 'When Cricket Was Fun!', ch. III, pp. 11–12.
13. Ibid., ch. III, p. 12.
14. Ibid., ch. IV, p. 2.
15. *Bulletin*, 12.xii.1934.
16. BA, 'When Cricket Was Fun!', ch. IV, p. 3.
17. Ibid., ch. IV, p. 4.
18. Ibid., ch. IV, pp. 5–6.
19. Ibid. pp. 8–9.
20. *Women's Cricket*, May 1935, vol. 6, no. 1, p. 8.
21. BA, 'When Cricket Was Fun!', ch. IV, p. 10. Brian Penton at the time was a columnist with the *Daily Telegraph*, of which he became editor. He also wrote two novels, *Landtakers* and *Inheritors*, and the pamphlet *Think—or Be Damned*.
22. *Sydney Morning Herald*, 17.xii.1934.
23. *Courier-Mail*, 21.xii.1934.
24. *Courier-Mail*, 24.xii.1934.
25. *Daily Mail* (Manchester), 3.x.1934.
26. Stan Phillips, *Telegraph* Sporting Supplement, 28.12.1934.
27. BA, 'When Cricket Was Fun!' ch.V, pp. 12–13.
28. Ibid., ch.V, p. 15.
29. *Sunday Mail* (Brisbane), 23 December 1934.
30. Marjorie Pollard, *Morning Post* (London), 23.i.1935.
31. BA, interview, 5.vi.1990.
32. BA, 'When Cricket Was Fun!', ch.VI, p. 3.
33. 'A Male', *Sydney Morning Herald* Women's Supplement, 24.i.1935.
34. BA, 'When Cricket Was Fun!', ch.VIII, pp. 2–3.
35. Myrtle Maclagan, interview, 29.x.1991.
36. *Women's Cricket*, June 1935, vol. 6, no. 2, p. 32.

37. BA, 'When Cricket was Fun!', ch.VI, p. 15.
38. Ibid., ch.VI, p. 16.
39. Ibid., ch.VI, p. 23.
40. Ibid., ch.VII, pp. 4–5.
41. Ibid., ch.VII, p. 16.
42. BA, interview, 13.viii.1991.
43. Maclagan, interview, 29.x.1991.
44. *Sydney Morning Herald*, 13.vi.1935.

Chapter 10: The Road From Jarrow

1. Betty D.Vernon, *Ellen Wilkinson, 1891–1947*, Croom Helm, 1982, p. 6.
2. BA, interview, 12.vi.1990.
3. Vernon, *Ellen Wilkinson*, p. 140.
4. Ibid., p. 142.
5. Ibid.
6. Ibid., p. 153, n. 56.
7. 'The Northern Pageant' column, *Newcastle Sunday Sun* (UK), 16.v.1937.
8. Vernon, *Ellen Wilkinson*, p. 136.
9. BA, *Indiscretions of a Headmistress*, Angus & Robertson, 1972, p. 18.
10. BA, interview, 12.iii.1992.
11. *Perth Daily News*, 24.viii.1936.
12. Felicity Charles, interview, 5.xi.1991.
13. Audrey Collins, interview, 1.xi.1991.
14. Janna Bruce, interview, 10.x.1991.
15. Ibid.
16. Nancy Lord, interview, 2.xi.1991.
17. Bruce, interview, 10.x.1991.
18. Lord, interview 2.xi.1991.
19. HA, 'An Interfering Female', unpublished ms, ch. X, pp. 8–10.
20. Ibid. ch.XI, pp. 8–13.
21. Ibid. ch.XV, p. 4.
22. Ibid. ch. XV, pp. 4–6.
23. Nancy Lord and Cecil Western, interview, 2.xi.1991.

Chapter 11: Wrens in the Tropics

1. Madge Dawson and Heather Radi, eds, *Against the Odds*, Hale & Iremonger, 1984, p. 263.
2. BA, interview, 12.vi.1990.
3. BA, interview, 4.xii.1990.
4. BA, interview, 12.vi.1990.
5. BA, interview, 12.vi.1990.
6. BA, letter to HA, 2.i.1941.
7. BA, diary, 21.i.1941.
8. Elizabeth Miller, unpublished ms, ch. 5, pp. 58–9.
9. Ibid., ch.VI, p. 63.
10. Miller, ch.VI, pp. 66–7.
11. BA, interview, 12.vi.1990.
12. BA, letter to HA, 25.iii.1941.

13. Miller, ch. IX, pp. 104–6.
14. Phyll Puttick, interview, 9.xi.1991.
15. Mary Heathcott, *Singapore Free Press*, 30.vii.1941.
16. *Singapore Free Press*, 2.xii.1941.
17. BA, letter to HA, 27.x.1941.
18. Miller, ch. XII, pp. 146–7.
19. BA, letter to HA, 16.viii.1941.
20. Phyll Puttick, interview, 9.xi.1991.
21. Ibid.
22. Vera Laughton Matthews, letter to HA, 9.ix.1941.
23. BA, letter to HA, 15.vii.1943.
24. BA, letter to HA, 3.x.1941.
25. BA, letter to HA, 21.vii.1941.
26. Miller, ch. XV, p. 178.
27. Phyll Puttick, interview, 9.xi.1991.
28. Miller, ch. XV, p. 179.
29. Phyll Puttick, interview 9.xi.1991.
30. BA, letter to HA, 24.xii.1941.
31. Miller, ch. XV, pp. 188–90.
32. *Evening Standard*, 11.xii.1941.
33. Miller, ch. XVI, p. 195.
34. BA, letter to HA, 6.i.1942.
35. Women's College Union Oral History Project, 10.xi.1986.
36. BA, letter to HA, 2.iv.1942.
37. Miller, ch. XVIII, p.216.
38. BA, interview, 12.vi.1990.
39. BA, letter to HA, 3.iv.1942.
40. *Ceylon Daily News*, 7.iv.1942.
41. Ceylon newspaper cutting.
42. Phyll Puttick, interview, 9.xi.1991.
43. Ibid.
44. Miller, ch. XX, pp. 248–53.
45. Phyll Puttick, interview, 9.xi.1991.
46. Miller, chs XXI-XXII, pp. 266–74.
47. BA, letter to HA, 12.vi.1990.
48. BA, letter to HA, 29.vii.1942.
49. BA, diary, 26.vii.1942.
50. BA, letter to HA, 31.viii.1942.
51. BA, diary, 5.ix.1942.
52. BA, diary, 16.ix.1942.
53. Miller, ch. XXII, pp. 275–6.
54. BA, letter to her Wrens, 29.ix.1942.
55. AA, letter to HA, 26.ix.1942.
56. BA, diary, 24.x.1942.
57. BA, letters to HA, 8.ii.1943 and 14.ii.1943.
58. AA, letter to HA, 28.x.1942.
59. Eileen Crompton, letter to BA, 22.xii.1942.
60. BA, letter to HA, quoting Sister Young's letter of 7.iv.1943.

61. BA, letter to HA, 4.v.1943.
62. Ibid.
63. BA, letter to HA, 8.ii.1943.
64. Press officer for D.WRNS, letter to BA, 25.vi.1945.
65. BA, letter to HA, 11.vi.1943.
66. BA, letter to HA, 26.ix.1943.
67. R. Gleadowe to BA.
68. Citation for MBE, 1.i.1944.
69. Phyll Puttick, interview, 9.xi.1990.
70. AA, letter to HA, 11.ii.1944.

Chapter 12: Women's College
1. BA, interview, 13.ix.1990.
2. BA, letter to HA, 26.ix.1945.
3. BA, letter to HA, 20.x.1945.
4. BA, interview, 5.vi.1990.
5. BA, letter to HA, 15.ii.1946.
6. BA, interview, 24.vii.1990.
7. Newspaper clipping headline, 'Sydney's Talking About … ', 1947.
8. Janet Hay, interview, 30.iii.1994.
9. Ibid.
10. Margaret Ford, letter headed 'Random Memories of Betty Archdale' to Women's College, University of Sydney, 1999.
11. Jo Bastian, interview, 12.x.1994.
12. BA interview in *Newcastle Herald*, 27.ii.1947.
13. Marie Bashir, interview, 12.iv.1994.
14. Geoffrey Blainey, 'Turning Point, How the Forties Changed Us Forever', *The Australian Magazine*, 12–13.x.1996.
15. Peter Coleman, *The Australian Weekend Review*, 28–9.x.1995.
16. Charles Birch, telephone interview, 24.ii.1998.
17. Margaret Ford, letter to Women's College, University of Sydney, 1999.
18. Helen Buchanan, interview, 23.iii.1994.
19. BA letter to HA, 3.iv.1946.
20. AA, letter to HA, 27.v.1945.
21. Colin Munro, interview, 5.iv.1992.
22. Aline Fenwick, telephone interviews, 1994 and 1997.
23. Elizabeth Wilkinson, interview, 12.iv.1994.
24. Verna Coleman, *Adela Pankhurst: The Wayward Suffragette, 1885–1961*, Melbourne University Press, 1996, pp. 171–5.
25. Elizabeth Hake, interview, 14.vi.1991.
26. BA, interview, 8.v.1992.
27. Barbara Edmonson, telephone interview, 23.ii.1998.
28. Council Minutes, Women's College, University of Sydney, 21.iv.1949.
29. Ibid., 23.vi.1949.
30. BA, letter to HA, 17.vii.1949.
31. BA, telegram to HA, 14.vii.1949.
32. BA, letter to HA, 17.vii.1949.
33. BA, letter to HA, 11.viii.1949.

34. BA, interview, 26.vi.1990.
35. Nancy Lord, interview, 2.xi.1991.
36. Ibid.
37. HA, will, 29.x.1935.
38. Council Minutes, Women's College, University of Sydney, 7.viii.1952.
39. Liz Palmer, interview, 30.iii.1994.
40. Speech at Reunion Dinner, Women's College, University of Sydney, 24.ix.1983.
41. Liz Palmer (née McGrath), Janet Hay (Cowper), Helen Campbell (Kenyon), Elizabeth Hassall (Ferris), Prue McCullagh (Docker), group interview, 30.iii.1994.
42. Ibid.
43. Heather Morgan, Senior Student Report, Council Minutes, Women's College, University of Sydney, 30.x.1951.
44. Marie Bashir, interview, 12.iv.1994.
45. Ibid.
46. Janet Hay et al., interview, 30.iii.1994.
47. BA, letter to Miss Cohen, Council Minutes, Women's College, University of Sydney, 26.iii.1954.
48. Marie Bashir, interview, 12.iv.1994.
49. Council Minutes, Women's College, University of Sydney, 11.xi.1954.
50. Ibid., 17.ii.1955.
51. BA, speech, 80th birthday party, Abbotsleigh, 20.viii.1987.
52. Marie Bashir, interview, 12.iv.1994.
53. Violet Lee, Senior Student Report, Michaelmas Term, Council Minutes, Women's College, University of Sydney, 1955.
54. BA, 'England and Australia —A Comparison', A.B.C. Weekly Magazine, vol. 19, no. 1, 5.i.1957, and no. 2, 12.i.1957.
55. BA, interview, 19.vi.1990.
56. Meg Mulvey and Helen Buchanan, interview, 23.iii.1994.
57. Ibid.
58. Ibid.
59. BA, interview, 28.viii.1990.
60. BA letter, Council Minutes, Women's College, University of Sydney, 15.xi.1956.
61. Madge Dawson and Heather Radi, eds, Against the Odds, Hale & Iremonger, p. 267.
62. Janet McCredie, Senior Student Report, Council Minutes, Women's College, University of Sydney, 11.xii.1956.
63. Colin Munro, interview, 5.iv.1992.
64. BA, 'Claims to The Antarctic', The Year Book of World Affairs, 1958, vol. 12, The London Institute of World Affairs, Stevens & Sons, 1958.
65. BA, 'Too Much Woman', speech at Lachlan Divisional Convention of the Agricultural Bureau, 14.iii.1957, recorded in The Land newspaper.
66. Canon M. Newth, interview, 20.iii.1998.
67. BA, interviews, 26.vi.1990 and 3.vii.1990.
68. BA, interview, 19.iii.1991.
69. BA, interview, 26.vi.1990.

Chapter 13: Alec and Galston

1. BA, interview, 8.v.1990.
2. BA, interview, 9.x.1990.

3. Audley Nicholas Archdale, interview, Liphook, 4.xi.1991.
4. Ibid.
5. AA, 'Northis, a Pisé House', unpublished ms, p. 6.
6. Colin Munro, Eulogy for Alexander Archdale, Sydney, 19.v.1986
7. Cecil Western, interview, 2.xi.1991.
8. 'Low Cost Houses You Can Build Yourself', *Women's World*, 16.x.1974, p. 25.
9. AA, 'Northis, a Pisé House', p. 7.
10. AA, 'Take One Actor', unpublished ms, p. 91.
11. Ruth Cracknell, telephone interview, 10.iii.1998.
12. Leo McKern, *Sydney Morning Herald*, 2.viii.1986, p. 47.
13. BA, unpublished letter to editor, *Sydney Morning Herald*, 4.viii.1986.
14. BA, interview, 18.vii.1990.
15. AA, 'Take One Actor', p. 111.
16. Ibid., pp. 111–12.
17. Ibid., p. 114.
18. Ibid., p. 115.
19. Ibid., p. 118.
20. Ibid., p. 130.
21. Ibid., p. 148.
22. Ibid., p. 219.
23. Lyn Marchant-Willliams, interview, 30.iii.1994.
24. AA, letter to Mr Burnett, 7.x.1977.
25. Ruth Cracknell, interview, 10.iii.1998.
26. Lyn Marchant-Williams, interview, 30.iii.1994.
27. BA, interview, 22.v.1990.
28. Joyce Cole, interview, 11.ix.1995.
29. Pat Garrow, *Sunday Times*, 1.x.1985.
30. Nancy Lord, interview, 2.xi.1991.

Chapter 14: Abbotsleigh
1. BA, interview, 28.xii.1998.
2. Abbotsleigh Council Minutes, 25.iii.1957.
3. Meredith Burgmann, interview, 19.v.1994.
4. BA, interview, 14.iii.1994.
5. Janna Bruce, interview, 10.x.1991.
6. Abbotsleigh Council Minutes, 15.vii.1957.
7. Canon M. Newth, interview, 20.iii.1998.
8. Jane Plasto (Parkinson), interview, 12.v.1994.
9. Janna Bruce, interview, 10.x.1991.
10. Canon M. Newth, interview, 20.iii.1998.
11. Charles Higham, *Bulletin*, 2.x.1965.
12. Meredith Burgmann, interview, 19.v.1994.
13. Wendy Blaxland, letter to BA, 26.i.1990.
14. Elva Julien, interview, 9.xi.2001.
15. *The Weaver*, Abbotsleigh School Magazine, 1964.
16. Ibid., 1960.
17. Christine Fox (Carter), interview, 4.vi.1994.
18. Ellis Blain, interview with BA, ABC Radio, 1969.

19. Jenny Rowe (Oswin), interview, 23.iv.1994.
20. Annabelle Schmidt (Higgins), telephone interview, 1998.
21. Glynis Johns, interview, 23.iv.1994.
22. Susan Anthony, *Sydney Morning Herald*, 12.iv.1995.
23. Francis James, *Nation*, 21.xii.1968, p. 8.
24. Wendy Blaxland, letter to BA, 26.i.1990.
25. Bill Farram at BA's 80th birthday luncheon, Abbotsleigh, 20.viii.1987.
26. Rosie Hoskins, conversation, 1991.
27. Joyce Cole, interview, 11.ix.1995.
28. Penny Figgis, interview, 19.v.1994.
29. BA, 'Thoughts on Tertiary Education', *Union Recorder*, 4.iii, year not noted.
30. Jill Auld (Cowper), interview, 12.v.1994.
31. Christine Fox (Carter), interview, 4.vi.1994.
32. Meredith Burgmann, interview, 19.v.1994.
33. Caroline de Costa (Downes), interview, 15.iv.1994.
34. Francis James, *Nation*, 21.xii.1968.
35. BA, interview, *Sun-Herald*, 1.vii.1984.
36. Caroline de Costa (Downes), interview, 15.iv.1994.
37. BA, interview with Jane Singleton on *City Extra*, ABC Radio, 7.v.1985.
38. Mary Smith, BA's 80th birthday luncheon, Abbotsleigh, 20.viii.1987.
39. Joyce Cole, interview, 11.ix.1995.
40. BA, interview with Jill Lennon on *Education Now*, ABC Radio, 11.iii.1982.
41. Elva Julien, interview, 9.xi. 2001.
42. Bill Farram at BA's 80th birthday luncheon, Abbotsleigh, 20.viii.1987.
43. Abbotsleigh Council Minutes, 9.xi and 14.xii.1966.
44. BA, talk given in Careers Week, University of Sydney, 1969, in an undated university publication amongst BA's papers.
45. Judy Copeland, conversation, 1.ii.1998.
46. BA, interview with Jill Lennon on *Education Now*, ABC Radio, 11.iii.1982.
47. Lyn Marchant-Williams, interview, 30.iii.1994.
48. Val Street, interview, 2.ix.1994.
49. Lyn Marchant-Williams, interview, 30.iii.1994.

Chapter 15: Against the Wind
1. *Daily Telegraph*, 13.xi.1964.
2. Aline Fenwick, telephone interviews, 1994 and 1997.
3. John Gorton, letter to BA, 15.v.1968.
4. Dorothy Ellison, interview, 20.ix.1994.
5. Peter Duly, interview, 3.iii.1997.
6. Janna Bruce, interview, 10.x.1997.
7. Val Street, interview, 2.ix.1994.
8. Caroline de Costa (Downes), interview, 15.iv.1994.
9. Jane Plasto (Parkinson), interview, 12.v.1994.
10. *Women's Day*, 2.v.1968.
11. Wendy Blaxland, letter to BA, 26.i.1990.
12. Kim McConchie (Brown), interview, 12.v.1994.
13. Francis James, *Nation*, 21.xii.1968.
14. Helen Campbell (Kenyon), interview, 30.iii.1994.

15. BA, *Indiscretions of a Headmistress*, Angus & Robertson, 1972, p. 131.
16. BA, *School Family*, April/May 1971.
17. Jill Auld (Cowper), interview, 12.v.1994.
18. Christine Fox (Carter), interview, 4.vi.1994.
19. Michelle Judzewitsch (Cotton), interview, 11.vii.2000.
20. Kerry Taylor (Bremner), interview, 12.v.1994.
21. Charles Higham, *Bulletin*, 2.x.1965.
22. Ibid.
23. Freda Whitlam, interview, 8.xi.2001.
24. BA, 'What Easter Means to Me', *Sunday Australian*, 2.iv.1972, p. 17.
25. Susan Bures (Klein) at a 1993 school reunion.
26. BA, 'Religion in Church Schools: The Classroom, the Girls' Point of View', undated, BA's papers.
27. Meredith Burgmann, interview, 19.v.1994.
28. BA, 'Religion in Church School'.
29. Christine Fox (Carter), interview, 4.vi.1994.
30. Glynnis Johns, interview, 23.iv.1994.
31. Canon Newth, interview, 20.iii.1998.
32. Peter Duly, interview, 3.iii.1997.
33. *Canberra Times*, 26.x.1985.
34. BA, *Indiscretions of a Headmistress*, p. 98.
35. BA, interview, 26.vi.1990.
36. Jill Auld (Cowper), interview, 12.v.1994.

Chapter 16: Controversies

1. Jo Bastian, interview, 12.x.1994.
2. Charles Higham, *Bulletin*, 2.x.1965.
3. Kath McCredie, interview, 21.xi.1994. In fact the headline quoting BA was, 'I'm a Virgin: But not All Singles Girls Have to Be', *Mirror*, 23.iii.1974.
4. Ellis Blain, interview with BA, ABC Radio 1969.
5. *Australian* 18.ix.1969, p. 17.
6. *Daily Telegraph*, 17.iv.1952.
7. James Franklin, 'Corrupting The Youth: Australian Philosophers and Their Students', unpublished ms.
8. University of Sydney Archives, 8.vii.1961.
9. *Mirror*, 6.iv.1972.
10. Higham, *Bulletin*, 2.x.1965.
11. *Mirror*, 6.iv.1972.
12. BA, *Women's World*, 10.x.1973.
13. Glynis Johns, interview, 23.iv.1994.
14. Jennifer Rowe (Oswin), interview, 23.iv.1994.
15. Meg Matthews (Giblin), interview, 4.vi.1994.
16. BA, 'Teenage Dating', *Woman's World*, 10.x.1973, including quote from John A. T. Robinson, *Honest to God*, SCM Press, 1963, p. 119.
17. Abbotsleigh Council Minutes, 13.vii.1966.
18. Richard Neville, *Hippie Hippie Shake*, Minerva, 1996, pp. 40–1.
19. Ibid., p. 38.
20. *Sydney Morning Herald*, 25.vii.1964.

21. Francis James, *Nation*, 21.xii.1968.
22. Neville, *Hippie Hippie Shake*, p. 53.
23. *Sydney Morning Herald*, 17.x.1964.
24. Abbotsleigh Council Minutes, 13.vii.1966.
25. *Sunday Telegraph*, 13.ix.1970.
26. Quoted in Abbotsleigh Council Minutes, 9.x.1963.
27. Ted Noffs, letter to BA, quoted in Abbotsleigh Council Minutes, 9.ix.1964.
28. Joy Lang, letter to Deirdre Macpherson, 11.vii.1994.
29. Peter Duly, interview, 3.iii.1997.
30. Ibid.
31. Ibid.
32. BA, obituary of Miss Filose, *The Weaver*, 1968.
33. Tim Bowden interview with BA, *Personal Imprint*, ABC Radio, 11.ix.1977.
34. BA, *Indiscretions of a Headmistress*, Angus & Robertson, 1972, p. 220.
35. Merrilyn Brice, telephone conversation, 17.viii.1994.
36. Abbotsleigh Council Minutes, 4.xii.1968.
37. Ibid., 10.vi.1970.
38. Dianne V. Henshaw, 'Betty Archdale: A Description and Analysis of the Role of an Australian Independent School Headmistress', Master of Educational Administration dissertation, 1992.
39. Susan Mitchell, *Weekend Australian*, 7.x.1995.
40. Janet Hawley, *Australian*, 6.xii.1968.
41. *Mirror*, 6.xii.1968.
42. *Sun*, 8.xii.1969.
43. BA, paper, 'Schools: The Need for Change', undated.
44. BA, *Portfolio*, January 1987 and 14.viii.1975.
45. BA, 'Schools: The Need For Change'.
46. BA, interview with Jill Lennon, *Education Now*, ABC Radio, 11.iii.1982.
47. BA, letter to Professor Taylor, Abbotsleigh Council Minutes, 12.iv.1969.
48. BA et al., letter to *Australian*, 17.v.1978.
49. BA, letter to Abbotsleigh Council, 10.ix.1969.
50. BA, letter to Abbotsleigh Council, 11.iii.1970.
51. Kath McCredie, interview, 21.xi.1994.
52. BA, interview, 3.vii.1990.
53. BA, interview, 23.x.1990.
54. Peter Duly, interview, 3.iii.1997.
55. BA, interview with Barbara Sinclair (not broadcast), October 1975, ABC Archives.
56. BA, interview with Ellis Blain, ABC Radio, 1969.
57. Jill Auld (Cowper), interview, 12.v.1994.
58. Joyce Cole, interview, 11.ix.1995.
59. Freda Whitlam, interview, 8.xi.2001.
60. Kath McCredie, interview, 21.xi.1994.
61. *Mirror*, 8.v.1970.

Chapter 17: Freewheeling
1. When I went with Betty to one of these readings she lent me an edition of Shakespeare which, I was startled to discover, had been printed in the early 1700s.
2. *Sun-Herald*, 1.x.1967.

3. BA, *Indiscretions of a Headmistress*, Angus & Robertson, 1972, p. 225.
4. *Sunday Australia*, 2.iv.1972.
5. *Gazette*, University of Sydney, vol. 4, no. 9, September 1984.
6. BA, interview, 18.vii.1990.
7. Ken Coles, letter to BA, 5.vi.1984.
8. BA, letter to John Kerr, undated, after 1975.
9. Richard Walsh, letter to BA, 31.vii.1973.
10. *Border Morning Mail*, 29.iv.1978.
11. *Australian Women's Weekly*, 18.x.1978.
12. BA, interview, 13.ix.1990.
13. BA, interview, 22.v.1990.
14. BA, interview with Caroline Jones on *The Search for Meaning*, ABC Radio, 11.ii.1988.
15. BA, interview, 19.iii. 1991.
16. BA, interview, 14.iii.1994.
17. BA, interview, 22.v.1990.
18. Paul Berry, letter to BA, 7.i.1975.
19. BA, interview, 16.iv.1991.
20. *Sydney Morning Herald*, 2.v.1974.
21. BA, letter to John Kerr, 13.xi.1975 or 76, the year not noted.
22. Colin Munro, interview, 5.iv.1992.
23. *Sydney Morning Herald*, 30.vii.1979.
24. *Daily Liberal* (Dubbo), 24.vi.1975.
25. *Sydney Morning Herald*, 19.i.1980.
26. *Women's Day*, 14.v.1973.
27. BA, Occasional Address, Macquarie University, 2.v.1995.
28. BA, conversation, 17.iii.1999.
29. Elizabeth Hake, interview, 14.vi.1991.
30. Janna Bruce, interview, 10.x.1991.
31. *Sunday Australian*, 2.iv.1972.
32. BA, interview, 7.viii.1990.
33. *Sydney Morning Herald*, 4.viii.1990.
34. *Sydney Morning Herald*, 14.ix.1990.
35. BA, letter to the Rev. Father James Bromley, Vicar-General, Anglican Catholic Church, Diocese of Australia, 28.ix.1990.
36. BA, interview with Barbara Sinclair, *Coming Out Ready or Not* show, ABC Radio, 6.x.1975.
37. BA, interview with Barbara Sinclair (not broadcast), October 1975, ABC Archives.

Chapter 18: Goodbye Galston
1. Northis remains, now painted mission brown. It looks insignificant in relation to the large brick homestead built further down the block.

Chapter 19: Towards the End
1. Morris West, letter to BA, 16.ii.1993.
2. BA, interview with Cheryl Szatow, 1986.
3. BA, interview with Caroline Jones on *The Search for Meaning*, ABC Radio, 11.ii.1988.

SELECT BIBLIOGRAPHY

Abbotsleigh Council Minutes, 1957–70.
Abbotsleigh Girls School Archives, newspaper clipping, 'School Row Brewing', 1957.
ABC Radio and Television Archives.
Archdale, Alexander, letters to Helen Archdale throughout the World War II.
Archdale, Alexander, 'Northis, a Pisé House', unpublished ms.
Archdale, Alexander, 'Take One Actor', unpublished ms
Archdale, Betty, 'Claims to the Antarctic', *The Year Book of World Affairs, 1958*, vol. 12,
    London Institute of World Affairs, Stevens & Sons, 1958.
Archdale, Betty, diaries 1934–5, 1941, 1942.
Archdale, Betty, 'England and Australia—A Comparison', *A.B.C. Weekly Magazine*, vol.
19, no.1, 5.i.1957 and no. 2, 12.i.1957.
Archdale, Betty, *Girls at School*, The Happy Family Series, Hodder & Stoughton, 1970.
Archdale, Betty, 'Religion in Church Schools: The Classroom, The Girls' Point of View',
undated, Betty Archdale's papers.
Archdale, Betty, 'Too Much Woman', speech at Lachlan Divisional Convention of the
Agricultural Bureau, 14.iii.1957, recorded in *The Land* newspaper.
Archdale, Betty, *Indiscretions of a Headmistress*, Angus & Robertson, Sydney, 1972.
Archdale, Betty, interview with Caroline Jones on *The Search For Meaning*, ABC Radio,
    11.ii.1988.
Archdale, Betty, letters to Helen Archdale throughout the war and her early days at the
University of Sydney.
Archdale, Betty, Occasional Address, Macquarie University, 2.v.1995.
Archdale, Betty, *Portfolio*, January 1987 and *Portfolio*, 14.viii.1975.
Archdale, Betty, 'Teenage Dating', *Woman's World*, 10.x.1973, including quote from John
A. T. Robinson, *Honest to God*, SCM Press, London, 1963, p. 119.
Archdale, Betty, 'The Women's International Movement in Relation to General
    Internationalism', Australian Quarterly, December 1948.
Archdale, Betty, 'Thoughts on Tertiary Education', *Union Recorder*, 4.iii. year not noted.
Archdale, Betty, 'Schools: The Need for Change', undated.
Archdale, Betty, 'What Easter Means to Me', *Sunday Australian*, 2.iv.1972, p. 17.
Archdale, Betty, 'When Cricket Was Fun!', unpublished ms.
Archdale, Helen, 'An Interfering Female', unpublished ms.
Archdale, Henry Blackwood, *Memoirs of the Archdales, With the Descents of Some Allied*

Families, Impartial Reporter Office, Enniskillen,1925.

Archdale, Theodore Montgomery, diaries, 1895–1917 (years 1904 to 1913 missing).

Australian, 'Sex, Drugs and Politics', 3.iii.1993, with excerpts from Janet McCulman, *Journeyings: The Biography of a Middle Class Generation, 1929–1990*, Melbourne University Press, Melbourne, 1993.

Australian Womens Weekly, 18.x.1978.

Blainey, Geoffrey, 'Turning Point, How the Forties Changed Us Forever', *The Australian Magazine*, 12–13.x.1996.

Border Morning Mail, 29.iv.1978.

Bulletin, Sydney, 1934, 1965.

Campion, Edmund, *Sydney Morning Herald*, 1.vii.1972.

Canberra Times, 26.x.1985.

Castle Archdale Museum Display, exhibition notes.

Ceylon Daily News, 1942.

Citizen, St Andrews, 1935.

Coffey, H. W., and M. J. Morgan, *Irish Families in Australia and New Zealand*, revised vol. 1, *Abbott-Dynan, 1788–1983*, self-published.

Coleman, Peter, *The Australian Weekend Review*, 28–9.x.1995

Coleman, Verna, *Adela Pankhurst: The Wayward Suffragette, 1885–1961*, Melbourne University Press, Melbourne, 1996.

Courier-Mail (Brisbane), 1934.

Daily Liberal (Dubbo), 24.vi.1975.

Daily Mail (Manchester), 1934.

Daily Telegraph (Sydney).

De Berg, Hazel, taped interview with Betty Archdale for the National Library, 1972.

Dawson, Madge, and Heather Radi, *Against the Odds*, Hale & Iremonger, Sydney, 1984.

East Anglian Daily Times (Ipswich), 1934.

Eoff, Shirley M., *Viscountess Rhondda: Equalitarian Feminist*, Ohio State University Press, Columbus, 1991.

Evening Standard (London),1934, 1941.

Franklin, James, 'Corrupting the Youth: Australian Philosophers and Their Students', unpublished ms.

Garrow, Pat, *Sunday Times* (UK), 1.x.1985.

Gazette (Montreal), 1929.

Gazette (University of Sydney), September 1984.

Hawes, Joan L., *Women's Test Cricket: The Golden Triangle, 1934–1984*, The Book Guild Ltd., Lewes, 1987.

Hawley, Janet, *The Australian*, 6.xii.1968.

Henshaw, Dianne V., 'Betty Archdale: A Description and Analysis of the Role of an Australian Independent School Headmistress', Master of Educational Administration dissertation, 1992.

Herald (Melbourne), 1934, 1936.

Irish Times, 1918.

James, Francis, *Nation*, 21.xii.1968.

Judd, Alan, *Writers and Their Houses*, Hamish Hamilton, London, 1993.

Landed Gentry of Ireland, 1958.

'Low Cost Houses You Can Build Yourself', *Women's World*, 16.x.1974.

Macaulay, J.S.A., ed., *St Leonard's School*, St Leonard's School, St Andrews, 1977.

Mackenzie, Midge, *Shoulder to Shoulder*, Alfred A. Knopf, New York, 1976.

Magnusson, Magnus, *The Glorious Privilege: The History of 'The Scotsman'*, Nelson, London, 1967.

Miller, Elizabeth, unpublished ms.
Mirror (Sydney).
Mitchell, Susan, *Weekend Australian*, 7.x.1995.
Mombasa Times, 1942.
Montreal Daily Star, 1927.
Morning Post (London), 1935.
Natal Mercury (Durban), 1934.
Neville, Richard, *Hippie Hippie Shake*, Minerva, Melbourne, 1996.
Newcastle Herald (Australia), 1947.
Newcastle Sunday Sun (UK), 1937.
O'Brien, Anne, 'Sins of Omission, Women in the History of Australian Religion and
    Religion in the History of Australian Women', *Australian Historical Studies*, 108, 1997.
Perth Daily News, 1936.
Phillips, Mary, *The Militant Suffrage Campaign in Perspective*, Edward O. Beck, London,
    1957.
Rogers, Mary, *Living By Lough Erne*, self-published, 1910.
St Andrews Citizen, 1928.
Scots Ancestry Research Society Report on Paternal Ancestry of Helen Russel, 1.x.91.
Singapore Free Press, 1941.
Star (London), 1934.
Sunderland Echo, 1935.
Tate, Audrey, *Fair Comment: The Life of Pat Jarrett, 1911–1990*, Melbourne University
    Press, Melbourne, 1956.
The Scotsman, 1876.
Thompson, Roger C., 'Women and the Significance of Religion in Australian History',
    Australian Historical Studies, 108, 1997.
Sun-Herald, 1.x.1967.
Sun (Sydney), 1962, 1965.
Sunday Australian, 2.iv.1972.
Sunday Referee (UK).
Sydney Morning Herald, 1934, 1935, 1974, 1980.
Telegraph Sporting Supplement, 1934.
Time and Tide.
University of Sydney Archives, 8.vii.1961.
Vernon, Betty D., *Ellen Wilkinson, 1891–1947*, Croom Helm, London, 1982.
Vicinus, Martha, *Independent Women: Work and Community for Single Women, 1850–1920*,
    Virago, London, 1985.
Viscountess Rhondda, *This Was My World*, Macmillan & Co., London, 1933.
Walsh, Adela P. (née Pankhurst), two letters to Helen Archdale.
Ward, Ian, and Ralph Modder, *Malaya and Singapore, December 1941–February 1942*,
    Media Masters, 1989.
Ward, Ian, and Ralph Modder, *The Japanese Conquest of Malaya and Singapore, December
    1941–February 1942*, Media Masters, 1989.
West Australian, 1934.
The Weaver, Abbotsleigh School Magazine, 1957–70.
Wetherall, D., and C. Carr-Gregg, *Camilla: C.H. Wedgwood, a Life, 1901–1955*, NSW
    University Press, Kensington, 1990.
Women's College Union, University of Sydney, Oral History Project, 1986.
Women's College, University of Sydney, Council Minutes, 1946–57.
Womens Cricket, May 1935 and June 1935.
Women's Day, 2.v.1968 and 14.v.1973.

INDEX